Presented to

_____

By

_____

On the Occasion of

_____

Date

_____

SHOW ME YOUR LOVE

Daily Devotional Insights from Classic Christian Writings

COMPILED BY JOHN HUDSON TINER

BARBOUR
PUBLISHING

Published by Barbour Publishing, Inc., P.O. Box 719, Uhrichsville, Ohio 44683
www.barbourbooks.com

Our mission is to publish and distribute inspirational products offering exceptional value and biblical encouragement to the masses.

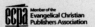 Member of the
Evangelical Christian
Publishers Association

Printed in the United States of America.
5 4 3 2 1

Introduction

Show Me Your Love—Daily Devotional Insights from Classic Christian Writings presents devotions from the finest gospel writers who have explored the Bible thoroughly and gone to the heart of love.

Presented are selections by more than forty pioneering men and women: talented writers, Bible scholars, beloved pastors, passionate religious reformers, gifted preachers, determined missionaries, and ordinary citizens of God's kingdom. Writers include John Bunyan, John Wycliffe, Charles Spurgeon, William Tyndale, D. L. Moody, Mary Slessor, and approximately three dozen others. They turned their considerable talents into giving people an understanding of God's love. This roll call of the faithful reveals, by everyday stories and interesting Bible examples, the meaning of love.

Often the names of these towering individuals are known, but their works are not easily accessible to modern readers. *Show Me Your Love* fulfills a very evident need by presenting the best of their ideas as daily inspirational readings for a full year. The devotions feature an easy-to-read updating of the original works.

The 366 powerful devotions in *Show Me Your Love* are certain to give greater comfort and deeper insight into the love of God. All of them sparkle with a rainbow of love. Tested by time, proven by the gospel, set before you by the hand of the world's greatest writers, these devotions will make your life fuller, happier, and closer to God.

Amazing things can happen when you learn the full meaning of "God is Love."

Renewed to Love

The LORD, your God, is in your midst,
a warrior who gives victory;
he will rejoice over you with gladness,
he will renew you in his love;
he will exult over you with loud singing.

ZEPHANIAH 3:17 NRSV

Without a renewal of faith, Christians are blind to the state of sinners. Their hearts are hard as marble. The truths of the Bible appear like a dream. They admit it to be all true; their conscience and their judgment assent to it, but their faith does not see it standing out in bold relief in all the burning realities of eternity.

But when they enter into a revival, they see things in that strong light which will renew the love of God in their hearts. This will lead them to labor zealously to bring others to Him. They will feel grieved that others do not love God, when they love Him so much. And they will set themselves to persuade their neighbors to give Him their hearts.

So their love to men will be renewed. They will be filled with a tender and burning love for souls. They will have a longing desire for the salvation of the whole world. They will be in an agony for individuals whom they want to have saved—their friends, relations, enemies. They will not only be urging them to give their hearts to God, but they will carry them to God in the arms of faith, and with strong crying and tears beseech God to have mercy on them and save their souls from endless burnings.

CHARLES FINNEY

What Is Love?

Praise the LORD, O my soul, and forget not all his benefits—
who forgives all your sins and heals all your diseases,
who redeems your life from the pit
and crowns you with love and compassion.

PSALM 103:2–4 NIV

Let us ask what *love* is—what is the true meaning of the word? And that we may be under no possibility of mistake, we will not at all trust the definition to the judgment of men but go to our Lord Himself for an account of the nature of love.

The love that our Lord requires in all His followers is the love of God and man—of God for His own sake and of man for God's sake. Now, what is it to love God but to delight in Him, to re-joice in His will, to desire continually to please Him, to seek and find our happiness in Him, and to thirst day and night for a fuller enjoyment of Him?

As to the measure of this love, our Lord has clearly told us, "You shall love the Lord your God with all your heart." But we are not to love or delight in none but Him. He has commanded us to love our neighbor—that is—all people as ourselves. We are to desire and pursue their happiness as sincerely and steadily as our own. We are to love in the strictest sense: to delight in them and to enjoy them. Love in such a way and measure will prepare us for the enjoyment of Him.

JOHN WESLEY

Beautiful Love

If I speak in the tongues of men and of angels,
but have not love,
I am only a resounding gong or a clanging cymbal.

1 CORINTHIANS 13:1 NIV

Everyone has asked the great question: What is the supreme good? You have life before you. Once only you can live it. What is the noblest object of desire, the supreme gift to covet?

Paul says, "If I have all faith, so that I can remove mountains, and have not love, I am nothing." Love was not Paul's strong point. The observing student can detect a beautiful tenderness growing and ripening all through his character as Paul gets old; but the hand that wrote, "The greatest of these is love," when we meet it first, is stained with blood.

Nor is this letter to the Corinthians peculiar in singling out love as the supreme good. Peter says, "Above all things have fervent love among yourselves." Above all things! And John goes farther, "God is love." And you remember the profound remark which Paul makes elsewhere, "Love is the fulfilling of the law." Did you ever think what he meant by that? In those days, people were working their passage to heaven by keeping the Ten Commandments and the many other commandments that they had manufactured out of them. Christ said, "I will show you a more simple way." If you do one thing, you will do these many things without ever thinking about them. If you love, you will unconsciously fulfill the whole law. Love is the rule for fulfilling all rules.

HENRY DRUMMOND

Love That Understands

*O LORD, you have examined my heart
and know everything about me.*

PSALM 139:1 NLT

There are times when severe fever makes us utterly unaware of the presence of our most careful and tender nurses. A child in delirium will cry out in anguish for its mother. The child is being attended with the untold tenderness of a mother's love. Disease has hidden the mother from the child, but it has not hidden the child from the mother. In the same way, it is with our God and us. The darkness of our fears, sorrows, or despairs cannot hide us from God, although it often hides Him from us.

If we think of Him as a stern tyrant, intent only on His own glory, we shall be afraid of His continual presence. If we think of Him as a tender, loving Father, intent only on our blessing and happiness, we shall be glad and thankful to have Him with us. For the presence and the care of love can never mean anything but good to the one being loved.

Our God knows us and understands us, and is acquainted with all our ways. No one else in all the world understands us. Others misinterpret our actions and misjudge our motives. No one makes allowances for our ill health. No one realizes how much we have to contend with. But our heavenly Father knows it all. He understands us, and His judgment of us takes into account every element, conscious or unconscious, that goes to make up our character and to control our actions. Only an all-comprehending love can be just, and our God is just.

HANNAH WHITALL SMITH

The Absent Bridegroom

All night long on my bed I looked for the one my heart loves;
I looked for him but did not find him.
SONG OF SONGS 3:1 NIV

The betrothed bride has learned to love her lord, and no other companionship than his can satisfy her. His visits may be occasional and may be brief, but they are precious times of enjoyment. Their memory is cherished in the intervals, and their repetition longed for. There is no real satisfaction in his absence, and yet he comes and goes. As the ever-changing tide, her experience is an ebbing and flowing one. It may even be that unrest is the rule, satisfaction the exception. Is there no help for this? Must it always continue so? Has he created these unquenchable longings only to tantalize them? Strange indeed it would be if this were the case.

Yet, are there not many of the Lord's people whose habitual experience corresponds with hers? They know not the rest and the joy of abiding in Christ. They know neither how to attain to it nor why it is not theirs. Are there not many who look back to the delightful times of their first espousals, who, so far from finding richer inheritance in Christ than they then had, are even conscious that they have lost their first love?

Poor mistaken one! The Bridegroom is waiting for you all the time. The conditions that prevent His approach are all of your own making. Take the right place before Him, and He will be most ready, most glad to satisfy your deepest longings, to meet, supply your every need.

HUDSON TAYLOR

Love Calls Missionaries

These proclaim Christ out of love,
knowing that I have been put here
for the defense of the gospel.

PHILIPPIANS 1:16 NRSV

The obstacles to carrying the gospel among the heathen must arise, I think, from either their distance from us, their primitive manner of living, the danger of being killed by them, the difficulty of acquiring the necessaries of life, or the lack of understanding of their languages.

As to their distance from us, there are trading companies whose commerce lies in many of the places where these people dwell. Every fresh account of their ignorance should call forth our pity, and excite us to concur with divine guidance in seeking their eternal good.

Their primitive way of living can be no objection to any except those whose love of ease renders them unwilling to expose themselves to inconveniences for the good of others. The apostles and their successors went among foreign people. They did not wait for the ancient inhabitants of other realms to be educated before they could be converted to Christianity. Dealing with them provokes no objection to commercial men. We should have as much love to the souls of our fellow sinners as they have for the profits arising from a few otter skins. After all, the uneducated state of the heathen, instead of affording an objection against preaching the gospel to them, ought to furnish an argument for it.

Does not the goodness of the cause, the duties incumbent on us as Christians call upon us to venture all and use every effort for their benefit?

WILLIAM CAREY

Future Love

Those who sow in tears will reap with songs of joy.
PSALM 126:5 NIV

It seems perfectly reasonable that God should have given us a glimpse of the future, for we are constantly losing some of our friends by death, and the first thought that comes to us is, *Where have they gone?* When a loved one is taken away from us, how that thought comes up before us! How we wonder if we will ever see them again and where and when it will be! Then it is that we turn to this blessed Book, for there is no other book in all the world that can give us the slightest comfort. No other book can tell us where the loved ones have gone.

Not long ago, I met an old friend, and as I took him by the hand and asked about his family, the tears came trickling down his cheeks as he said, "I haven't any now. I am left here desolate and alone."

Would anyone take from that man the hope that he will meet his dear ones again? Would anyone persuade him that there is not a future where the lost will be found? No, we need not forget our dear loved ones. But we cling forever to the enduring hope that there will be a time when we can meet unfettered, and be blessed in that land of everlasting suns, where the soul drinks from the living streams of love that roll by God's high throne.

DWIGHT LYMAN MOODY

Love Is a Fact

But God demonstrates his love for us by t
he fact that Christ died for us
while we were still sinners.

ROMANS 5:8 ISV

It is of vital importance for us to understand that the Bible is a statement, not of theories but of actual facts. Things are not true because they are in the Bible, but they are only in the Bible because they are true. A little boy, who had been studying at school about the discovery of America, said to his father one day, "Father, if I had been Columbus, I would not have taken all that trouble to discover America."

"Why, what would you have done?" asked the father.

"Oh," replied the little boy, "I would have just gone to the map and found it."

This little boy did not understand that maps are only pictures of already known places, and that America did not exist because it was on the map, but it could not be on the map until it was already known to exist. Similarly, the Bible is, like the map, a simple statement of facts. When it tells us that God loves us, it is only telling us something that is a fact, and that would not be in the Bible if it had not been already known to be a fact.

It was a great discovery to me when I grasped this idea. It seemed to take all uncertainty and all speculation out of the revelation given us in the Bible of the salvation of the Lord Jesus Christ, and to make all that is written concerning Him to be simply a statement of incontrovertible facts.

HANNAH WHITALL SMITH

Spirit of Love

"A new command I give you:
Love one another.
As I have loved you,
so you must love one another."
JOHN 13:34 NIV

You have not the spirit of love until you have a will to do all goodness at all times and on all occasions. You may indeed do many works of love and delight in them, especially at such times as they are not inconvenient to you, or contradictory to your state or temper. But the spirit of love is not in you until it is the spirit of your life, until you live freely, willingly, and universally according to it.

Every spirit acts with freedom and universality according to what it is. It needs no command to live its own life, or be what it is, no more than you need to bid wrath to be wrathful. Therefore, the spirit of love can only love, wherever it is or goes.

As the sparks know no motion but that of flying upwards, whether it be in the darkness of the night or in the light of the day, so the spirit of love is always in the same course. It knows no difference of time, place, or persons, whether it gives or forgives, bears or forbears; it is equally doing its own delightful work. For the spirit of love is its own blessing and happiness because it is the truth and reality of God in the soul; and therefore, it is in the same joy of life everywhere and on every occasion.

WILLIAM LAW

Merciful Love

Be mindful of your mercy, O LORD,
and of your steadfast love,
for they have been from of old.

PSALM 25:6 NRSV

Adam and Eve had eaten the fruit of which God had commanded them that they should not eat. When arraigned before God, they could not be brought to confess it. What reason can be given as to why sentence of death should not be pronounced against the prisoners at the bar? How can God, consistently with His justice, possibly forgive them? Yet mercy cries: Spare these sinners, spare the work of Your own hands! Look then, wisdom contrives a scheme how God may be just and yet be merciful.

An amazing scene of divine love here opens to our view, which had been from all eternity hid in the heart of God! Although Adam and Eve were repentant and did not so much as put up one single petition for pardon, God immediately passes sentence upon the serpent and reveals to them a Savior.

Adam and Eve stood by as criminals, and God could not indulge them because they had broken His covenant. God the Father and God the Son had entered into a covenant concerning the salvation of the elect from all eternity. The first Adam proved false. Therefore, to secure the second covenant from being broken, God puts it into the hands of the second Adam, the Lord from heaven. Adam after the fall stood no longer as our representative. He and Eve were only private persons, as we are, and were only to lay hold on the declaration of mercy contained in this promise by faith.

GEORGE WHITEFIELD

Love in His Presence

And they said one to another,
Did not our heart burn within us,
while he talked with us by the way,
and while he opened to us the scriptures?
LUKE 24:32 KJV

Now the poor soul complains, "I wish that I could love Christ more!" Then you cannot but love Him. Now, you know little of His agreeableness and therefore love little; then, your eyes will affect your heart, and the continual viewing of that perfect beauty will keep you in continual joy of love.

Christians, does it not now stir up your love to remember all the experiences of His love? Does not kindness melt you and the sunshine of divine goodness warm your frozen hearts? What will it do then, when you shall live in love, and have all in Him who is all? Christians, you will be then brimful of love; yet, love as much as you can, you shalt be ten thousand times more beloved.

Were not the arms of the Son of God open upon the cross and an open passage made to His heart by the spear? Will not His arms and heart be open to you in glory? Did not He begin to love before you loved and will not He continue now? Did He love you an enemy, you a sinner, you who even loathed yourself? Did He accept you when you did disclaim yourself? And will He not now immeasurably love you as a son, as a perfect saint? He that in love wept over the old Jerusalem when near its ruin, with what love will He rejoice over the new Jerusalem in her glory!

RICHARD BAXTER

Father Love

> *Praise be to the God and Father of our Lord Jesus Christ,*
> *the Father of compassion*
> *and the God of all comfort.*
>
> 2 CORINTHIANS 1:3 NIV

A father loves his child; therefore, whether it is a smile or a rebuke, it is for the good of the child. God's chastening is not to destroy but to reform. God cannot hurt His children, for He is a tenderhearted Father. Will a father seek the ruin of his child, the child that came from himself, that bears his image? All his care and contrivance is for his child. Whom does he settle the inheritance upon, but his child?

God is an everlasting Father. Before we were children, God was our father, and He will be our father to eternity. A father provides for his child while he lives; but if the father dies, then the child may be exposed to injury. But God never ceases to be a father. You who are a believer have a Father who never dies; and if God be your father, all things must work for your good.

The words "thy God" also imply the relation of a husband. This is a near and sweet relation. The husband seeks the good of his spouse. There is a marriage relation between God and His people. If He be a husband whose heart is full of love, then He will seek the good of His spouse. Either He will shield off an injury or will turn it to the best. God entirely loves His people.

THOMAS WATSON

Love and Discipline

*"Those whom I love I rebuke and discipline.
So be earnest, and repent."*
REVELATION 3:19 NIV

Christ will have His favored church walk with great care, and if she will not follow Him fully by being shown wherein she has erred and will not repent when kindly counseled, He then takes some sharper means.

It is a very solemn thing to be dearly loved by God. It is a privilege to be coveted. But the person who is so honored occupies a position of great delicacy. The Lord your God is a jealous God, and He is most jealous where He shows most love. If the Lord gives a church a special blessing, He expects more of it—more care of His honor and more zeal for His glory. When He does not find it, what will happen? Because of His very love, He will rebuke it with hard sermons, sharp words, and painful blows to the conscience.

The chastening is a blessing and a token of love. Sorrow is often brought upon Christians by the sins of their fellow-members. Many brothers and sisters love the Lord and want to see souls converted, but they can only sigh and cry because nothing is done. They are the ones who bear the burden of a lukewarm church.

The best remedy for churches in relapse is increased spiritual fellowship with Christ. Christ is outside the church, driven there by her unkindness, but He has not gone far away; He loves His church too much to leave her altogether. He longs to come back, and therefore He waits and knocks at the door.

CHARLES HADDON SPURGEON

Hope and Love

He rekindles burned-out lives with fresh hope,
restoring dignity and respect to their lives.

1 SAMUEL 2:8 TM

In the three attributes of admiration, hope, and love, a person's personality abides. Gain them, and you win the person! All three attributes must be regarded in permanent union. The quality of each depends upon the presence of all. Strike out one, and you maim the rest. There is an imperfect love in which there is no admiration. There is an imperfect admiration in which there is no love. Perfect love admires, perfect admiration loves, and love and admiration are ever associated with the gracious spirit of hopeful aspiration. These three constitute the very marrow of life—the deep, secret springs of character and conduct. We live by admiration, hope, and love.

There is no need to be sensational. The sensational is never the parent of fruitful love. Gethsemane was very quiet, and all we need to do is walk very softly, taking others with us and letting them gaze upon the Sufferer as He bows amid the olive groves on that most eventful night.

Let us bear in mind the manner of our living. Those who are to gain others for the Master must be careful how they live. The detection of inconsistency is fatal to the reception of our message. "I say" may count for little or nothing. "I know" may count for very little more. "I am" is the personification that gives the defense and confirmation to the gospel, and reveals something of a reflected beauty of the glorious lover Himself.

JOHN HENRY JOWETT

Rebellion and Love

They refused to obey, and were not mindful of the wonders
that you performed among them. . . . But you are a God
ready to forgive. . .and abounding in steadfast love.
NEHEMIAH 9:17 NRSV

A boy was sick a little time before, and the mother had watched over him so faithfully and tenderly that she had caught his sickness. She had brought him back to health, but she was lying very sick. She had told the boy and his sister that they could go out into the garden, and said, "There are some flowers out there about which I am very careful. I do not want you to pick them."

So Johnny and Mary go out, and Johnny goes to work to do just what he was asked not to do. His sister says, "Johnny, did you not hear Mother tell us not to pick those flowers? Why pick them?"

"Because," says Johnny, "she loves me so, Mary. Don't you know how she loves me; how when I was sick, Mother gave up sleep and everything, and watched over me through the nights? Don't you know that she is sick there now because she loves me so? And so I am now going to do the very thing she told me not to do."

What would you think of a boy like that? And what do you think of the man or woman who make their boast of the love of God, and because God loves them, make God's love an excuse for rebellion against Him, and make God's love a reason for a worldly life?

REUBEN ARCHER TORREY

Unchangeable Love

*Now I beg you, brethren, through the Lord Jesus Christ,
and through the love of the Spirit, that you strive together
with me in prayers to God for me.*

ROMANS 15:30 NKJV

This evening I was walking in our little garden, meditating on the fact that Jesus Christ is the same yesterday, today, and forever. While meditating on His unchangeable love, power, and wisdom, I turned my meditation, as I went on, into prayer concerning myself. While applying likewise His unchangeable love, power, and wisdom both to my present spiritual and earthly circumstances— all at once the present need of the orphanage was brought to my mind. Immediately I was led to say to myself, *Jesus in His love and power has previously supplied me with what I have needed for the orphans. In the same unchangeable love and power, He will provide me with what I may need for the future.* A flow of joy came into my soul while realizing the unchangeableness of our adorable Lord.

About one minute after, a letter was brought to me, enclosing an amount of money. In it was written: "Will you apply the amount of the enclosed money to the furtherance of the objects of your Scriptural Knowledge Society, or of your Orphan Establishment, or in the work and cause of our Master in any way that He Himself, on your application to Him, may point out to you. It is not a great sum, but it is a sufficient provision for the requirements of today." This money allowed me to meet the expenses of the orphanages that came upon me four days later.

GEORGE MÜLLER

The Object of Love

"Yet the LORD chose your ancestors as the objects of his love."
DEUTERONOMY 10:15 NLT

This is an ancient graveyard with the names Adam, Sheth, and Enosh. The names of past generations who were born and died, who loved and suffered, who stormed and fought through the world, are engraven on these solid slabs. But there is no inscription to record their worth or demerit. Just names and nothing more.

How strange to think that if Christ tarry, our names will be treated with the same apathy as these! So far as this world is concerned, we and all our generation shall pass away. But each of these lives fulfilled a necessary part in the progress of the human race. Each was in turn parent and child. Each passed on the torch of life. Each contributed something to the fabric of humanity, rising like coral islands from unknown depth. The hilltops would not be possible but for their lower courses which touch the valleys. We could not have the somebodies without an immense number of nobodies.

But each person was the object of the love of God. Each was included in the redemptive purpose of our Lord. Each is living yet somewhere. Each will have to stand before the judgment bar of God. It is a stupendous thought to imagine the whole human race rooted in Adam like one vast far-spreading tree. Ah, reader, be sure that you art taken out of the first Adam and grafted into the second—the Lord Jesus.

F. B. MEYER

Love and the Rainbow

Like the appearance of a rainbow in a cloud on a rainy day,
so was the appearance of the brightness all around it.
This was the appearance of the likeness of
the glory of the LORD.

EZEKIEL 1:28 NKJV

Glory belongs to the Father and the Son: to the Father that He so loved the world that He gave His only begotten Son, to the Son that He so loved the world as to give up Himself. But there is equal glory due to the Holy Spirit for He is that love of the Father and the Son to the world. Just so much as the first two persons of the Godhead glorify Themselves by showing the astonishing greatness of Their love and grace, just so much is that wonderful love and grace glorified by the Holy Spirit.

Christ purchased for us that we should have the favor of God and might enjoy His love, but this love is the Holy Spirit, which is but the indwelling of the Holy Spirit in the heart. Christ purchased for us spiritual joy and comfort, which is in a participation of God's joy and happiness, which joy and happiness is the Holy Spirit. The Holy Spirit is the sum of all good things.

The various sorts of rays of the sun and their beautiful colors do well represent the Spirit. They well represent the love and grace of God and were made use of for this purpose in the rainbow after the flood, and I suppose also in that rainbow that was seen round about the throne by Ezekiel, and round the head of Christ by John in Revelation 10:1.

JONATHAN EDWARDS

Wonderful Love

"As the Father has loved me,
so have I loved you.
Now remain in my love."
JOHN 15:9 NIV

Have you ever noticed the difference between work and fruit? A machine can do work; only life can bear fruit. A law can compel work; only love can spontaneously bring forth fruit. Work implies effort and labor. The essential idea of fruit is that it is the silent, natural, restful produce of our inner life. The gardener may labor to give his apple tree the digging, watering, and pruning it needs. But he can do nothing to produce the apple: Healthy life bears much fruit. All that the vine does for the branch, it does under a law of nature. There is no personal living love to the branch.

We are in danger of looking to Christ as a Savior and a supplier of every need, appointed by God, accepted and trusted by us, without any sense of the intensity of the personal affection in which Christ embraces us. He leads us to Himself to show us how identical His own life is with ours. Even as the Father loved Him, Jesus loves us. If we are to live like Him, as branches to be truly like the vine, we must share in this, too. Our life must have its breath and being in a heavenly love as much as His. What the Father's love was to Him, His love will be to us. If that love made Him the true vine, His love can make us true branches.

ANDREW MURRAY

Walking in God's Love

*And Enoch walked with God:
and he was not;
for God took him.*

GENESIS 5:24 KJV

Walking with God implies our making progress or advances in the divine life. Walking, in the very first idea of the word, seems to suppose a progressive motion. A person who walks, though he moves slowly, yet he goes forward and does not continue in one place. So it is with those who walk with God.

In one sense, the divine life admits of neither increase nor decrease. When a soul is born of God, to all intents and purposes he is a child of God. Though he should live to the age of Methuselah, yet he would then be only a child of God after all. But in another sense, the divine life admits of decays and additions. Hence, it is that we find the people of God charged with backslidings and losing their first love.

Believers keep up and maintain their walk with God by reading of His holy Word. "Search the scriptures," says our blessed Lord, "for these are they that testify of Me." If we cease making the written Word of God our sole rule both as to faith and practice, we shall soon lie open to all manner of delusion and be in great danger of making shipwreck of faith and a good conscience.

If you would walk with God, you will associate and keep company with those who do walk with Him. The primitive Christians, no doubt, kept up their vigor and first love by continuing in fellowship one with another.

GEORGE WHITEFIELD

Love That Destroys

For men shall be. . .
lovers of pleasures more than lovers of God.
2 TIMOTHY 3:2, 4 KJV

Youth is the time when our passions are strongest—and, like unruly children, cry most loudly for indulgence. Youth is the time when we have generally our most health and strength. Death seems far away, and to enjoy ourselves in this life seems to be everything. Youth is the time when most people have few earthly cares or anxieties to take up their attention. And all these things help to make young people think of nothing except pleasure.

Time would not permit me to tell you all the fruits this love of pleasure produces, and all the ways in which it may harm you. All things that give a feeling of excitement for the time— all things that drown thought and keep the mind in a constant whirl, and all things that please the senses and delight the flesh—these are the sort of things that have mighty power at your time of life. They owe their power to the love of pleasure. There is no surer way to get a seared conscience and a hard heart toward the things of God than to give way to the desires of the flesh and mind.

The violation of the seventh commandment against sexual immorality is the sin that leaves deeper scars upon the soul than any other sin that a person can commit. It is a sin that destroys thousands of young people, and has even overthrown a few of the saints of God in the past. Samson and David are fearful proofs.

J. C. RYLE

Rainbow of Love

Love is patient, love is kind. It does not envy,
it does not boast, it is not proud.
Love does not delight in evil but rejoices with the truth.

1 CORINTHIANS 13:4, 6 NIV

Love is like light. You have seen a scientist take a beam of light and pass it through a prism. You have seen it come out on the other side of the prism broken up into its component colors—red, orange, yellow, green, blue, violet, and all the colors of the rainbow. In the same way, Paul passes this thing, love, through the magnificent prism of his inspired intellect. It comes out on the other side broken up into its elements. And in these few words we have what one might call the spectrum of love, the analysis of love.

Will you observe what its elements are? Will you notice that they have common names. They are virtues that we hear about every day. They are things that can be practiced by every person in every stage of life. Will you notice how, by a multitude of small things and ordinary virtues, the supreme thing is made up?

The spectrum of love has nine ingredients: patience, kindness, generosity, humility, courtesy, unselfishness, good temper, guilelessness, and sincerity. These make up the supreme gift, the stature of the perfect Christian. You will observe that all are in relation to men, in relation to life, in relation to the known today and the near tomorrow, and not to the unknown eternity.

HENRY DRUMMOND

Led by Love

Keep yourselves in the love of God;
look forward to the mercy of our Lord Jesus Christ
that leads to eternal life.
JUDE 21 NRSV

Consider the everlasting love of God to my soul when I was in great distress! When my troubles were great, then was His love exceedingly great. All honor and glory be to You, Lord of Glory!

The Lord gently led me along and let me see His love, which was endless and eternal, surpassing all the knowledge that men have in the natural state or can obtain from history or books. His love let me see myself as I was—without Him.

I found that there were two thirsts in me—the one after the creature comforts and the other after the Lord, the Creator, and His Son Jesus Christ. I saw that all the world could do me no good. If I had had a king's diet, palace, and attendance, all would have been as nothing because nothing gave me comfort but the Lord by His power. I saw the great love of God and was filled with admiration at the infiniteness of it.

One day, when I had been walking alone and came home, I was taken up in the love of God. I could not but admire the greatness of His love. While I was in that condition, I clearly saw that all these troubles were good for me for the trial of my faith. I saw all through these troubles and temptations that my living faith was raised.

GEORGE FOX

The Lord Is Good

Now that you have tasted that the Lord is good.

1 PETER 2:3 NIV

I shall never forget the hour when I first discovered that God was really good. It had never dawned on me that it meant He was actually and practically good, with the same kind of goodness He has commanded us to have. The expression "the goodness of God" had seemed to me nothing more than a sort of heavenly statement, which I could not be expected to understand. Then one day in my reading of the Bible I came across the words "O taste and see that the Lord is good" and suddenly they meant something. What does it mean to be good?

To be good is to do the best we know. I saw that since God has total knowledge He must know what is the best and highest good of all; therefore, His goodness must necessarily be beyond question.

I can never express what this meant to me. I had such a view of the actual goodness of God that I saw nothing could possibly go wrong under His care, and it seemed to me that no one could ever be anxious again. Over and over, when appearances have been against Him, and when I have been tempted to question whether He had been unkind or neglectful or indifferent, I have been brought up short by the words "the Lord is good." I have seen that it was simply unthinkable that a God who was good could have done the bad things I had imagined.

HANNAH WHITALL SMITH

Love Written on the Heart

And we know that all things work together
for good to them that love God,
to them who are the called according to his purpose.

ROMANS 8:28 KJV

There are two things that I have always looked upon as difficult. The one is to make the wicked sad, and the other is to make the godly joyful. Dejection in the godly arises from a double source: either because their inward comforts are darkened or their outward comforts are disturbed. To cure both these troubles, I have put forth this ensuing piece, hoping by the blessing of God it will buoy up their desponding hearts and make them look with a more pleasant aspect. I would prescribe them to take, now and then, a little of this cordial, this comfort for the heart: "All things work together for good to them that love God."

To know that nothing hurts the godly is a matter of comfort. To be assured that all things that happen shall cooperate for their good, that their crosses shall be turned into blessings, that showers of affliction shall water the withering root of their grace and make it flourish; this may fill their hearts with joy until they run over.

It is not a matter wavering or doubtful. The apostle does not say, "We hope." A Christian may come not merely to a vague opinion, but to a certainty of what he holds. Though a Christian has not a perfect knowledge of the mysteries of the gospel, yet he has a certain knowledge. The Spirit of God imprints heavenly truths upon the heart as with the point of a diamond.

THOMAS WATSON

Love and the Cannibals

"Because he loves me," says the LORD,
"I will rescue him;
I will protect him, for he acknowledges my name."

PSALM 91:14 NIV

One day, while working as a missionary on the Pacific Island of Tanna, I heard an unusual bleating among my few remaining goats, as if they were being killed. I rushed to the goat house and found myself instantly surrounded by a band of armed men. Their weapons were raised, and I expected the next moment to die. But God moved me to talk to them firmly and kindly. I warned them of their sin and its punishment. I showed them that only my love and pity led me to remain there seeking their good, and that if they killed me, they killed their best friend. I further assured them I was not afraid to die, for at death my Savior would take me to heaven and that I would be far happier than on earth. My only desire to live was to make them happy by teaching them to love Jesus Christ my Lord.

I then lifted up my hands and eyes to the heavens and prayed aloud for Jesus to bless all the Tannese and to protect me or take me to heaven as He saw to be for the best. One after another, they slipped away from me, and Jesus restrained them again. Did ever a mother run more quickly to protect her crying child in danger's hour than the Lord Jesus hastens to answer believing prayer and send help to His servants?

JOHN G. PATON

Simple Expressions of Love

*I am generously supplied with the gifts
you sent me with Epaphroditus.
They are a sweet-smelling sacrifice that is acceptable to God
and pleases him.*
PHILIPPIANS 4:18 NLT

My little five-year-old daughter came to me with a curious little birthday gift in her hand. "Papa, I haven't bought you a birthday present," said she. "I thought you would rather have something I made myself."

How glad I was that she should think that something she could make would be more precious to me than any purchased gift! But what the curious little gift could be intended for I was quite at a loss to discover. She had found a small piece of wood and had bored a hole in it with her scissors, in which she had inserted a peg and on the top had hung half a cockleshell. I took my dear child on my knee and, kissing her, said, "Papa is so pleased to have a birthday present of your own making. What is it my darling has made for me?"

"Why, don't you know, Papa? I thought you would like best a ship to take you to China!"

The dear child was right. Probably no gift I ever received gave more pleasure or was as carefully treasured. When that dear child had become old enough to engage in missionary work in China herself, I remembered the little ship. She was surprised that I should remember it. But it had never passed from my memory, and the recollection of it is a pleasure still. It is not hard to please those who love us.

HUDSON TAYLOR

Love or Money?

> *"You shall not covet your neighbor's house.*
> *You shall not covet your neighbor's wife,*
> *or his manservant or maidservant, his ox or donkey,*
> *or anything that belongs to your neighbor."*
>
> EXODUS 20:17 NIV

The Bible says that the love of money is a root of all kinds of evil. The tenth commandment against coveting has therefore been properly called a "root extractor" because it would tear up and destroy this root. Matthew tells us that the deceitfulness of riches chokes the Word of God. Isn't that true of many business people today? They are so engrossed with their affairs that they have no time for religion. They lose sight of their souls and their eternal welfare in their desire to amass wealth. They do not even hesitate to sell their souls to the devil. People say, "We must make money, and if God's law stands in the way, brush it aside."

Greed for money leads people to commit violence and murder, to cheat, deceive, and steal. It turns the heart to stone, devoid of all natural affection, cruel, and unkind. The scramble for a share of the wealth smashes them to pieces. Because of covetousness of rank and position in society, parents barter sons and daughters in ungodly marriages.

Recall how Judas's love of money lured him into the betrayal of his divine friend into the hand of His murderers. You ask me how you are to cast this unclean spirit out of your heart. Make up your mind that by the grace of God you will overcome the spirit of selfishness. You must overcome it, or it will overcome you.

DWIGHT LYMAN MOODY

Love and Steadfast Faith

But let all who take refuge in you be glad;
let them ever sing for joy.
Spread your protection over them,
that those who love your name may rejoice in you.

PSALM 5:11 NIV

Faith is likened to the North Star, for it showed the port of grace to men rowing in the sea of this world. Faith is a stone lying in the foundation of a strong building that bears up all the work. For as the building stands firmly that is well grounded upon a stone, so each virtuous deed is strong when it is grounded upon the solidity of belief.

A man who has lost his right eye is unable to defend himself in battle because his shield hides his left eye, and so he has no sight to defend himself from the enemy. In the same way, he who has lost the right eye of true faith is unable to withstand or fight against his spiritual enemy, the devil.

We must trust steadfastly that nothing may harm us any more than He will allow it, and all things that He sends come for the best. And let no wealth of this failing world, neither tribulation, draw our hearts from firm belief in God. Let us not put our belief or trust in charms or in dreams or any other fantasies, but only in Almighty God.

To believe in God, as St. Augustine says, is in belief to cling to God through love, and to seek actively to fulfill His will. For no man truly believes in God except he who loves God.

JOHN WYCLIFFE

Trust and Love

But I am like an olive tree flourishing in the house of God;
I trust in God's unfailing love for ever and ever.

PSALM 52:8 NIV

Trust, like life, is feeling, although much more than feeling. An unfelt life is a contradiction; an unfelt trust is a misnomer, a delusion, and a contradiction. Trust is the most felt of all attributes. It is all feeling, and it works only by love. An unfelt love is as impossible as an unfelt trust. The trust of which we are now speaking is a conviction. An unfelt conviction? How absurd!

Trust sees God doing things here and now. Yes, and more. It rises to a lofty eminence and, looking into the invisible and the eternal, realizes that God has done things and regards them as being already done. Trust brings eternity into the annals and happenings of time, transmutes the substance of hope into the reality of fulfillment, and changes promise into present possession. We know when we trust just as we know when we see, just as we are conscious of our sense of touch. Trust sees, receives, and holds. Trust is its own witness.

Yet, quite often, faith is too weak to obtain God's greatest good immediately. It has to wait in loving, strong, prayerful, and pressing obedience until it grows in strength and is able to bring down the eternal into the realms of experience and time. Trust, in a historical fact or in a mere record, may be a very passive thing, but trust in a person vitalizes the quality, makes it productive, and makes it known with love.

EDWARD MCKENDREE BOUNDS

Yield to Love

Surely it was for my benefit that I suffered such anguish.
In your love you kept me from the pit of destruction;
you have put all my sins behind your back.
ISAIAH 38:17 NIV

Since the ungodly do not know that they are governed by God's hand, they think that most of their troubles happen by chance. The ungodly are like a wrongheaded young man, who leaves his father's house and wanders far away. When he all but perishes from hunger, cold, and other evils, he admits that he has met the just punishment of his stupidity. He does not understand that his troubles are the chastisement of his father. So the ungodly, having alienated themselves from God and His household, do not understand that they are still within the reach of God's hand.

Let us keep in mind that we cannot taste the love of God in our afflictions unless we are persuaded that they are rods with which our Father chastises us for our sins. Although God's hand falls upon those in His house and those outside, it falls upon the former to show His special care for them. The true solution of our problem is as follows: Anyone who knows and is persuaded that God reprimands him must promptly go on to consider that God afflicts him because He loves him. For if God did not love him, He would not care about his salvation. God offers Himself as a Father to all those who endure correction. In short then, when God corrects us, He does so only as our Father, provided we yield and obey.

JOHN CALVIN

The Meaning of Love Your Neighbor

The commandments, "Do not commit adultery,"
"Do not murder," "Do not steal," "Do not covet,"
and whatever other commandment there may be,
are summed up in this one rule:
"Love your neighbor as yourself."

ROMANS 13:9 NIV

A man ought to love his neighbor equally and fully as well as himself because his neighbor is equally created of God and is fully redeemed by the blood of our Savior Jesus Christ. Out of which commandment of love spring these: Kill not your neighbor, defile not his wife, bear no false witness against him. You must not only avoid doing these things in deed, but you must also not covet in your heart his house, his wife, his manservant, maidservant, ox, donkey, or whatsoever is his. These laws, pertaining unto our neighbor, are not fulfilled in the sight of God except with love. For the commandment is "Though your neighbor's wife be ever so fair and you have ever so great opportunity given you, and she consent or provoke you (as Potiphar's wife did Joseph), yet see that you love your neighbor so well for that very love you cannot find in your heart to do that wickedness."

For he who has trust in anyone, whether in heaven or in earth, save in God and His Son Jesus, can see no cause to love God with all his heart. And likewise, against this law, "Love your neighbor as yourself," I may obey no worldly power to do anything to hurt my neighbor even if he is an unbeliever.

WILLIAM TYNDALE

The Sword of Love

Disregarding another person's faults preserves love;
telling about them separates close friends.
PROVERBS 17:9 NLT

Can a person hate the world enough to change it, and yet love it enough to think it worth changing? Can he look up at its colossal evil without feeling despair? I want to love my neighbor not because he is I, but precisely because he is not I. I want to adore the world, not as a person likes looking at his image in a mirror because it is one's self, but as one loves a woman because she is entirely different. If souls are separate, love is possible. A man may be said loosely to love himself, but he can hardly fall in love with himself.

And it is just here that Christianity is on the side of humanity, liberty, and love. Love desires personality; therefore, love desires differences. It is the instinct of Christianity to be glad that God has broken the universe into little pieces, because they are living pieces. It is Christianity's innate nature to say "Little children love one another," rather than to tell one large person to love himself.

Christianity is a sword that separates and sets free. No other philosophy makes God actually rejoice in the separation of the universe into living souls. But according to Christianity, this separation between God and man is sacred, because this is eternal. For a person to love God, it is necessary that there should be not only a God to be loved, but a person to love Him.

GILBERT K. CHESTERTON

Academy of Love

I revere your commandments, which I love,
and I will meditate on your statutes.

PSALM 119:48 NRSV

The first requirement of real life is something to love, and the second requirement is something to revere. Each of the elements is essential. Each deprived of the other is robbed of its dynamic. Neither can lift if the other be absent. Love without reverence becomes a purely carnal sentiment and resides in the channels of the flesh. Reverence without love is like cold moonlight and will never enrich the heart with the presence of gracious flowers. Love without reverence is a destructive fever; reverence without love is a perpetual frost. True love kneels in reverence; true reverence yearns in love. Each, I say, is essential to the other, and both are needful in the creation of worthy and wealthy life.

Now, where can love and reverence be best produced? Where can we find the atmosphere most fitted for their creation? Where can we learn to love and revere in such a way that they shall become the spontaneous exercises of the soul?

I sometimes take down from my bookshelves a little book of devotions and read one of its quaint and engaging titles: "Calvary is the true academy of love." If I want a school where love is taught and revealed, I must seek the academy of Calvary! The teaching is superlatively impressive, and even the dullest scholar makes progress in the school. We are to go into the academy of Calvary, which is the all-excelling school of love.

JOHN HENRY JOWETT

Bobby the Missionary

"Yes," replied Jesus, "have you never read,
" 'From the lips of children and infants
you have ordained praise'?"
MATTHEW 21:16 NIV

We have a little boy of six years old in our St. Thomas' Hospital—
we often have such abandoned children. He was brought in
cursing and swearing. He had never heard a good word in all his
life. He had an abscess in his back. That was about a year ago,
and he can only just stand now.

The head nurse of the ward did not scold or preach to
Bobby—he goes by the name of Bobby because no one knows his
name. She was very gentle with him and very loving. By degrees,
she taught him little prayers. And now if she is busy, he calls,
"Sister, Sister, I have not said my prayers." It is a real speaking to
God with him. The new patients stop and listen to hear him.

Now he has his real little mission in the ward—although he
never preaches—he is not goody and is quite a little "elf." But it
is as Christ meant when He said that the little child might be the
best preacher of us all. So he is a little missionary and quite an
influence among the rough men patients, and they take care of
him. Never a word is spoken now to him that a little child ought
not to hear. One of the poor men who had to be taken into a
medical ward sent a message to Bobby from his deathbed. Bobby
has the real thing in his heart, the true religion.

FLORENCE NIGHTINGALE

Grounded in Love

Not to us, O LORD, not to us,
but to your name give glory,
for the sake of your steadfast love
and your faithfulness.
PSALM 115:1 NRSV

Why should anything have my heart but Christ? He loves me; He loves me with love that goes beyond knowledge. He loves me, and He shall have me. He loves me, and I will love Him. His love stripped Him of all for my sake. Lord, let my love strip me of all for Your sake. I am a son of love, an object of love, a monument of love, of love freely given, of distinguishing love, of special love, and of love that passes knowledge. I walk in love—in love to God, in love to men, in holy love, and in genuine love.

Let the upright speak of love that is taken with love, that is captivated with love, that is carried away with love. If the upright speaks of love, his speaking signifies something. The powers and bands of love are upon him, and he shows to all that he knows what he is speaking of. But the very mentioning of love in the mouth of the profane is like a parable in the mouth of fools or as salt unsavory.

If you would improve this love, keep yourself in it. He who would live a sweet, comfortable, joyful life must live a very holy life. To this end, you must take root and be grounded in love; that is, you must be well settled and established in this love, if indeed you would improve it.

JOHN BUNYAN

Ride on the Train of Love

Guide me down the road of your commandments;
I love traveling this freeway!
PSALM 119:35 TM

At a train station, a little girl about eight years old came aboard. The conductor came along collecting tickets and fare. "Where are you going?" the conductor asked.

"I am going to heaven," she answered. "My mother used to sing of Jesus on the heavenly railroad, and that He paid the fare for everybody. But my mother don't sing to me any more. Nobody sings to me now, and I thought I'd take the cars and go to Mother. Mister, do you sing to your little girl about the railroad that goes to heaven? You have a little girl, haven't you?"

He replied, "No, my little dear, I have no little girl now. I had one once, but she died some time ago and went to heaven."

"Did she go over this railroad, and are you going to see her now?" she asked. Hearing some person say that she was an angel, the little girl earnestly replied, "Yes, my mother used to say that I would be an angel sometime." Addressing herself once more to the conductor, she asked him, "Do you love Jesus? I do, and if you love Him, He will let you ride to heaven on His railroad. I am going there, and I wish you would go with me. I know Jesus will let me into heaven when I get there, and He will let you in, too, and everybody who will ride on His railroad—yes, all these people. Wouldn't you like to see heaven and Jesus and your little girl?"

S. B. SHAW

Love and Prayers

*"But I tell you:
Love your enemies and
pray for those who persecute you."*

MATTHEW 5:44 NIV

I recommend to you the importance of intercession in our prayers. We are all selfish by nature, and our selfishness is very apt to stick to us even when we are converted. There is a tendency in us to think only of our own souls, our own spiritual conflicts, our own progress in religion, and to forget others. Against this tendency, we all have need to watch and strive, and not the least in our prayers. We should try to bear in our hearts the whole world, the unbelievers, the body of true believers, the churches, the country in which we live, the congregation to which we belong, the homes in which we visit, the friends, and the relations we are connected with. For each and all of these, we should plead. This is the highest love. They love me best who love me in their prayers.

I commend to you the importance of thankfulness in prayer. It is of mercy that we still live and have opportunities of glorifying God for that free grace by which we live and for that loving-kindness which endures forever. Never was there an eminent saint who was not full of thankfulness. St. Paul hardly ever writes a letter without beginning with thankfulness.

I offer these points for your private consideration. I do it in all humility. I know no one who needs to be reminded of them more than I do myself. But I believe them to be God's own truth, and I desire myself and all I love to feel them more.

J. C. RYLE

Talking to God

Hold fast the form of sound words,
which thou hast heard of me,
in faith and love which is in Christ Jesus.
2 TIMOTHY 1:13 KJV

Sojourner Truth's mother talked to her of God. From these conversations, her mind drew the conclusion that God was a great man and, being located high in the sky, could see all that transpired on the earth. She believed He not only saw but also noted down all her actions in a great book.

At first, she heard Jesus mentioned in reading or speaking, but had received from what she heard no impression that He was any other than an eminent man, like a Washington or a Lafayette. Now He appeared to her so mild, so good, and so every way lovely, and He loved her so much! And, how strange that He had always loved her and she had never known it! And how great a blessing He conferred, in that He should stand between her and God! And God was no longer a terror and a dread to her.

She stopped not to argue the point, even in her own mind, whether He had reconciled her to God or God to herself, being but too happy that God was no longer to her as a consuming fire and Jesus was altogether lovely. Her heart was now full of joy and gladness, as it had been of terror and at one time of despair. In the light of her great happiness, the world was clad in new beauty, the very air sparkled as with diamonds and was redolent of heaven.

SOJOURNER TRUTH

Image of Christ

If you have any encouragement from being united with Christ,
if any comfort from his love, if any fellowship with the Spirit,
if any tenderness and compassion, then make my joy complete
by being like-minded, having the same love,
being one in spirit and purpose.

PHILIPPIANS 2:1–2 NIV

When Christians have sunk down into a low state, they neither have nor can have the same love and confidence toward each other as when they are all alive and active and living holy lives. If Christian love is the love of the image of Christ in His people, then it can be exercised only where that image really exists. Merely knowing that they belong to the church, or seeing them occasionally at the Communion table, will not produce Christian love unless they see the image of Christ.

Nothing but a revival can restore Christian love and confidence among church members. There is no other way to wake up that love of Christians for one another which is sometimes felt, when they have such love as they cannot express. You cannot have such love without confidence, and you cannot restore confidence without such evidence of piety as is seen in a revival.

So if a member of the church finds his brethren cold toward him, there is but one way to restore it. It is by being revived himself, and pouring out from his eyes and from his life the splendor of the image of Christ. This spirit will catch and spread in the church, confidence will be renewed, and brotherly love prevail again.

CHARLES FINNEY

The Best of the Three

And now faith, hope, and love abide, these three;
and the greatest of these is love.

1 CORINTHIANS 13:13 NRSV

The apostle says love is greater than the other two—that is, faith and hope—for the more richly love dwells in a man, the better the man in whom it dwells. For when we ask whether someone is a good man, we are not asking what he believes or hopes, but what he loves. He who loves rightly believes and hopes rightly. Likewise, he who does not love believes in vain, even if what he believes is true. An example of this would be if a man hopes for life eternal—and who is there who does not love that?—and yet does not love righteousness without which no one comes to life eternal.

The true faith of Christ is faith that works through love. And what faith yet lacks in love, it asks that it may receive, it seeks that it may find, and knocks that it may be opened unto it. For faith achieves what the law commands.

If a man begins to be led by the Spirit of God, then the mightier power of love struggles against the power of the flesh. And although there is still in man a power that fights against him, yet the righteous man lives by faith and lives righteously insofar as he does not yield to evil desires, conquering them by his love of righteousness.

AUGUSTINE

Love and the Saint's Rest

Put me on trial, LORD, and cross-examine me.
Test my motives and affections.
For I am constantly aware of your unfailing love,
and I have lived according to your truth.

PSALM 26:2–3 NLT

Christian, believe this and think on it: You shalt be eternally embraced in the arms of that love which was from everlasting and will extend to everlasting. You will be embraced by that love which brought the Son of God's love from heaven to earth, from earth to the cross, from the cross to the grave, from the grave to glory. You will be in the arms of that love which was weary, hungry, tempted, scorned, scourged, buffeted, spit upon, crucified, and pierced; which did fast, pray, teach, heal, weep, sweat, bleed, and die. It will be loving and rejoicing, not loving and sorrowing. Yes, it will make Satan's court ring with the news that the saints are arrived safe at the bosom of Christ, out of the reach of hell forever.

Know this, believer, to your everlasting comfort: If those arms have once embraced you, His love to you will not be as yours was on earth to Him—seldom and cold. He who would not cease nor abate His love for all your enmity, unkind neglects, and churlish resistances, can He cease to love you when He has made you truly lovely? He who keeps you so constant in your love to Him that you can challenge tribulation, distress, persecution, famine, nakedness, peril, or sword, how much more will He Himself be constant!

RICHARD BAXTER

Sunny Love

For I am persuaded that neither. . .
height nor depth, nor any other created thing,
shall be able to separate us
from the love of God which is in Christ Jesus our Lord.
ROMANS 8:38–39 NKJV

The nature of God, as testified by John, is love. Nothing but love can bind the universe together; therefore, God, the life, the spring of all, must be love. Wrath, the opposite of love, is that which disunites; therefore, it cannot really exist in God. There can be nothing in God contrary to love; else, He would be divided. If God's nature is love, then He must be just, faithful, true, merciful, and so on.

The sun shines, not to show itself, but to give light to creation. So the love of God flows in eternal, unchangeable streams upon all creation, to give light, life, and happiness to all. Although the sun shines invariably the same, those in a deep dungeon are kept from receiving its influence or deriving any comfort from it. So, too, the love of God. While Lucifer and his angels remained in a holy state, they received light, life, glory, and happiness from the ever-beaming streams of infinite love. But when they sinned, fear, torment, condemnation, and wrath took place in their hearts and prevented the influence of God's love.

Adam and Eve enjoyed the unceasing streams of love. But sin filled them with fear, torment, condemnation, and wrath. These would have eternally kept them for receiving any influence of eternal love. But Jesus came to destroy the works of the devil, and to prepare our hearts for receiving again the happiness and comfort of God's eternal love.

BARTON W. STONE

Obedient Love

"Choose to love the LORD your God and to obey him and commit yourself to him, for he is your life.
DEUTERONOMY 30:20 NLT

It is a very great thing to obey, to live under a superior and not to be one's own master, for it is much safer to be subject than it is to command. Many live in obedience more from necessity than from love. Such become discontented and dejected on the slightest pretext. They will never gain peace of mind unless they subject themselves wholeheartedly for the love of God.

Go where you may; you will find no rest except in humble obedience to the rule of authority. Dreams of happiness expected from change and different places have deceived many. Everyone, it is true, wishes to do as he pleases and is attracted to those who agree with him. But if God be among us, we must at times give up our opinions for the blessings of peace.

Furthermore, who is so wise that he can have full knowledge of everything? Do not trust too much in your own opinions, but be willing to listen to those of others. If, though your own be good, you accept another's opinion for love of God, you will gain much more merit; for I have often heard that it is safer to listen to advice and take it than to give it. It may happen, too, that while one's own opinion may be good, refusal to agree with others when reason and occasion demand it is a sign of pride and obstinacy.

THOMAS À KEMPIS

Surrendered Love

Therefore, my brothers and sisters,
whom I love and long for,
my joy and crown, stand firm in the Lord in this way,
my beloved.
PHILIPPIANS 4:1 NRSV

What should we think of a betrothed one whose conceit and self-will prevented not only the realization of her own joy but also of his who had given her his heart? She does not care to give up her own rights and possessions and her own will to him who has become necessary for her happiness. She would claim him fully without giving herself fully to him. But it can never be. She may not promise to love and honor if she will not also promise to obey. Until her love reaches that point of surrender, she must remain an unsatisfied lover.

Could there be a sadder proof of the extent and reality of the Fall than the deep-seated distrust of our loving Lord and Master, which makes us hesitate to give ourselves entirely up to Him. The real secret of an unsatisfied life lies too often in an unsurrendered will. And yet how foolish this is!

Do we fancy that we are wiser than He, that our love for ourselves is more tender and strong than His, or that we know ourselves better than He does? What would be the feelings of an earthly bridegroom if he discovered that his bride-elect were dreading to marry him, for fear that when he had the power, he should render her life insupportable? Yet how many of the Lord's redeemed ones treat Him just so! No wonder they are neither happy nor satisfied!

HUDSON TAYLOR

Fortress of Love

Keep me as the apple of the eye,
hide me under the shadow of thy wings.
PSALM 17:8 KJV

Our ignorance of God gives us all sorts of wrong ideas about Him. We think He is an angry judge who is on the watch for our slightest faults, or a harsh taskmaster determined to exact from us the uttermost service, or a self-absorbed deity demanding His full measure of honor and glory, or a far-off sovereign concerned only with His own affairs and indifferent to our welfare. Who can wonder that such a God can neither be loved nor trusted? Who could expect Christians with such ideas concerning Him to be anything but full of discomfort and misery?

But I can assert boldly and without fear of contradiction that it is impossible for anyone who really knows God to have such uncomfortable thoughts about Him. Plenty of outward discomforts there may be and many earthly sorrows and trials, but through them all, the soul that knows God cannot but dwell inwardly in a fortress of perfect peace. If we would really listen unto God, which means not only hearing Him but believing what we hear, we could not fail to know that, just because He is God, He cannot do other than care for us as He cares for the apple of His eye. All that tender love and divine wisdom can do for our welfare must be and will be unfailingly done. Not a single loophole for worry or fear is left to the soul that knows God.

HANNAH WHITALL SMITH

Whole-Hearted Love

*"If you want to be my follower you must love me
more than your own father and mother, wife and children,
brothers and sisters—yes, more than your own life.
Otherwise, you cannot be my disciple."*
LUKE 14:26 NLT

In Jacksonville at the house in which I stayed, my attention was attracted by a little boy, who bore a different name from the household. Yet, in all respects he was treated as one of themselves.

I asked the lady of the house who he was. She told me the father of the boy was a missionary in India. Some years before, the father and mother had come home with their five children to have them educated. It was arranged that the children should be received into various families—treated as part of them—and that the father and mother should return to India. The mother came to this friend's home and stayed a few days along with the boy. The night before she had to leave, sitting with the lady of the house, she told her how she wished to leave him without a tear at parting. The struggle this would cost, the lady well knew.

Next morning, passing the door of the mother's room, the lady overheard a sobbing, struggling prayer for strength to do what was on her heart to do. In a short time, the mother came down with a smiling, cheerful face; and looking so, she took leave of her boy. She went with her husband to India. A short year later, she met her Savior. And would not a welcome await her there, who had so loved Him here and so cheerfully served Him?

DWIGHT LYMAN MOODY

Love and the Dove

And the Holy Spirit descended on him
in bodily form like a dove.
And a voice came from heaven:
"You are my Son, whom I love;
with you I am well pleased."

LUKE 3:22 NIV

We may learn by the Word of God that the Godhead does subsist in love. I think it is plainly revealed to us that the Holy Spirit is that love. Seeing we have God's Spirit dwelling in us, we have God dwelling in us. It is evident also by this that God's dwelling in us and His love being in us are the same thing. The scripture seems in many places to speak of love in Christians as if it were the same with the Spirit of God in them. The apostle argues that Christian liberty does not make way for fulfilling the lusts of the flesh in biting and devouring one another and the like, because a principle of love that was the fulfilling of the law would prevent it.

This is confirmed by the symbol of the Holy Spirit; that is, a dove, which is the emblem of love or a lover and is so used in scripture, and especially often so in Solomon's Song (Song of Songs). The dove alone of all birds was appointed to be offered in sacrifice because of its innocence and because it is the emblem of love, love being the most acceptable sacrifice to God. It was under this similitude that the Holy Spirit descended from the Father on Christ at His baptism, signifying the infinite love of the Father to the Son.

JONATHAN EDWARDS

Triumphant Love

My God in his steadfast love will meet me;
my God will let me look in triumph on my enemies.
PSALM 59:10 NRSV

Would you know the blessing of all blessings? It is this God of love dwelling in your soul and killing every root of bitterness that is the pain and torment of every earthly, selfish love. For all wants are satisfied, all disorders of nature are removed, no life is any longer a burden, every day is a day of peace. Everything you meet becomes a help to you because everything you see or do is all done in the sweet, gentle element of love. For as love has no selfish purposes, wills nothing but its own increase, so everything is as oil to its flame.

Everything naturally helps love to live in its own way and to bring forth its own work. The spirit of love does not want to be rewarded, honored, or esteemed. Its only desire is to propagate itself and become the blessing and happiness of everyone who wants it. Therefore, it meets wrath, evil, hatred, and opposition with the same will as light meets the darkness, only to overcome it. Did you want to avoid the wrath and ill-will or to gain the favour of any persons, you might easily miss your goals; but if you have no will but to all goodness, everything you meet, be it what it will, must be forced to be assistant to you. For the wrath of an enemy, the treachery of a friend, and every other evil only helps the spirit of love to be more triumphant.

WILLIAM LAW

The Bridegroom's Friends

*In love of the brethren be tenderly affectioned one to another;
in honor preferring one another.*

ROMANS 12:10 ASV

If we are married to Jesus Christ, we shall not only reverence the bridegroom, but we shall also love and honor the bridegroom's friends. Jesus says, "By this, shall all men know that you are My disciples, if you love one another."

"By this we know," says the beloved disciple, "that we have passed from death to life because we love the brethren." Observe love for the brethren without limit of whatever denomination. This was the case of the primitive Christians. They were all of one heart and of one mind. It was said of them (Oh, that it could be said of us!): "See how these Christians love one another!"

They were of the same spirit as a good woman of Scotland was, who saw a great multitude coming from various parts to receive the blessed sacrament. She saluted them with a "Come in, ye blessed of the Lord, I have a house that will hold a hundred of you, and a heart that will hold ten thousand." Let us go and do likewise.

Once more: Persons who are married, take one another for better or for worse, for richer or for poorer, to love and to cherish each other in sickness and in health. And if we are married to Jesus Christ, we shall be willing to bear His cross as well as to wear His crown. They will cry out, "Crown Him, crown Him," when others are crying out, "Crucify Him, crucify Him."

GEORGE WHITEFIELD

The Call of Love

"But the hour is coming, and now is,
when the true worshipers will worship
the Father in spirit and truth;
for the Father is seeking such to worship Him."
JOHN 4:23 NKJV

There is no life like that of one who lives in the favor of God. To receive everything as a gift preserves the mind from self-righteous pride and from self-accusing despair. It makes the heart grow warm with grateful love. It creates a feeling in the soul that is infinitely more acceptable to God than anything that can possibly come of slavish fear. Those who hope to be saved by trying to do their best know nothing of that devout joy in God, which comes with salvation given freely. The slavish spirit of self-salvation is no match for the joyous spirit of adoption.

Faith is spiritual, and God who is a spirit delights in it for that reason. Years of prayer saying, church going, or ceremonies may only be displeasing in the sight of Jehovah if done with self-righteous pride. But a glance from the eye of true faith is spiritual, and it is therefore dear to Him.

Your own heart will not prosper unless it is filled with intense concern to bless your fellow men. The life of your soul lies in faith. Its health lies in love. He who does not long to lead others to Jesus has never been under the spell of love himself. Get to the work of the Lord—the work of love. Begin at home. Next, visit your neighbors. Then, enlighten the village or the street in which you live.

CHARLES HADDON SPURGEON

Excessive Love?

I love those who love me,
and those who seek me diligently find me.
PROVERBS 8:17 NRSV

You may love the world but receive hatred for your love. Would it not annoy one to lay out money upon a piece of ground that, instead of bringing forth corn or grapes, should yield nothing but nettles? So it is with all earthly things. We love them, and they bring nettles that sting. We meet with nothing but disappointment. While we love the things of the earth, fire comes out of this bramble to devour us; but if we love God, He will not return hatred for love. God may chastise, but He cannot hate. Every believer is part of Christ, and God can as well hate Christ as hate a believer.

You may overlove the things of the earth. You may love wine too much and silver too much, but you cannot love God too much. If it were possible to exceed, excess here would be a virtue, but it is because of our sin that we cannot love God enough. So it may be said, "How weak is our love to God!" If we could love God far more than we do, yet it would not be proportional to His worth. There is no danger of excess in our love to God.

You may love worldly things, and they die and leave you. Riches take wings. Relations drop away. There is nothing here abiding. But if you love God, He is called a sun for comfort, a rock for eternity. He abides forever. We see it is better to love God than the world.

THOMAS WATSON

Active Love

Be kind and compassionate to one another,
forgiving each other, just as in Christ God forgave you.
EPHESIANS 4:32 NIV

We hear much of love to God, but Christ spoke much of love to man. The supreme thing, love, is not a thing at all, but the giving of a further finish to the extensive words and acts that make up the sum of every common day.

Love is patience. This is the normal attitude of love. Love is calm. It is ready to do its work when the summons comes, but meantime it is wearing the ornament of a meek and quiet spirit. Love suffers long. For love understands and therefore waits.

Love is active. Have you ever noticed how much of Christ's life was spent in doing kind things? Run over it with that in view, and you will find that He spent a great proportion of His time simply in making people happy—in doing good turns to people. What God has put in our power is the happiness of those about us, and that is largely to be secured by our being kind to them.

"The greatest thing," says someone, "a man can do for his heavenly Father is to be kind to some of His other children." I wonder why it is that we are not all kinder than we are. The world needs it. How easily it is done. How instantaneously it acts. How infallibly it is remembered. How superabundantly it pays itself back—for there is no debtor in the world so honorable, so superbly honorable, as love. Love is success, love is happiness, love is life.

HENRY DRUMMOND

Teaching Children Love

> *[Jesus] said to them, "Let the little children come to me,
> and do not hinder them, for the kingdom of God
> belongs to such as these."*
>
> MARK 10:14 NIV

To win a child's love and admiration and hope is to grip his entire being and conquer all the powers of his soul. If Jesus, the great Lover, can win these, the pursuit will be followed by the wedding. How can we so represent Him that this triumph shall be won?

We live by love. By admiration, too! Our children must not only find in Jesus their Savior; they must find in Him their hero, too. Say to yourself, "I will so present my Master as a hero as to attract the adoring homage of my children." Would you be without any heroic subject matter? Your eyes are closed and sealed if you do not see the heroic glowing upon every page of the sacred story! His splendid bravery; His tremendous hatred of all meanness and sin; His magnificent solitude in the night; His strenuous refusal of a popular crown, when the sovereignty would mean compromise with the powers of darkness! Let these be unfolded with the same tremendous effort and vivid realization which we make when we seek to unveil the heroism of earthly achievers, and our boys and girls will go on their knees before the unveiling with reverent admiration and homage.

The glorious Lord will become the children's staff of life. Their worship will become their desire. Their loving will become their longing. Their admiration will become aspiration. Their faith will become their hope.

JOHN HENRY JOWETT

Unfolding Love

*For this very reason, make every effort to add to your
faith goodness; and to goodness, knowledge; and to knowledge,
self-control; and to self-control, perseverance; and to perseverance,
godliness; and to godliness, brotherly kindness;
and to brotherly kindness, love.*

2 PETER 1:5–7 NIV

So long as sin is in the world, love must make war against it. The
first step of love is the offer of pardon through the atoning blood
of Jesus Christ. But a pardoned criminal is not necessarily a
good citizen. Pardon has changed his relation to the law but not
his hostility toward the governor. A change must take place
within him.

The second step in the conquest of the soul by love divine
is regeneration, or the New Birth. It is a change wrought within
the soul by the power of the Holy Spirit, creating within the soul
a new spiritual life, a life of loyalty and love. It implies future
germination, growth, and bearing of fruit. It is to spread its
branches until it fills the heart, and by absorbing all the fertility
of the soil and by completely overshadowing all other plants,
destroys their life.

Up to this point, the old nature, though dying, has lingered
and mingled with the new. Dying unto sin and living unto God
have coexisted. The destructive and the reconstructive processes
have gone on side by side. There is an absolute end to the former when there is nothing more to be destroyed. There is no
end to the latter. The positive work of spiritual adornment,
strength, and growth must go on so long as the soul is capable
of advancement.

DANIEL STEELE

The Devil Despises Love

This is how we know who. . .the children of the devil are:
Anyone who does not do what is right is not a child of God;
nor is anyone who does not love his brother.

1 JOHN 3:10 NIV

About the time that I first began to preach, I lived for about two months in free lodgings provided for students of divinity in an orphanage. About that time, I was still so weak in faith that I fell repeatedly into open sins. Yet, I could not continue in them, no, not even for a few days without sorrow of heart, confession before God, and fleeing to the blood of the Lamb.

I formed a close friendship with a brother who was also a divinity student. Because we loved one another so much and were so happy in one another's company, we thought to rent lodging to share, and that in this way we might mutually help one another. Accordingly, I left the free lodgings in the orphanage and lived with him.

Unfortunately, we were not aware that because God is greatly glorified by the love and union of His people, Satan particularly hates it and will, therefore, in every possible way seek to divide them. We ought to have especially prayed that the Lord would keep us together in brotherly love. Instead, I do not think that we at all feared disunion, as we loved one another so much. Our great adversary soon got an advantage by our neglecting prayer concerning this point, and we were disunited. Unity was not fully restored between us until after we had been for some time separated.

GEORGE MÜLLER

Stand on Love

Don't just pretend that you love others. Really love them.
Hate what is wrong. Stand on the side of the good.
ROMANS 12:9 NLT

The prophet Nehemiah had a perfect right to take tax money from the people, but he did not. Not a word could be said even by his critics, if he did. He was doing a priceless work and might justly claim his support. On the other hand, the people were very poor, and he would have a larger influence over them if he were prepared to stand on their level and to share with them.

Often we must forego our evident rights and liberties in order to influence others for Christ. Do not always stand on your rights. Instead, live for others, making any sacrifice in order to save some—even as Christ loved us and gave Himself for us. What ought we to do for love? Love is more relentless than law. Its demands are more stringent and searching. Are we doing as much for love of Jesus as generations before did simply out of duty? But what Jesus does get is infinitely sweet to Him insofar as love prompts it.

All around you, people are doing things that they say are perfectly legitimate. They call you narrow-minded and bigoted because you do not join with them. They are always arguing with you in an effort to prove you are wrong. But your supreme law is your attitude to your Master: "I cannot do otherwise for the love of Jesus."

F. B. MEYER

True Christian Love

And watch as I take those who call themselves true believers
but are nothing of the kind,
pretenders whose true membership is in the club of Satan—
watch as I strip off their pretensions
and they're forced to acknowledge it's you that I've loved.

REVELATION 3:9 TM

I held my Sabbath school at the house of a free colored man, whose name I deem it imprudent to mention. I had at one time over forty scholars, and those of the right sort, ardently desiring to learn. We loved each other, and to leave them at the close of the Sabbath was a severe cross indeed.

They not only possessed loving hearts but also brave ones. I loved them with a love stronger than anything I have experienced since. It is sometimes said that we slaves do not love and confide in each other. In answer to this assertion, I can say I never loved any or confided in any people more than my fellow-slaves. I believe we would have died for each other.

What I have said respecting and against religion, I mean strictly to apply to the slaveholding religion of this land and with no possible reference to Christianity proper. I love the pure, peaceable, and impartial Christianity of Christ. Sincerely and earnestly hoping that this little book may hasten the glad day of deliverance to the millions of my brethren in bonds—faithfully relying upon the power of truth, love, and justice for success in my humble efforts, I subscribe myself—Frederick Douglass.

FREDERICK DOUGLASS

Receive and Give Love

*"I have obeyed my Father's commands
and remain in his love."*
JOHN 15:10 NIV

Jesus has said that by obedience we live in His love. He tells that this was the way He lived in the Father's love. As the vine, so is the branch. His life, strength, and joy had been in the love of the Father.

He was made like us in all things, that we might be like Him in all things. He opened up a path in which we may walk even as He walked. He took our human nature to teach us how to wear it. He showed us how obedience is the only way to live in the favor of God and enter into His glory. And now He comes to instruct and encourage us, and asks us to keep His commandments, even as He kept His Father's commandments and lived in His love.

God's will is the very center of His divine perfection. As revealed in His commandments, it opens up the way for us, His creation, to grow into the likeness of the Creator. In accepting and doing His will, we rise into fellowship with Him. Our life is to be the exact complement of Christ's life.

Dear Lord, I am only beginning to comprehend how exactly the life of the vine is to be that of the branch, too. You are the vine, because the Father loved You and poured His love through You. My life as a branch is to be like You, a receiving and a giving out of heavenly love.

ANDREW MURRAY

Tears of Love

Jesus wept. Then the Jews said, "See how he loved him!"
But some of them said, "Could not he who opened the eyes
of the blind man have kept this man from dying?"

JOHN 11:35–37 NIV

Jesus wept at the tomb of Lazarus to show us that it was no sin to shed a tear of love and resignation at the grave of a deceased friend. He wept to see what havoc sin had made in the world and how it had reduced man—by making him subject to death—to a level with the beasts that perish.

Above all, He wept at the foreknowledge of the people's unbelief. He wept to think how many then present would not only not believe on Him but would be hardened and have their prejudices increased more and more against Him, though He should raise Lazarus from the dead before their eyes.

For then the bystanders said, "Behold, how He loved him." But all were not well affected at seeing Jesus weep! For we are told that some of them said, "Could not this man, who opened the eyes of the blind, have caused that even this man should not have died?" One would imagine that Satan himself could scarce have uttered a more perverse speech. "Is not this a sufficient proof that He is a cheat? Is it likely that He really helped others when He could not help His own friend?"

How patient ought the servants of our Lord to be! And how may they expect to be censured and have their good deeds questioned!

GEORGE WHITEFIELD

Love and Salvation

May those who love your salvation always say,
"The LORD be exalted!"
PSALM 40:16 NIV

Will you say that you are afraid to come to God? Your fear is needless. You shall not be cast out, if you will but come in the way of faith in Christ. Our God is not an austere man. Our Father in heaven is full of mercy, love, and grace. I yield to none in desire to promote the love, mercy, and tenderness of God the Father.

We know that God is holy. We know He is just. We believe that He can be angry with them who go on still in sin. But we also believe that to those who draw near to Him in Christ Jesus, He is most merciful, most loving, most tender, and most compassionate. We tell you that the cross of Jesus Christ was the result and consequence of that love.

The cross was not the cause and reason of God's mercy, but the result and consequence of the everlasting love of God the Father, God the Son, and God the Holy Ghost toward a poor, lost, and bankrupt world. Draw near in faith by that living way, Christ Jesus to the Father. Think not for a moment that in drawing near to God the Father by Christ, God the Father will not receive you. He will receive you gladly. As the father did to the prodigal son when he ran to meet him—fell on his neck and kissed him—so will God the Father do to that soul who draws near to Him in the name of Christ.

J. C. RYLE

Love and Sacrifice

If I. . .surrender my body to the flames,
but have not love,
I gain nothing.

1 CORINTHIANS 13:3 NIV

Paul contrasts love with sacrifice and martyrdom. And I beg the little band of would-be missionaries—and I have the honor to call some of you by this name for the first time—to remember that though you give your bodies to be burned and have not love, it profits nothing. Nothing! You can take nothing greater to the heathen world than the impression and reflection of the love of God upon your own character.

Love is the universal language. It will take you years to speak in Chinese or in the dialects of India. From the day you land in a foreign country, that language of love, understood by all, will be pouring forth its unconscious eloquence. It is not your words but your character that is the message.

In the heart of Africa, I have come across men and women who remembered the only white man they ever saw before—David Livingstone. As you cross his footsteps in that continent, men's faces light up as they speak of the kind doctor who passed there years ago. They could not understand him, but they felt the love that beat in his heart. Take into your new sphere of labor that simple charm, and your lifework must succeed. You can take nothing greater; you need take nothing less. You may take every accomplishment, you may be braced for every sacrifice, but if you have not love, it will profit you and the cause of Christ nothing.

HENRY DRUMMOND

Affectionate Love

*Surely goodness and love will follow me all the days of my life,
and I will dwell in the house of the LORD forever.*
PSALM 23:6 NIV

Great pains had been taken by my parents to instill the doctrines of Christianity into my mind, and I had no difficulty in understanding the theory of our free salvation by the atonement of our Savior. I really began to feel the necessity and value of a personal application of the provisions of that atonement to my own case.

The change was like what may be supposed would take place were it possible to cure a case of "color blindness." The perfect freeness with which the pardon of all our guilt is offered in God's Book drew forth feelings of affectionate love to Him who bought us with His blood. A sense of deep obligation to Him for His mercy has influenced my conduct ever since. But I shall not again refer to the inner spiritual life, which I believe then began, nor do I intend to specify with any prominence the evangelistic labors to which the love of Christ has since impelled me. I will speak, not so much of what has been done, as of what still remains to be performed, before the gospel can be said to be preached to all nations.

In the glow of love, which Christianity inspires, I soon resolved to devote my life to the alleviation of human misery. Turning this idea over in my mind, I therefore set myself to obtain a medical education, in order to be qualified for that enterprise.

DAVID LIVINGSTONE

Love without Doubt

For the one who doubts is like a wave of the sea,
driven and tossed by the wind.

JAMES 1:6 NRSV

I knew one devoted Christian whose religious life was one long torment of doubt. He thought that perfect confidence could only arise from a feeling that he was good enough to be worthy of God's love, but he felt this would be presumptive. But our confidence does not come from our own goodness but from the goodness of God. While we never can be and never ought to be satisfied with goodness in ourselves, there cannot possibly be any question to one who believes the Bible as to the all-sufficiency of God's goodness.

A wavering Christian is a Christian who trusts in the love of God one day and doubts it the next, and who is alternately happy or miserable. He mounts to the hilltop of joy at one time, only to descend at another time into the valley of despair. He is driven to and fro by every wind of doctrine, is always striving and never attaining, and is a prey to each changing influence, caused by his state of health or by the influences around him or even by the state of the weather.

If you believe one day that God loves you and is favorable to you and the next day doubt His love, and fear that He is angry with you, does it not stand to reason that you must waver in your experience from joy to misery? Only a steadfast faith in His love and care could give you an unwavering experience.

HANNAH WHITALL SMITH

Love at the Core

May the Lord direct your hearts to the love of God
and to the steadfastness of Christ.
2 THESSALONIANS 3:5 NRSV

Love is the very heart and spirit of the Christian religion. Love is an expansion of soul by which a Christian breathes after God as the supreme and sovereign good. Love sets the soul going toward God, as the wings by which we fly to heaven. By love, we cleave to God as the needle to the loadstone.

We cannot love that which we do not know. That our love may be drawn forth to God, we must know that He has a fullness of grace to cleanse us and a fullness of glory to crown us. He has a fullness not only of sufficiency but also of redundancy. He is a sea of goodness without bottom and banks. God has an innate propensity to dispense mercy and grace. He drops them as honey from the honeycomb.

We set a high value upon God as being the most sublime and infinite good. The stars vanish when the sun appears. All other things vanish in our thoughts when the sun of righteousness shines in His full splendor. The soul who loves God rejoices in Him as in his treasure, and rests in Him as in his center. The heart is so set upon God that it desires no more. We desire that His interest may prevail. Our prayer is that His name may be held in honor and that His gospel, which is the rod of His strength, may, like Aaron's rod, blossom and bring forth fruit.

THOMAS WATSON

Inseparable Love

Many waters cannot quench love;
rivers cannot wash it away.
If one were to give all the wealth of his house for love,
it would be utterly scorned.

SONG OF SONGS 8:7 NIV

Love is inseparable when a man's mind is inflamed with great love and clings to Christ by inseparable thought. Such a man does not allow Christ to be any moment out of his mind. As though he were bound in the heart, he thinks upon and draws his spirit from God. Therefore, the love of Christ so grows in the heart of the lover of God and despiser of the world that it may not be overcome by any other affection or love. When a man clings to Christ continuously, thinking upon Him, forgetting Him for no other occasion, then man's love is said to be inseparable and everlasting.

Love moves a soul in which it dwells to sing of his beloved. Love unites the lover and the beloved. Love is the desire of the heart, ever thinking on that which it loves. Love is a stirring of the soul to love God for Himself and all other things for God. This love puts out all other love that is against God's will. Love is a right will, turned from all earthly things, and joined to God without departing, accompanied with the fire of the Holy Spirit.

In this manner shall a lover of Jesus Christ be. He shall so burn in love that he shall be wholly turned into the fire of love. He shall so shine in virtues that no part of him will be dark in vices.

JOHN WYCLIFFE

Love's Counterfeit

Flee the evil desires of youth, and pursue righteousness,
faith, love and peace, along with those who
call on the Lord out of a pure heart.

2 TIMOTHY 2:22 NIV

Lust is the devil's counterfeit of love. There is nothing more beautiful on earth than a pure love, and there is nothing so blighting as lust. I do not know of a quicker, shorter way down to hell than by adultery and the kindred sins. The Bible says that with the heart man believeth unto righteousness, but lust will drive all natural affection out of a man's heart. For the sake of some vile harlot, a man will trample on the feelings and entreaties of a sainted mother, beautiful wife, and godly sister.

Young man, are you leading an impure life? Are you fit for the kingdom of heaven? You know very well that you are not. When you look upon that pure wife or mother, you say, "What a vile wretch I am! The harlot is bringing me down to an untimely and dishonored grave."

May God show us what a fearful sin it is! The idea of making light of it! I do not know of any sin that will make a man run down to ruin more quickly. I am appalled when I think of what is going on in the world, of so many young men living impure lives, and talking about the virtue of women as if it didn't amount to anything. This sin is coming in upon us like a dark shroud at the present day.

DWIGHT LYMAN MOODY

Love and Language

Out of the same mouth proceedeth blessing and cursing.
My brethren, these things ought not so to be.

JAMES 3:10 KJV

People often ask, "How can I keep from swearing?" I will tell you. If God puts His love into your heart, you will have no desire to curse Him. I was preaching one day in the open air, when a man drove up in a fine carriage, and after listening a little while, he put the whip to his fine-looking steed, and away he went.

Later, I visited him at his home. "I am told that God has blessed you above all men in this part of the country. He has given you wealth, a beautiful Christian wife, and seven lovely children. I do not know if it is true, but I hear that all He gets in return is cursing and blasphemy."

The man said, "What you say is true. But you don't know anything about a businessman's troubles. When he is harassed and tormented the whole time, he can't help swearing."

"Yes," I said, "he can. I used to swear myself." I began to tell him about Christ in the heart and how that would take the temptation to swear out of a man. At the next church prayer meeting, the man was there. He said, "My friends, I want to have you pray for my salvation."

Thirty-odd years later I spoke to the man. He said, "I have never had a desire to swear since then. It was all taken away." He was not only converted but became an earnest, active Christian, and all these years has been serving God.

DWIGHT LYMAN MOODY

Teach Children Love

Jesus said, "Let the little children come to me,
and do not hinder them,
for the kingdom of heaven belongs to such as these."
MATTHEW 19:14 NIV

Dear Alice Hepworth,

Please accept the Bible which has been waiting for you so long. I need not tell you again, my dear child, to whom I wish all the highest blessings of that book which tells us how Christ loves us so much that He will even come and dwell in us and make us live and love like Himself.

Perhaps that very gain of a certain assured progress in essentials at Lea Infant School will enable the nice lessons you once practiced in St. Thomas' Hospital to be introduced. I am speaking of the little moral tales that you used to give your scholars once a week at St. Thomas.

Would there be time now for giving the religious morning instruction with little talks? Perhaps you always do this. I do not know exactly what the children's religious instruction is. It may be necessary to give a good deal of learning scripture by heart. But then if scripture is really to tell on the children's lives—the only thing that Christ cares about and that Christ came to live and die for—and still lives for—the mother must explain by little stories and illustrations.

Do the children know that Christ loved little children and that He was always meek and gentle? Are they more or less gentle and loving with each other? Or do they tell tales of each other instead of themselves? God bless you and all your children. Ever yours sincerely, Florence Nightingale.

FLORENCE NIGHTINGALE

Cheerful and Obedient Love

I prayed to the LORD my God and confessed:
"O Lord, the great and awesome God,
who keeps his covenant of love
with all who love him and obey his commands."

DANIEL 9:4 NIV

In principle, obedience to God is the same quality as obedience to earthly parents. It implies the giving up of one's own way and following that of another. Commands from our heavenly Father are directed by love. All such commands are in the best interests of those who are commanded. God's commands are issued neither in severity nor tyranny. They are always issued in love and in our interests, and so it is proper for us to heed and obey them.

Obedience is love fulfilling every command, and love expressing itself. Obedience, therefore, is not a hard demand made upon us. Love delights to obey and please whom it loves. There are no hardships in love. There are no impossible tasks for love. Obedience runs ahead of all and every command. It is love obeying by anticipation. They greatly err, and even sin, who declare that people are bound to commit iniquity, either because of environment or heredity or tendency. God's commands are ways of pleasantness, and their paths peace.

Loving obedience puts us where we can ask anything in His name with the assurance that He will do it. Loving obedience brings us into the prayer realm and makes us beneficiaries of the wealth of Christ and of the riches of His grace. Cheerful obedience to God qualifies us to pray effectually. This obedience must be loving, constant, always doing the Father's will, and cheerfully following the path of God's commands.

EDWARD MCKENDREE BOUNDS

Love's Foundation

Righteousness and justice are the foundation of your throne;
steadfast love and faithfulness go before you.
PSALM 89:14 NRSV

Our minds cannot come to rest in tranquillity unless they arrive at the free love of God. Since we are not to seek the base of our salvation anywhere but in Christ, we must try to find out where He came to us from and why He was offered up to be our Savior. Scripture distinctly teaches both truths: Faith in Christ means life to all people, and Christ had this life because God loved mankind and would not let us perish. When it is a question of the source of our salvation, we must consider the inborn and wicked ambition of our nature, which traps us into the devilish fancy that we deserve to be saved. Therefore, we imagine that God is good to us because He judges us worthy of His favor. But scripture praises everywhere His pure and unmixed mercy, which does away with all merit.

Christ means to do nothing else than establish the love of God as the foundation of our salvation. When we try to go beyond this, the Spirit Himself slams the door in our face. God's love is founded in His own will and purpose. Christ does not declare that He was led to deliver us because He found us worthy of such a blessing. On the contrary, He attributes the glory of our deliverance solely to His love. Faith looks to Christ rightly when it sees in Him the heart of God overflowing with love.

JOHN CALVIN

Love and the First Commandment

You shall love the LORD your God with all your heart,
and with all your soul, and with all your might.

DEUTERONOMY 6:5 NRSV

It is not possible to sin any sin at all, except a person break the first commandment beforehand. Now the first commandment is divided into two verses: "Your Lord God is one God; and you shalt love your Lord God with all your heart, with all your soul, with all your power, and with all your might." The whole cause why I sin against any secondary decree is that this love is not in my heart. If this love were written in my heart and were it full and perfect in my soul, it would keep my heart from consenting unto any sin.

The whole and only cause why this love is not written in our hearts is that we believe not the first part that "our Lord God is one God." He made all and rules all, and whatsoever is done to me, whether it be good or bad, is yet His will and that He only is the Lord who rules and does it. If my heart believed and felt the infinite benefits and kindness of God toward me, and understood and earnestly believed the many covenants of mercy wherewith God has bound Himself to be mine wholly with all His power, love, mercy, and might, then should I love Him with all my heart, soul, power, and might. Because of that love I should always keep His commandments.

WILLIAM TYNDALE

Keep Love Burning

*"And because of the increase of lawlessness,
the love of many will grow cold."*
MATTHEW 24:12 NRSV

You who have love to God, labor to preserve it. As you would have God's love to be continued to you, let your love be continued to Him. Love, as fire, will be ready to go out. Satan labors to blow out this flame, and through neglect of duty we lose it. A tender baby's body without clothes is likely to get cold. So when we leave off duty, we cool in our love to God. Of all graces, love is most apt to fade; therefore, we need to be the more careful to preserve it. It is sad to see believers declining in their love to God.

When duties of religion are performed in a dead, formal matter, this is a sad symptom of decay in our first love. If the strings of a violin are slack, the violin can never make good music. Believers who grow slack in duty can never make any harmonious sound in God's ears. When spiritual action is slow and the pulse of the soul beats low, it is a sign that Christians have left their first love.

Watch your hearts every day. Take notice of the first declining in love. Observe yourselves when you begin to grow dull and listless, and use all means for quickening. Be much in prayer, meditation, and holy discussion. When the fire is going out, you throw on fuel. So when the flame of your love is going out, make use of gospel principles and promises as fuel to keep the fire of your love burning.

THOMAS WATSON

Truly Live in Love

Do not lag in zeal, be ardent in spirit, serve the Lord.

ROMANS 12:11 NRSV

If we mean truly to live, we have got to find time for the highest of all exercises, meditation upon the eternal things of God. We have to go to Calvary and reverently contemplate the unveilings of redemptive grace. How many of the people ever open their Bibles for private meditation from Monday morning to Saturday night? Love and reverence are not the uncertain products of chance. They are the sure and stately products of thought. If our thought is steadily directed, love and reverence will follow.

Let us go, then, into the school of Calvary with eyes and ears alert and activated that we may see and hear. We shall get into the secret places of the Most High, and we shall observe the marvelous unveiling of infinite love. We shall hear that wondrous Christian gospel that Pascal heard, and which melted his heart, and hallowed all his years: "I love you more ardently than you have loved your sin."

I know how I have sinned. I know how I have clung to my sin. I know how I have pursued it at any cost. And, now in the school of Calvary, my Master takes up my strenuous and overwhelming passion for sin, and contrasts it with His passion for me: "I love you more ardently than you have loved your sin." If in some quiet moment that grand message swept through our souls in heavenly strains, we should fall in love with the lover.

JOHN HENRY JOWETT

The Redeemer's Affection

He who loves his brother abides in the light,
and there is no cause for stumbling in him.
1 JOHN 2:10 NKJV

Through eternal ages, the Son of God became in the fullness of time the Son of Man. He became the Light of the world as well as the Lamb of God. In each aspect of doing the will as well as the work of God, He thus revealed the wondrous love and grace of the Father and His own perfect Sonship. The Father's will included Christ's glad reception of all who come to Him, His meeting all their needs, saving, sanctifying, satisfying, keeping, raising up at the last day, His giving Himself for, and giving Himself to all those given to Him of the Father.

Time would fail us to count the various objects and acts of typical service that were all fulfilled in Him. The Son of God is the Kinsman who has the right to redeem, the Friend who sticketh closer than a brother, the One who has come not only to be the Light of the world, but in a special sense to be the Light of His own redeemed ones.

The Friend who sticketh closer than a brother is precious at all times, but never so valued as in times of adversity. The very expression "the Light of the world" tells us of the darkness not only around but also within. The shining of the face of the Son dispels the darkness and the gloom, manifests the presence of the Friend in need, and shows us the Redeemer.

HUDSON TAYLOR

Our Love

> *For men shall be lovers of their own selves,*
> *covetous, boasters, proud, blasphemers,*
> *disobedient to parents, unthankful, unholy.*
>
> 2 TIMOTHY 3:2 KJV

It is common for equals to love and for superiors to be beloved. But for the King of princes, for the Son of God, for Jesus Christ to love man—this is amazing. Those beloved by Him are called transgressors, sinners, and enemies. Yet this great, this high, this glorious person loves such.

The love that is in Christ is different from the love that is in us. Love in us is a passion of the soul and, being such, is subject to ebb and flow and be extreme in both ways. For whatever is a passion of the soul, whether love or hatred, joy or fear, is more likely to exceed or come short than to keep within its due bounds. Often that which is loved today is hated tomorrow. Yes, and that which should be loved with bounds of moderation is loved to the drowning of both soul and body in perdition and destruction.

Besides, love in us is likely to choose to itself undue and unlawful objects. Love in us requires that something pleasing and delightful be in the object loved. Love in us decays if the object of our love disappoints our expectation. All this we know to be true. Our love is weak, unorderly, fails and miscarries, either by being too much or too little. The love that is in Christ is not love of the same nature as is love in us. Love in Him is essential to His being.

JOHN BUNYAN

The Measure of Love

And this is love: that we walk in obedience to his commands.
As you have heard from the beginning,
his command is that you walk in love.
2 JOHN 6 NIV

We must be careful that our love to God is sweet, even, and full of tranquillity, having in it no violence. A new beginner in religion has passionate desires. But they must not be the measure of his actions. He must consider his spiritual strength, and not go to storm a strong fort or attack a potent enemy or do heroic actions that are fit for giants in religion. Indiscreet and untimely actions are the rocks of religion against which tender spirits often suffer shipwreck.

Let our love be prudent and without illusion; that is, that it express itself in such instances which God has chosen or which we choose ourselves by proportion to His rules and measures. Love turns into doting when religion turns into superstition. No degree of love can be imprudent, but the expressions may. We cannot love God too much, but we may proclaim it in an indecent manner.

Let our love be firm, constant, and inseparable. Let it not be coming and returning like the tide, but descending like a never-failing river, ever running into the ocean of divine excellency, passing on in the channels of duty and a constant obedience. Let our love never cease to be what it is until it is turned into sea and vastness, even the immensity of a blessed eternity.

JEREMY TAYLOR

Rescue the Lost

*He has rescued us from the dominion of darkness
and brought us into the kingdom of the Son he loves.*

COLOSSIANS 1:13 NIV

It is not surprising that God made such sacrifice to save us.
Listen to a humble father as he relates an incident:

My name is Anthony Hunt. About ten years ago, I rode back
home after selling cattle in town and buying a doll for Dolly, my
little girl. Night set in. A storm that had been brewing broke,
and the rain fell in torrents. Suddenly, I heard a little cry, like a
child's voice. I couldn't see a thing. Then I became suspicious. I
thought it might be a trap. How could a real child be out on the
prairie in such a night at such an hour?

Sure enough, I found a little dripping child bundled in wet
clothes. I tucked the little soaked child under my coat as best I
could. When I arrived home, I saw something was the matter. The
room was full of neighbors and my wife amid them weeping.

"Oh, don't tell him," she said. "It will kill him."

"What is it, neighbors?" I cried.

One asked, "What's that in your arms?"

"A poor lost child," I said. "I found it on the road." And I
lifted the sleeping child and saw the face of my little Dolly. It
was my darling who I had picked up on the drenched road. My
little child had wandered out to meet Papa and the doll while
her mother was at work, and for her they were lamenting as for
one dead.

S. B. SHAW

Love Is Patient

Charity suffereth long, and is kind.
1 CORINTHIANS 13:4 KJV

The Apostle Paul describes the effects of love in 1 Corinthians 13. These properties are unfailing marks whereby any man may judge himself, whether he has this love or has it not. These properties deserve our deepest consideration.

Love is long-suffering. If you love your neighbor for God's sake, you will bear long with his shortcomings. If he lacks wisdom, you wilt pity and not despise him. If he is in error, you will mildly try to correct him without any sharpness or reproach. If he is overtaken in a sin, you will labor to restore him in the spirit of meekness. You will have patience with him. God may bring him at length to the knowledge and love of the truth. In all provocations, you will show in yourself a pattern of gentleness and meekness. Let no one deceive you with vain words: He who is not long-suffering has not love.

Love is kind. Whosoever feels the love of God and man in his heart feels an ardent and uninterrupted thirst after the happiness of all his fellow human beings. His soul melts away with the very fervent desire to promote kindness. So that whether he thinks or speaks, or whatever he does, it all points to the same end—the advancing, by every possible way, the happiness of all his fellow human beings. Deceive not your own souls. He who is not kind has not love.

JOHN WESLEY

Growing in Faith

He has showed you, O man, what is good.
And what does the LORD require of you?
To act justly and to love mercy
and to walk humbly with your God.

MICAH 6:8 NIV

Think how grieved and alarmed you would be if you discovered any ebbing of affection for you in your wife, husband, or children, if you saw another engrossing their hearts and thoughts and time. Perhaps in such a case you would well nigh die with a just and virtuous jealousy. Now, God calls Himself a jealous God, and have you not given your heart to other loves and infinitely offended Him?

Growth in the knowledge of God is a condition of growth in His favor. We might grow in knowledge without growing in His favor, because we might not love and trust Him in accordance with the increased knowledge. We cannot love and trust Him more perfectly, unless we become more perfectly acquainted with Him. If our love and faith keep pace with our growing knowledge, we must grow in His favor. But growth in knowledge must be a condition of growth in love and faith.

When we are more and more affected by the mercies of God and by the kindnesses of those around us, when we more thoroughly appreciate manifestations of kindness in God, when we are more and more humbled by these kindnesses and find it more and more natural "to do justly, and to love mercy, and to walk humbly," and live gratefully, we have evidence that we are growing in favor with God.

CHARLES FINNEY

Love, Faith, and Benevolence

If I give away all my possessions. . .
but do not have love,
I gain nothing.
1 CORINTHIANS 13:3 NRSV

Paul contrasts love with other things that people in those days thought much of. He contrasts love with eloquence. What a noble gift it is, the power of playing upon the wills of people and rousing them to lofty purposes. Paul says, "If I speak with the tongues of men and of angels, and have not love, I am become as sounding brass, or a tinkling cymbal." And we all know why. We have all felt the brazenness of words without emotion, and the hollowness of eloquence behind which lies no love.

He contrasts it with faith. What is the use of faith? It is to connect the soul with God. And what is the object of connecting with God? That we may become like God. But God is love. Love, therefore, obviously is greater than faith.

Love is greater than benevolence. A charitable act is only a little bit of love, one of the innumerable avenues of love, and there may even be, and there is, a great deal of charity without love. It is a very easy thing to toss a coin to a beggar on the street. It is generally an easier thing than not to do it. Yet, love is just as often in the withholding. We purchase relief from the sympathetic feelings roused by the spectacle of misery at the coin's cost. It is too cheap—too cheap for us, and often too dear for the beggar. If we really loved him, we would either do more for him or less.

HENRY DRUMMOND

Revitalized Love

Consider how I love your precepts;
preserve my life according to your steadfast love.
PSALM 119:159 NRSV

God is the chief good, and all our happiness consists in His love. His love should be valued and sought above all things. He is our only Lord, and therefore chiefly to be served. We must love Him with all our heart, soul, and strength. Our great business in the world is to glorify God and obtain salvation. Are these beliefs seen in our practice? Or rather, do our works deny what our words affirm?

But no matter how much our principles inspire us to our work, we are sure we can never do too much. No person can obey or serve God too much. As long as we are swayed by the world, we can never be righteous too much. People of the world think that faithful diligence in the service of Christ is a foolish peculiarity. The time will come when they will easily confess that God could not be loved or served too much and that no one can be too earnest to save his soul. We may easily do too much for the world, but we cannot for God.

If you loved God, you would think nothing was too much that you could possibly do to serve Him and please Him. Love is ready, active, and attentive. If you loved Christ, you would keep His commandments and not accuse Him of too much strictness. If you had faith, it would revitalize and encourage you. If you had the hope of glory, it would, as the spring in the watch, set all the wheels of your soul going.

RICHARD BAXTER

Undertrusted Love

But I trusted in your steadfast love;
my heart shall rejoice in your salvation.
PSALM 13:5 NRSV

I was once talking to an intelligent agnostic. He said, "The Christians I meet seem to me to be the very most uncomfortable people anywhere around. They seem to carry their religion as a man carries a headache. He does not want to get rid of his head, but at the same time, it is very uncomfortable to have it."

This was a lesson I have never forgotten. It seemed, as one of my Christian friends said to me one day when we were comparing our experiences, "as if we had just enough religion to make us miserable."

I confess that being uncomfortable with religion was very disappointing. I had expected something altogether different. It seemed to me exceedingly odd that a religion whose fruits were declared in the Bible to be love, joy, and peace should so often work out practically in an exactly opposite direction and should develop the fruits of doubt, fear, unrest, conflict, and discomforts of every kind. Why should the children of God lead such utterly uncomfortable religious lives when He has led us to believe that His yoke would be easy and His burden light? Why do we find it so hard to be sure that God really loves us?

The religion of the Lord Jesus Christ was meant to be full of comfort, because "eye has not seen, nor ear heard, neither have entered into the heart of man the things which God has prepared for them that love Him." All the difficulty arises from the fact that we have underbelieved and undertrusted.

HANNAH WHITALL SMITH

Cross of Love

Then He said to them all,
"If anyone desires to come after Me,
let him deny himself,
and take up his cross daily, and follow Me."

LUKE 9:23 NKJV

This mortal life is marked with crosses on all sides. A man, though afflicted in many ways, is not without hope of consolation because he knows that great reward is coming to him for bearing his cross. When he carries it willingly, every ache of tribulation is changed into hope of solace from God. The more the flesh is distressed by affliction, so much the more is the spirit strengthened by inward grace.

It is the grace of Christ, and not the virtue of man, which can and does bring about that through fervor of spirit frail flesh learns to love and to gain what it naturally hates and shuns.

To carry the cross, to love the cross, to chastise the body and bring it to subjection, to flee honors, to endure contempt gladly, to despise self, to suffer any adversity and loss, to desire no prosperous days on earth—this is not man's way. If you rely upon yourself, you can do none of these things, but if you trust in the Lord, strength will be given you from heaven. The world and the flesh will be made subject to your word. You will not even fear your enemy, the devil, if you are armed with faith and signed with the cross of Christ. Set yourself, then, like a good and faithful servant of Christ, to bear bravely the cross of your Lord, who out of love was crucified for you.

THOMAS À KEMPIS

Unified Love

I have compared thee, O my love,
to a company of horses in Pharaoh's chariots.
SONG OF SOLOMON 1:9 KJV

Horses originally selected for Pharaoh's own chariot would not only be of the purest blood and perfect in proportion and symmetry, but also perfect in training—docile and obedient. They would know no will but that of the charioteer. The only object of their existence would be to carry the king whithersoever he would go. So should it be with the church of Christ: one body with many members, indwelt and guided by one Spirit, holding the Head, and knowing no will but His.

Many years ago, a beloved friend, returning from the East by the overland route, made the journey from Suez to Cairo in the ponderous stagecoach then in use. About a dozen wild young horses were harnessed with ropes to the vehicle. The driver took his seat and cracked his whip. The horses dashed off, some to the right, some to the left, and others forward, causing the coach to start with a bound and as suddenly to stop with the effect of first throwing those sitting in the front seat into the laps of those sitting behind, and then of reversing the operation. With the aid of sufficient men running on each side to keep these wild animals progressing in the right direction, the passengers were jerked and jolted, bruised and shaken, until, on reaching their destination, they were too wearied and sore to take the rest they so much needed.

Is not the church of God today more like these untrained steeds than a company of horses in Pharaoh's chariot?

HUDSON TAYLOR

Love the Law

Oh, how I love your law!
I meditate on it all day long.

PSALM 119:97 NIV

If we are lovers of God, we love what God loves. We love God's Word. David esteemed the Word for the sweetness of it above honey and for the value of it above gold. The lines of scripture are richer than the mines of gold. Well may we love the Word—it is a guiding star that directs us to heaven. That man who does not love the Word, but thinks it too strict and could wish any part of the Bible torn out, has not the least spark of love in his heart.

A gracious soul loves God's laws and is glad of the law because it checks his sinful excesses. The heart would be ready to run wild in sin if it had not some blessed restraints put upon it by the law of God. He who loves God loves His law—the law of repentance, the law of self-denial.

Many say they love God, but they hate His laws. God's precepts are compared to cords: They bind men to their good behavior, but the wicked think these cords too tight; therefore, they say, "Let us break them." They pretend to love Christ as a Savior, but hate Him as a king. Sinners would have Christ put a crown upon their head, but not a yoke upon their neck. He would be a strange king who should rule without laws.

THOMAS WATSON

Love the Bible

But as it is written, Eye hath not seen, nor ear heard,
neither have entered into the heart of man, the things which
God hath prepared for them that love him.
1 CORINTHIANS 2:9 KJV

Like all the other wonderful works of God, this Book bears the sure stamp of its author. It is like Him. Though man plants the seeds, God makes the flowers, and they are perfect and beautiful like Himself. Men wrote what is in the Bible, but the work is God's. All that is in the Bible about God, about man, about redemption, and about a future state, agrees with our own ideas of right, with our reasonable fears, and with our personal experiences.

All the historical things are told in the way that we know the world had of looking at them when they were written. People very often think that science is all fact and that religion is only fancy. A great many persons think the stars around us are inhabited, but they cannot bring themselves to believe that there is a life beyond this earth for immortal souls.

The true Christian puts faith before reason, and believes that reason always goes wrong when faith is set aside. If people would but read their Bibles more, and study what there is to be found there about Heaven, they would not be as worldly minded as they are. They would not have their hearts set upon things down here but would seek the imperishable things above.

DWIGHT LYMAN MOODY

Overwhelmed with Love

And the Word became flesh, and dwelt among us
(and we beheld his glory,
glory as of the only begotten from the Father),
full of grace and truth.

JOHN 1:14 ASV

The souls of the saints, when they leave their bodies at death, go to receive a glorious fellowship with Christ. They will know that He is their own Redeemer and beloved friend and bridegroom—the very same who loved them with a dying love and redeemed them to God by His blood. The nature of this glory of Christ will be such as will draw and encourage them. They will not only see infinite majesty and greatness, but infinite grace, mildness, gentleness and sweetness, all equal to His majesty.

The sight of Christ's great kingly majesty will be no terror to them but will only serve the more to heighten their pleasure and surprise. The souls of departed saints with Christ in heaven shall have Christ manifesting His infinite riches of love toward them. They shall be enabled to express their love to Him, in an infinitely better manner than ever they could while on earth. They shall eat and drink abundantly, swim in the ocean of love, and be eternally swallowed up in the infinitely bright, infinitely mild, and sweet beams of divine love—eternally receiving that light, eternally full of it, and eternally compassed round with it.

When He ascended into heaven, He took possession of heaven, not only for Himself but for His people. The saints in heaven have a joint participation with Christ in His glory and blessedness.

JONATHAN EDWARDS

Love—The Cure for Evil

Be not overcome of evil,
but overcome evil with good.
ROMANS 12:21 KJV

Nothing can live in God but as it lives in love. Look at every vice, pain, and disorder in human nature. It is in itself nothing else but the spirit of the creature turned from the universality of love to some self-seeking or own will. So that love alone is, and only can be, the cure of every evil.

He who lives in the purity of love is risen out of the power of evil into the freedom of the one spirit of heaven. The schools have given us very accurate definitions of every vice, whether it be covetousness, pride, wrath, envy, etc. But the Christian has a much shorter way of knowing their nature and power and what they all are and do in and to himself. For call them by what names you will, or distinguish them with ever so much exactness, they are all, separately and jointly, just that same one thing, and all do that same one work. If you would therefore have a true sense of the nature and power of pride, wrath, covetousness, envy, etc., they are in their whole nature nothing else but the murderers and crucifiers of the true Christ of God.

This therefore is a certain truth: That hell and death, curse and misery can never cease or be removed from the Creation till the will of the creature is again as it came from God and is only a spirit of love that wills nothing but goodness.

WILLIAM LAW

Charity Means Love

Love never fails.
But whether there are prophecies, they will fail;
whether there are tongues, they will cease;
whether there is knowledge, it will vanish away.

1 CORINTHIANS 13:8 NKJV

Nothing is more valuable and commendable, and yet not one duty is less practiced than that of charity. But before I go any further, I shall inform you what the apostle means by *charity,* and that is *love.* If there is true love, there will be charity. There will be an endeavor to assist, help, and relieve according to that ability wherewith God has blessed us.

We often pretend concern for the misery of our fellow-creatures, but yet we seldom commiserate their condition so much as to relieve them according to our abilities. But unless we assist them with what they may stand in need of—for the body as well as for the soul—all our wishes are no more than words of no value. When we hear of any deplorable circumstance in which our fellow-creatures are involved, be they friends or enemies, it is our duty as Christians to assist them to the utmost of our power.

St. Paul had been showing that spiritual gifts were diverse. Though there are these different spiritual gifts, they are all given for some wise end. We are not to hide those gifts, which God has given us. They are to be used for the glory of God and the good of immortal souls. After he had particularly illustrated this, St. Paul comes to show that all gifts, however great they may be in themselves, are of no value unless we have charity

GEORGE WHITEFIELD

The Right Charity

Now that you have purified your souls
by your obedience to the truth so that
you have genuine mutual love,
love one another deeply from the heart.
1 PETER 1:22 NRSV

Your charity is not of the right kind when it proceeds from worldly views. If it is to be seen of men, to receive any advantage from them, to be esteemed or to gain a reputation in the world, then it is all in vain. If you have any pride in it and expect to reap benefits from God merely for it, then it is all in vain. Your charity does not proceed from a right motive, but you are hereby deceiving your own souls. If you give alms purely to be observed by man, then you have not the glory of God or the benefit of your fellow-creatures at heart but merely yourself. This is not charity.

When we give anything to our fellow-creatures purely to indulge them in vice, this is so far from being charity that it is a sin, both against God and against our fellow-creatures.

Our charity comes from a right intention when it proceeds from love to God and for the welfare both of the body and soul of our fellow-creatures. When this is the sole end of relieving our distressed fellow-creatures, then our charity comes from a right reason. This is the charity that is pleasing to God. God is well pleased when all our actions proceed from love—love to Himself and love to immortal souls.

GEORGE WHITEFIELD

Beloved Friend

His mouth is most sweet;
Yea, he is altogether lovely.
This is my beloved, and this is my friend,
O daughters of Jerusalem.
SONG OF SOLOMON 5:16 ASV

The words "your God" imply the relation of a friend. A friend is, as St. Augustine says, half one's self. He is studious and desirous how he may do his friend good. He promotes his welfare as his own. Jonathan ventured the king's displeasure for his friend David. God is our friend; therefore, He will turn all things to our good. There are false friends. Christ was betrayed by a friend. But God is the best friend.

God is a faithful friend. He is faithful in His love. He gave His very heart to us, when He gave the Son out of His bosom. Here was a pattern of love without a parallel. He is faithful in His promises. He is faithful in His dealings.

God is a permanent friend. Friends often fail at a pinch. Many deal with their friends as women do with flowers; while they are fresh, they put them in their bosoms, but when they begin to wither, they throw them away. Accordingly, if prosperity shine on men, then friends will look upon them. But if there be a cloud of adversity on them, they will not come near them. But God is a friend forever. Although David walked in the shadow of death, he knew he had a friend by him. God, being such a friend, will make all things work for our good. A friend will seek the good of his friend. God never takes off His love wholly from His people.

THOMAS WATSON

Love That Acquits

Pursue a godly life, along with faith, love,
perseverance, and gentleness.
1 TIMOTHY 6:11 NLT

Jesus Christ came into the world to save sinners. I know that it is to me even to this day the greatest wonder that I ever heard of, that God should ever justify me. I feel myself to be a lump of unworthiness and a heap of sin apart from His almighty love. I know by a full assurance that I am justified by faith that is in Christ Jesus. Yet, by nature I must take my place among the most sinful. I am loved with as much love as if I had always been godly, although earlier I was ungodly. Who can help being astonished at this? Gratitude for such favor stands dressed in robes of wonder.

Have you lived without any love to God in your heart or regard to His commands in your life? You are the kind of person to whom this gospel is sent—this gospel which says that God justifies the ungodly. It is very wonderful, but it is available for you. It just suits you.

The salvation of God is for those who do not deserve it. The Lord only does that which is needful. Infinite wisdom never attempts that which is unnecessary. Jesus never undertakes that which is superfluous. To make him just who is just is no work for God. But to make him just who is unjust—that is work for infinite love and mercy. To justify the ungodly—this is a miracle worthy of a God.

CHARLES HADDON SPURGEON

The Nearby Love of Jesus

He looked up, saw Jesus walking nearby, and said,
"Here he is, God's Passover Lamb."

JOHN 1:36 TM

"There is a happy land, far, far away!" I do not think we greatly help the cause of the Lord by proclaiming the remoteness of His home. I have never been able to find out what we gain by teaching children the "far-offness" of the Savior's dwelling. I am afraid that the remoteness of the home tends to create a conception of the remoteness of the Lover; and, if the Lover is away, the invitation will be very mechanical and cold.

"There's a friend for little children, above the bright blue sky." That is the only line I don't like in that greatly beloved and very beautiful hymn. In my childhood, it helped to make me think that my Savior was an absentee. We shall perhaps best help the cause of the Lord if we teach that His home is very near, and that no clouds interpose between us and the place where He dwells.

Destroying all sense of remoteness, we must labor to bring the children into the immediate presence of the lover Himself. We have to reveal Jesus to the children, so that He captivates their love. We must strive to make it so real that the children, with their magnificently realistic imagination, shall feel that they are with Him among the flowers of the field. We must reveal Him watching the graceful flight of the birds in the air and His tender regard for the common sparrow. We must reveal Him as the approachable Jesus with groups of little children clustering about His knees and lovingly taking them into His arms to bless them.

JOHN HENRY JOWETT

What Would Jesus Do—The Minister

"Come, follow me," Jesus said,
"and I will make you fishers of men."
MATTHEW 4:19 NIV

Henry Maxwell paced his study back and forth. After a while he sat down at his desk and drew a large piece of paper toward him. He wrote: A number of things that Jesus would probably do in this parish.

Live in a simple, plain manner, without needless luxury on the one hand or undue severity on the other. Preach fearlessly to the hypocrites in the church, no matter what their social importance or wealth. Show in some practical form His sympathy and love for the common people as well as for the well-to-do, educated, refined people who make up the majority of the parish. Identify Himself with the great causes of humanity in some personal way that would call for self-denial and suffering. Preach against the saloon in Raymond. Become known as a friend and companion of the sinful people in the Rectangle, the slum district.

Maxwell was conscious, with a humility that was once a stranger to him, that his outline of Jesus' probable action was painfully lacking in depth and power, but he was seeking carefully for concrete shapes into which he might cast his thought of Jesus' conduct. Nearly every point he had put down meant, for him, a complete overturning of the custom and habit of years in the ministry. In spite of that, he still searched deeper for sources of the Christlike spirit. He did not attempt to write anymore, but sat at his desk absorbed in his effort to catch more and more the spirit of Jesus in his own life.

CHARLES SHELDON

Short Life of Love

He will swallow up death in victory;
and the Lord GOD will
wipe away tears from off all faces.

ISAIAH 25:8 KJV

I received the following letter from a former orphan who walked as a consistent believer for a considerable time before he left our care. The letter is written on the death of one of his sisters, a lovely Christian.

"My dear sir," the letter said. "It has pleased the Lord to take unto Himself my dear sister Elizabeth. I had lived in the fond hope of seeing her again, but it was the will of God that it should not be so. I now hope to meet her again with my dear father and mother in that happy land where God shall wipe away all tears from our eyes. It is now plainly to be seen what a mercy it was that we were taken to the orphanage where we all learned to know and love the Savior. It is three years since I left, and I can only say that goodness and mercy have followed me. I often need the help of God to overcome temptations, but in all my failings and wanderings, the hand of God has not suffered me to fall away. I have constant need of prayer. With love to all, I remain yours, gratefully and respectfully."

This was the last letter I had from this lovely youth who gave us great comfort while under our care. He walked as a most consistent Christian for the three years and a half he was employed. I learned from his Christian foreman that he died of typhus fever.

GEORGE MÜLLER

Constrained by Love

*"Should you help the wicked and
love those who hate the LORD?"*

2 CHRONICLES 19:2 NIV

Because God loved the world, He gave His well-beloved Son to be both prince and Savior. In knowing, loving, and serving Him, we can realize our supreme blessedness. Is Jesus your King? Never until He is so will you know the fullness of God's love. Those who question or refuse His authority are always in doubt about the love of God to themselves and to the world. Those, on the other hand, who acknowledge His claims and crown Him as King, suddenly find themselves admitted to a standpoint of vision in which doubts and disputations vanish. Then they experience divine love in its most entrancing characteristics. All is love where Jesus reigns.

There is a great tendency in the present day to boast in the closeness with which we can approach the world without injury. We join in the social life, read the same books, go to the same amusements, talk of the same themes. It is of little use to find fault with the outward as long as the heart is wayward. Love to the Lord Jesus is our only safeguard. The love of Christ must constrain us. Personal attachment to Christ will wean us away from this close identification with the world. But if we persist in identifying ourselves with the world, which God has doomed, we must not be surprised to find that wrath is on us from the Lord. He will chasten us for love's sake.

F. B. MEYER

Reform School Boys

*He who pursues righteousness and love
finds life, prosperity and honor.*
PROVERBS 21:21 NIV

A friend of mine was in charge of a reform school for boys. The effects produced on even the worst boys by the love shown them are really striking. The superintendent had long insisted that he did not want locks and bars to confine his boys. On one occasion the superintendent was to be absent two weeks. A director came to him urging that he must lock up the boys before he left for they would certainly run away. The superintendent replied, "I think not; I have confidence in those boys."

"But," responded the director, "give us some guarantee. Are you willing to pledge that if they do run away, your city lot goes to the reform school fund?"

After a little reflection he consented. "I will give you my lot—all the little property I have in the world—if any of my boys run away while I am gone."

He called all the boys together, explained to them his pledge, and asked them to look at his dependent family. He then appealed to their honor and their love for him. "Would you be willing to see me stripped of all my property? I think I can trust you."

He went and returned a little unexpectedly and late on one Saturday night. Scarce had he entered the yard when the word rang through the sleeping halls, "Our father has come!" and almost in a moment they were there greeting him and shouting, "We are all here! We are all here!"

Cannot Christ's love have as much power as that?

CHARLES FINNEY

Molded in Love

But we know that when he appears,
we shall be like him,
for we shall see him as he is.
1 JOHN 3:2 NIV

The first and chief need of our Christian life is fellowship with God. As I need every moment fresh air to breathe, as the sun every moment sends down its light, so it is only in direct living communication with God that my soul can be strong. Let God's love overwhelm you and bow you still lower down. Sink down before Him in humility, meekness, patience, and surrender to His goodness and mercy. Then accept and value your place in Christ Jesus. He loves you with a personal love. He looks every day for the personal response of your love. Look into His face with trust until His love really shines into your heart. Make His heart glad by telling Him that you do love Him. He offers Himself to you as a personal savior and keeper from the power of sin.

We have not only Christ's life in us as a power, and His presence with us as a person, but we have His likeness to be clearly apparent in us. He is to be formed in us so that His form and His likeness can be seen in us. The God who revealed Jesus in the flesh and perfected Him will reveal Him in you and perfect you in Him. The Father loves the Son, and delights to work out His image and likeness in you. Count upon it that this blessed work will be done in you as you wait on your God and hold fellowship with Him.

ANDREW MURRAY

The Bridegroom's Love

God gave the land of these kings as an inheritance—
His faithful love endures forever.

PSALM 136:21 NLT

Do you desire one who can love you? None can love you like Christ. His love is incomprehensible; His love passes all other love. The love of the Lord Jesus is first and without beginning; His love is free without any motive; His love is great without any measure; His love is constant without any change; His love is everlasting.

The love of the Lord Jesus Christ brought Him down from heaven and veiled His divinity in a human soul and body. It was love that made Him subject to hunger, thirst, and sorrow. His love carried Him back to heaven that He might make intercession for those whom He had redeemed.

If you have promised yourself to Christ, you will converse with Him. You will endeavor to promote His interest and advance His name in the world.

It is likewise your folly to refuse and neglect the gracious gifts of being the spouse of Christ. You forfeit all love that He would bestow upon you. You choose rags before robes, rubbish before gold, pebbles before jewels, wounds before healing, defilement before cleansing, deformity before comeliness, trouble before peace, slavery before liberty, the service of the devil before the service of Christ. You choose dishonor before a crown, death before life, hell before heaven, eternal misery and torment before everlasting joy and glory.

Consider who the Lord Jesus is, whom you are invited to embrace yourselves with. There is none comparable to Jesus Christ.

GEORGE WHITEFIELD

Where Love Is

And I have made mighty the house of Judah. . . .
And I have caused them to dwell, for I have loved them.
ZECHARIAH 10:6 YLT

Where love is, God is. He who dwells in love dwells in God. God is love. Therefore lavish love upon the poor, where it is very easy. Lavish it especially upon the rich, who often need it most. Lavish love upon our equals, where it is very difficult and for whom perhaps we each do least of all. There is a difference between trying to please and giving pleasure. Lose no chance of giving pleasure. For that is the ceaseless and anonymous triumph of a truly loving spirit.

I shall pass through this world but once. Any good thing, therefore, that I can do or any kindness that I can show to any human being, let me do it now.

Love envies not. Whenever you attempt a good work, you will find other people doing the same kind of work and probably doing it better. Envy them not. Envy is a feeling of ill will to those who are in the same line as ourselves. That most despicable of all the unworthy moods that clouds a Christian's soul assuredly waits for us on the threshold of every work unless we are fortified with this grace of generosity of spirit.

After having learned all that, you have to learn this further thing—humility. Put a seal upon your lips, and forget what you have done. After you have been kind, after love has moved quietly forth into the world and done its beautiful work, go back into the shade again and say nothing about it. Love hides even from itself. Love puts aside even self-satisfaction.

HENRY DRUMMOND

Mother's Love

*"How often I have longed to gather your children together,
as a hen gathers her chicks under her wings."*

MATTHEW 23:37 NIV

What a mother does for her foolish, careless, ignorant, but dearly loved little ones, this very thing our God does for us. When a mother is with her children, she thinks of their comfort and well-being always before her own. They must have comfortable seats where no cold air can reach them, no matter what amount of discomfort she may be compelled to endure. Their beds must be soft and their blankets warm; let hers be what they may. Their paths must be smooth and safe, although she is obliged to walk in rough and dangerous ways. Her own comfort, as compared with that of her children, is of no account in a loving mother's eyes. Surely our God has not made the mothers in this world more capable of a self-sacrificing love than He is Himself. He must be better and greater in love and self-sacrifice than any mother He ever made.

We may be perfectly sure that in even these little details of our lives we get the very best that His love, wisdom, and power can give us. He is so much better than any mother can be. His love is a wise love that sees the outcome of things and cares for our highest good. While a mother's weak love cannot see beyond the child's present comfort, and cannot bear to inflict or allow any discomfort, the strong, wise love of our God can permit the present discomfort for the sake of the future glory that is to result.

HANNAH WHITALL SMITH

Send the Word

Herein is our love made perfect,
that we may have boldness in the day of judgment:
because as he is, so are we in this world.
1 JOHN 4:17 KJV

I attached myself to the tribe called Bakuena, the chief of which was named Sechele. I was first struck by his intelligence, and by the marked manner in which we both felt drawn to each other. This remarkable man not only embraced Christianity but also expounded its doctrines to his people.

On the first occasion in which I held a public religious service, Sechele remarked that it was the custom, when any new subject was brought before his nation, to put questions on it. He begged me to allow him to do the same. On expressing my willingness, he inquired if my forefathers knew of a future judgment. I replied in the affirmative, and began to describe the scene of the "great white throne, and Him who shall sit on it, from whose face the heaven and earth shall flee away."

He said, "You startle me: These words make all my bones to shake. I have no more strength in me; but my forefathers were living at the same time yours were, and how is it that they did not send them word about these terrible things sooner? They all passed away into darkness without knowing whither they were going." I got out of the difficulty by explaining the geographical barriers in the North, and the gradual spread of knowledge from the South. I expressed my belief that, as Christ had said, the whole world would yet be enlightened by the gospel.

DAVID LIVINGSTONE

Christlike Love

I pray that. . .
Christ may dwell in your hearts through faith.
EPHESIANS 3:16–17 NIV

If Christ is dwelling in my heart, I must necessarily be Christlike. I cannot be unkind or irritable, self-seeking or dishonest. His gentleness, sweetness, tender compassion, and loving submission to the will of His Father must be manifested in my daily walk. The life of Jesus is to be made obvious in our lives. Are we so conformed to the image of Christ that people in seeing us see a glimpse of Him, also?

A minister's wife told me that at one time they had moved to a new place. Her little boy came in after the first afternoon of play. He exclaimed joyfully, "Mother, I have found such a lovely, good little girl to play with that I never want to go away again."

"I am very glad, darling," said the loving mother, delighted because of her child's happiness. "What is the little girl's name?"

The child replied with a sudden solemnity, "I think her name is Jesus."

"Frank!" exclaimed the mother. "What do you mean?"

He said deprecatingly, "She was so lovely that I did not know what she could be called but Jesus."

Are our lives so Christlike that anyone could have such a thought of us? Is it apparent to all around us that we have been with Jesus? Unfortunately, it is often just the contrary. Are some of us so cross and uncomfortable in our living that exactly the opposite thing would have to be said about us?

HANNAH WHITALL SMITH

Fervent Love

"So, because you are lukewarm—
neither hot nor cold—
I am about to spit you out of my mouth."
REVELATION 3:16 NIV

Our love to God must be complete, and it must be with the whole heart. God will have the whole heart. The true mother would not have the child divided, and God will not have the heart divided. God will not be an inmate, to have only one room in the heart and all the other rooms let out to sin. It must be an entire love.

Our love to God is sincere when it is pure and without self-interest. We must love Christ for Himself. God's beauty and love must be the two loadstones to draw our love to Him. Alexander the Great had two friends, Hephestion and Craterus, of whom he said, "Hephestion loves me because I am Alexander; Craterus loves me because I am King Alexander." The one loved his person; the other loved his gifts. We must love God more for what He is than for what He bestows. True love is not mercenary. You need not hire a mother to love her child. A soul deeply in love with God needs not be hired by rewards. It cannot but love Him for that luster of beauty that sparkles forth in Him.

Our love to God must be a fervent love. Saints must be burning in holy love. To love coldly is the same as not to love. The sun shines as hot as it can. Our love to God must be intense and ablaze like coals of juniper. Our love to God must flame forth.

THOMAS WATSON

Abuse of Love

*I am shocked that you are turning away so soon from God
who in his love and mercy called you to share
the eternal life he gives through Christ*

GALATIANS 1:6 NLT

Take heed of abusing the love of God. This exhortation seems
needless because love is such a thing that one would think none
could find in their heart to abuse. But I am of opinion that
nothing is more abused among believers this day than the love
of God. Lately, more light about the love of Christ broke out
than formerly. Every child now can talk of the love of Christ.
But this love of Christ has not been rightly applied by preachers
or else not rightly received by believers. For never was this grace
of Christ so turned into immorality as now.

But I say, let not this love of God and of Christ be abused.
It is unnatural to abuse love. To abuse love is a villainy condemned
of all. Yes, to abuse love is the most inexcusable sin of all. It is the
sin of devils to abuse the love of God and of Christ. And what can
one say for himself in the judgment who is charged with the abuse
of love? Christians, deny yourselves, your lusts, and the vanities of
this present life. Renounce the hidden things of dishonesty, walk
not in craftiness, nor handle God's word deceitfully. Devote yourselves to God. Become lovers of God and lovers of His ways. Then
shall you show to all people that you have not received the grace
of God in vain.

JOHN BUNYAN

Resurrected Love

Women received their loved ones back again from death.
But others trusted God and were tortured,
preferring to die rather than turn from God and be free.
They placed their hope in the resurrection to a better life.
HEBREWS 11:35 NLT

I did everything I could to bring him to Christ. He was a young man of considerable promise. But day by day, I preached to him as best I knew how. I think I never loved a man on earth as I loved that brother. Because he was sickly, that drew my love and sympathy toward him. How my heart yearned for his salvation!

After preaching one night, I said, "Now if any of this audience would like to take up his cross and follow Christ, I would like for him to rise." I cannot tell you what a thrill of joy filled my soul when that brother of mine arose! It seemed the happiest night of my life. I was full of joy and thankfulness. Afterward this brother and I worked together for a time.

After a year had passed, I went to Chicago. He was to come later. He bid me good-bye, and I said, "Samuel, I will see you in a few days, so I will only say good-bye till then." A few days after, a telegram came, saying, "Samuel is dead." I got more comfort out of that promise "I will raise him up at the last day" than anything else in the Bible. How it cheered me! How it lighted up my path!

DWIGHT LYMAN MOODY

Love and Idols

*Jesus said to Simon Peter, "Simon son of John,
do you truly love me more than these?"*

JOHN 21:15 NIV

You don't have to go to heathen lands today to find false gods. America is full of them. Whatever you love more than God is your idol. Many a man's heart is so full of idols that there is hardly room to turn around. Rich and poor, learned and unlearned, all classes of men and women are guilty of this sin. A man may make a god of some precious gift that God has bestowed upon him. He may forget the giver and let his heart go out in adoration toward the gift.

Many make a god of pleasure. If some old Greek or Roman came to life again and saw man in a drunken display, would he believe that the worship of Bacchus had died out? If he saw the streets of our large cities filled with prostitutes, would he believe that the worship of Venus had ceased? Others take fashion as their god. They give their time and thought to dress. Do not let us flatter ourselves to think that all idolaters are in heathen countries.

The atheist says that he does not believe in God. He denies His existence, but he can't help setting up some other god in His place. Has the human heart ever been satisfied with these false gods? Can pleasure or riches fill the soul that is empty of God? What do they look forward to? Nothing!

DWIGHT LYMAN MOODY

The Insurmountable Love of Jesus

Who shall separate us from the love of Christ?
Shall trouble or hardship or persecution
or famine or nakedness or danger or sword?
ROMANS 8:35 NIV

Unless a man is purified first by trials and sorrows, he may not come to the sweetness of God's love. Who else could give to me what I feel from You? Make my mind to drink deeply of Your sweet love that I, forgetting all evils, trivial thoughts, and disbelieving imaginations, may embrace You only, joyfully rejoicing in my Lord Jesus. Inflame my heart with Your love that shall forever burn upon Your altar.

Love is insurmountable when it cannot be overcome with any other love, trial, or temptation—when it gladly casts down all other hindrances and all temptations, and quenches fleshly desires. When a person suffers gladly and submissively all anguish for Christ, and is not overcome with any delight or flattering—so that whether you are in ease or in anguish, in sickness or in health, you would not for all the world anger God at any time—that is insurmountable love. And blessed is the soul that is in this state. Every labor is light to him who loves truly; neither can any man better overcome labor than by love.

Therefore take on love as the iron takes on the redness of fire, as air takes in the sun, as the wool absorbs the dye. The coal heats the iron in the fire so it is all fire. The air is infused by the sun so that it is all light. The wool takes the hue so that it changes all to the color.

JOHN WYCLIFFE

Love and Gratitude

I love the LORD, for he heard my voice;
he heard my cry for mercy.
Because he turned his ear to me,
I will call on him as long as I live.

PSALM 116:1–2 NIV

Thanksgiving is oral, positive, and active. It is the giving out of something to God. Thanksgiving comes out into the open. Gratitude is secret, silent, and passive. It does not show its being until expressed in praise and thanksgiving. Gratitude is felt in the heart. Thanksgiving is the expression of that inward feeling.

Thanksgiving is just what the word itself signifies—the giving of thanks to God. It is giving something to God in words that we feel in our heart for blessings received. Gratitude arises from serious meditation on the goodness of God. Both gratitude and thanksgiving have to do with God and His mercies. The heart is consciously grateful to God. The soul gives expression to that heartfelt gratitude to God in words or acts. Gratitude is born of meditation on God's grace and mercy. Herein we see the value of serious meditation. Praise is begotten by gratitude and a conscious obligation to God for mercies given. As we think of mercies past, the heart is inwardly moved to gratitude.

Love is the child of gratitude. Love grows as gratitude is felt and then breaks out into praise and thanksgiving to God. Answered prayers cause gratitude, and gratitude brings forth a love that declares it will not cease praying. Gratitude and love move us to increased praying.

EDWARD MCKENDREE BOUNDS

Love and Glory

"Father, I want those you have given me
to be with me where I am, and to see my glory,
the glory you have given me because you loved me
before the creation of the world."
JOHN 17:24 NIV

When the souls of the saints leave their bodies to go to be with Christ, they see His glory, the beauty of His perfection, His great majesty and almighty power, and His infinite wisdom, holiness, and grace. They have a most clear view of the unfathomable depths of the wisdom and knowledge of God. They see in a much clearer manner than the saints do here what is the length, depth, and height of the grace and love of Christ.

As they see the unspeakable riches and glory of the attribute of God's grace, so they most clearly see and understand Christ's eternal and unmeasurable dying love to them in particular. In short, they see everything in Christ that tends to kindle and inflame love, everything that tends to gratify love, and everything that tends to satisfy them. They see all of this in the most clear and glorious manner, without any darkness or delusion, without any impediment or interruption.

Now the saints while in the body see something of Christ's glory and love, as we in the dawning of the morning see something of the reflected light of the sun mingled with darkness. But when separated from the body, they see their glorious and loving Redeemer, as we see the sun when risen, and showing its whole disk above the horizon in a clear hemisphere and with perfect day.

JONATHAN EDWARDS

Beset with Love

Thou hast beset me behind and before,
and laid thine hand upon me.

PSALM 139:5 KJV

We are told in our Psalm that God besets our path. Some of us know what it is to be intruded upon by unwelcome and unpleasant people. Perhaps we never have thought that God besets us. He loves us so that He cannot leave us alone. Neither coldness nor rebuffs on our part can drive Him away. Yes, it is gloriously true!

Moreover, He besets us behind as well as before, just as a mother does. She goes after her children and picks up all they have dropped, and clears away all the litter they have left behind them. We mothers begin this in the nursery with the blocks and playthings, and we go on with it all our lives long. We are seeking continually to set straight that which our children have left crooked behind them. Often it is at the cost of much toil and trouble, but always with a love that makes the toil and trouble nothing in comparison to caring for the children we love.

What good mother ever turned away the poor little tearful darling who came with a tangled knot for her unraveling, or refused to help the eager, rosy boy to unwind his kite strings? Suppose it has been their own fault that the knots and tangles have come; still her love can sympathize with and pity the very faults themselves. All this and more does our God do for us from our earliest infancy, long even before we know enough to be conscious of it, until the very end of our earthly lives.

HANNAH WHITALL SMITH

Complete Love

No one has ever seen God;
but if we love one another,
God lives in us and his love is made complete in us.
1 JOHN 4:12 NIV

In general, people are always struggling with one another and are always ready to inflict injuries unless they change their natures. How is gentleness born? Truly it comes from the teaching of the gospel. The truth of the gospel has not reached us unless mutual love, friendliness, and the desire to do kindness prevails among us.

If we consider how little each one of us practices brotherly love, we shall rightly be ashamed of our negligence. Daily God declares Himself reconciled to us in His Son. Christ bears witness in this law of love that He is the giver of peace with God. He offers Himself for us, so that we may willingly be brothers to one another. We desire indeed to be enrolled as children of God and to enjoy the reconciliation won for us by the blood of Christ. Meanwhile we tear at one another; we sharpen our teeth; our minds are wholly ruthless. If we wish to prove ourselves disciples of Christ, we must heed this part of His teaching, and each one of us strive to help his neighbors.

This cannot be done without opposition from the flesh. We are prone to love ourselves and to seek too much our own private advantage. We must shed these immoderate and hurtful emotions of self-interest if brotherly love is to take their place. We are warned in scripture that it is not enough to refrain from doing injury; a man must be helpful to his brothers.

JOHN CALVIN

The Strength for Love

I love you, O LORD, my strength.

PSALM 18:1 NRSV

The law requires a free, a willing, and a loving heart. I may of my own strength refrain from hurting my enemy, but to love him with all my heart and put anger out of my mind, I cannot do of my own strength. I may refuse money of my own strength, but to put away love for riches out of my heart, I cannot do of my own strength. To abstain from adultery, as concerning the outward deed, I can do of my own strength; but not to desire in my heart is as impossible to me as to choose whether I will hunger or thirst. Yet the law requires it. Of our own strength the law is never fulfilled. We must have God's favor and His Spirit, purchased by Christ's blood.

Love of her own nature bestows all that she has, and even her own self, on that which is loved. You need not remind a kind mother to be loving unto her only son. Much less does spiritual love, which has eyes given to her by God, need human law to teach her to do her duty.

We should deal soberly with the consciences of the weak in faith, who do not yet understand the liberty of Christ perfectly enough. Favor them with Christian love, and do not use the liberty of faith as a hindrance but use it to edify the weak. Where love is perfect, there must be such a respect for the weak. It is a thing that Christ commanded and charged to be had above all things.

WILLIAM TYNDALE

The Face of Love

Let your face shine on your servant;
save me in your unfailing love.
PSALM 31:16 NIV

The face is perhaps the most wonderful part of the wonderful human body. Of all the faces that God has made, no two are exactly alike. We do occasionally meet with those who bear a very close resemblance, but intimate friends who know the play of the countenance are never mistaken. Why is this? Because God has so ordered it that the face shall reveal the character of the individual.

It is the purpose of God that the heart of Christ shall be revealed to His people. It is the will of God that "the light of the knowledge of the glory of God" should be revealed to us "in the face of Jesus Christ."

How well we know in actual life what the light of the countenance means! How the mother's smile brings light and gladness into the heart of the child! How the welcoming look of a friend is at once understood!

Where there is the shining of the face, we know there is more than forgiveness. There is favor and disposition to please. What a wonderful view of the light of His countenance the favored disciples must have had who were witnesses of His transfiguration. We are told that His face did shine as the sun. And so when the Lord makes the light of His countenance to shine upon any of His people, in the measure in which with unveiled face they discern the beauty of the Lord, there is a moral and progressive change into His likeness.

HUDSON TAYLOR

Love the Good Seed

*"I said, 'Plant the good seeds of righteousness,
and you will harvest a crop of my love.' "*

HOSEA 10:12 NLT

I would earnestly recommend all young missionaries to go at once to the real heathen. The Israelite slaves brought out of Egypt by Moses were not converted and elevated in one generation, though under the direct teaching of God Himself. We should not indulge in overwrought expectations as to the elevation that those who have inherited the degradation of ages may attain in our day.

Protestant missionaries of every denomination in South Africa all agree in one point, that no mere profession of Christianity is sufficient to entitle the converts to the Christian name. They are all anxious to place the Bible in the hands of the natives. With the ability to read that, there can be little doubt as to the future. We believe Christianity to be divine and equal to all it has to perform. Let the good seed be widely sown, and no matter to what sect the converts may belong, the harvest will be glorious.

Let nothing that I have said be interpreted as indicative of feelings unfavorable to any body of Christians, for I never, as a missionary, felt myself to be either Presbyterian, Episcopalian, or Independent, or called upon in any way to love one denomination less than another. My earnest desire is that those who really have the best interests of the heathen at heart should go to them. Assuredly, in Africa at least, self-denying labors among real heathen will not fail to be appreciated. Christians have never yet been disappointed in dealing fairly with the heathen.

DAVID LIVINGSTONE

Love for the Unlovely

But as touching brotherly love
ye need not that I write unto you:
for ye yourselves are taught of God
to love one another.

1 THESSALONIANS 4:9 KJV

It is in our daily life and conduct that the fruit of the Spirit is love. From that comes all the graces and virtues in which love is manifested. I have often thought that if we had written this we would have put in the foreground the manly virtues, such as zeal, courage, and diligence. But we need to see how the gentler virtues—kindness, humbleness, meekness, and long-suffering—are specially connected with dependence upon the Holy Spirit. They never were found in the heathen world. Christ was needed to come from heaven to teach them to us.

I cannot see God, but as a compensation I can see my brother. If I love him, God dwells in me. Loving my brother is the way to real fellowship with God. Suppose there is a brother, a most unlovable man. He worries you every time you meet him. He is of the very opposite disposition to yours. You have to deal with him in your business. He is most untidy and unbusinesslike. You say, "I cannot love him." Friend, you have not learned the lesson that Christ wanted to teach above everything. Let a man be what he will, you are to love him. Yes, listen! If a man loves not his brother whom he hath seen—if you don't love that unlovable man whom you have seen—how can you love God whom you have not seen? If the love of God is in your heart, you will love your brother.

ANDREW

Gentle Love

What do you prefer?
Shall I come to you with a whip,
or in love and with a gentle spirit?

1 CORINTHIANS 4:21 NIV

The triumph of God's gentle goodness will be our song forever. In those far-distant ages when we look back on our earthly course as a grown man on his boyhood, we shall recognize that the hand that guided us was as gentle as our mother's. The things we craved, but failed to receive, were withheld by His gentle goodness.

The apostle earnestly sought the Corinthian converts by the gentleness of Christ. Although there were abuses amongst them that seemed to call for stringent dealing, he felt that the abuses could be best removed by the gentle love that he had learned from the heart of Christ. The wisdom that is from above is gentle as well as pure.

In dealing with the sin that chokes our growth, it is probable that gentleness will do more than severity. The gentleness is the furnace before which the foul ingredients of our hearts are driven out never to return. We might challenge the lion, but we are conquered by the Lamb. We could withstand the scathing look of scorn, but when the gentle Lord casts on us the look of inexpressible tenderness, we go out to weep bitterly.

He has borne with us so lovingly. He has filled our lives with mercy even when compelled to correct. He has returned our rebuffs and slights with meekness and forbearance. He has never wearied of us. This is an everlasting tribute to the gentleness that makes great.

F. B. MEYER

Love Is Not Prideful

But let those who boast boast in this,
that they understand and know me,
that I am the LORD; I act with steadfast love, justice,
and righteousness in the earth.
JEREMIAH 9:24 NRSV

Another property of love is "Love is not puffed up." You cannot wrong one you love. Therefore, if you love God with all your heart, you cannot so wrong Him as to rob Him of His glory by taking to yourself what is due to Him only. You will admit that all you are and all you have is His. Without Him, you can do nothing. He is your light and your life, your strength and your all. You will admit that you are nothing, yes, less than nothing, before Him.

If you love your neighbor as yourself, you will not be able to prefer yourself before him. You will not be able to despise anyone, any more than to hate him. As the wax melts away before the fire, so does pride melt away before love. All haughtiness, whether of heart, speech, or behavior, vanishes away where love prevails. It brings down the high looks of him who boasts in his strength and makes him as a little child—humble of himself, willing to hear, glad to learn, easily convinced, easily persuaded. And whoever is otherwise minded, let him give up all vain hope: He is puffed up and so has not love.

Whatever we do and whatever we suffer, if we are not renewed in the spirit of our mind by the love of God shed in our hearts by the Holy Ghost, we cannot enter into life eternal.

JOHN WESLEY

Love Across the Ages

"For God so loved the world,
that he gave his only begotten Son,
that whosoever believeth in him should not perish,
but have everlasting life."
JOHN 3:16 KJV

Long before He formed a moral universe, He knew perfectly what it must cost Him to redeem sinners, and He knew that the result would amply justify all the cost. He knew that a wonder of mercy would be wrought—that the suffering demanded of Christ, great as it was, would be endured—and that results infinitely glorious would accrue therefrom.

He looked down the track of time into the distant ages—where there might be seen the joys of redeemed saints, who are singing their songs and striking their harps anew with the everlasting song, and was not this enough for the heart of infinite love to enjoy?

When you come to see Him face-to-face and tell Him what you think of it—when you are some thousands of years older than you are now—will you not adore that wisdom that manages this scheme, and the infinite love in which it had its birth?

God wants volunteers to help on this great work. God has given Himself, and given His Son, and sent His Spirit. More laborers still are needed. What will you give? Say not, "I have nothing to give." You can give yourself—your eyes, your ears, your hands, your mind, your heart, all. How many young men are ready to go? and how many young women? Whose heart leaps up, crying, "Here am I! Send me!"

CHARLES FINNEY

Love and Pity

*But the stranger that dwelleth with you
shall be unto you as one born among you,
and thou shalt love him as thyself.*
LEVITICUS 19:34 KJV

Consider what Christ did toward the saving of souls. He thought them worth His blood. Shall we not think them worth our breath? Will you not do a little where Christ has done so much? Consider what fit objects of concern ungodly people are to us. They are dead in trespasses and sins and have not hearts to feel their miseries or to regret their own condition. If others do not take pity on them, they will have no pity. It is the nature of their disease to make them pitiless to themselves. Yes, they are their own most cruel destroyers.

It was God's argument to the Israelites to be kind to strangers because they themselves had been strangers in the land of Egypt. So should you pity them who are strangers to Christ, because you were once strangers to Him yourselves. Consider your relation to them. They are your neighbors, your brothers, whom you are bound to love as yourself. He who loves not his brother, whom he sees daily, does not love God, whom he never saw. And does he love his brother who will go to hell and never restrain him?

This is the misery of man's nature: Though every man naturally hates sorrow and loves the most merry and joyful life, yet few love the way to joy or will endure the pains by which it is obtained. They will be content with earthly pleasures rather than ascend to heaven to seek a joyful life.

RICHARD BAXTER

Trusting Love

> " 'I will save my flock,
> and they will no longer be plundered.
> I will place over them one shepherd,
> my servant David, and he will tend them;
> he will tend them and be their shepherd.' "
>
> EZEKIEL 34:22–23 NIV

Great truths are so often found in the simplest texts in the Bible. Those texts, which were used by those who loved us to explain the love of our heavenly Father, contain in their simple statements the whole story. We all need to get back into the nursery and take up our childish verses once more. Repeat these familiar words over to yourselves: "The Lord is my shepherd; I shall not want."

Centuries before Jesus came to be the shepherd, the Father said: "And I will set up one shepherd over them, and He shall feed them." I catch a glimpse of the Father's yearning love as I read these words. None therefore who are in this flock need fear any evil.

If our faith will but claim Him in this blessed and wondrous relationship, He will care for us according to His love, His wisdom, and His power, and not according to our poor comprehension of it. Enter into this relationship with Christ and really be a helpless, docile, trusting sheep, and believe Him to be your shepherd with all the love, care, and tenderness that that name involves. If you will follow Him wherever He leads, you will soon lose all your old spiritual discomfort, and will know the peace of God that passes all understanding to keep your hearts and minds in Christ Jesus.

HANNAH WHITALL SMITH

Love Simple Truth

"You are a king, then!" said Pilate.
Jesus answered, "You are right in saying
I am a king. In fact, for this reason I was born,
and for this I came into the world,
to testify to the truth.
Everyone on the side of truth listens to me."
JOHN 18:37 NIV

Truth, not eloquence, is to be sought in reading the holy scriptures. Every part must be read in the spirit in which it was written. For in the scriptures we ought to seek profit rather than polished diction.

Likewise, we ought to read simple and devout books as willingly as learned and profound ones. We ought not to be swayed by the authority of the writer, whether he be a great literary light or an insignificant person, but by the love of simple truth. We ought not to ask who is speaking but mark what is said. Men pass away, but the truth of the Lord remains forever. God speaks to us in many ways without regard for persons.

Our curiosity often hinders our reading of the scriptures, when we wish to understand and mull over what we ought simply to read and pass by. If you would profit from it, therefore, read with humility, simplicity, and faith, and never seek a reputation for being learned.

O Lord, let Your truth teach me. Let it guard me, and keep me safe to the end. Let it free me from all evil affection and badly ordered love, and I shall walk with You in great freedom of heart.

THOMAS À KEMPIS

Intercede in Love

I exhort therefore, first of all,
that supplications, prayers, intercessions,
thanksgivings, be made for all men.

1 TIMOTHY 2:1 ASV

If we inquire why there is so little love to be found among Christians, we shall find it owing to a neglect of that excellent part of prayer: intercession—imploring divine grace and mercy in behalf of others.

Some forget this duty of praying for others because they seldom remember to pray for themselves. Even those who are constant in praying to their Father are often so selfish in their addresses that they do not enlarge their petitions for the welfare of their fellow Christians.

Intercession will fill your hearts with love one to another. He who every day heartily intercedes at the throne of grace for all mankind cannot but in a short time be filled with love and charity to all. The frequent exercise of his love in this manner will gradually enlarge his heart. He will be filled with joy, peace, meekness, long-suffering, and all other graces of the Holy Spirit. By frequently laying his neighbor's wants before God, he will be touched with a fellow-feeling for them. Every blessing bestowed on others, instead of exciting envy in him, will be looked on as an answer to his particular intercession and fill his soul with joy unspeakable and full of glory.

Abound therefore in acts of general and particular intercessions. You cannot imagine what a blessed alteration this practice will make in your heart, and how much you will increase day by day in the spirit of love and meekness toward all mankind!

GEORGE WHITEFIELD

Love and Ill Temper

The LORD is gracious and merciful,
slow to anger and abounding in steadfast love.
PSALM 145:8 NRSV

No form of vice, not worldliness, not greed of gold, not drunkenness itself, does more to un-Christianize society than evil temper. For embittering life, for breaking up communities, for destroying the most sacred relationships, for devastating homes, for withering up men and women; in short, for sheer gratuitous misery-producing power, this influence stands alone. Look at the prodigal son's elder brother. He was moral, hardworking, patient, and obedient—let him get all credit for his virtues—look at this man sulking outside his own father's door. "He was angry," we read, "and would not go in." Look at the effect upon the father, upon the servants, and upon the happiness of the guests. Judge the effect upon the prodigal son—and how many prodigals are kept out of the kingdom of God by the unlovely characteristics of those who profess to be inside?

Jealousy, anger, pride, uncharity, cruelty, self-righteousness, touchiness, and sulleness—these are the ingredients of this dark and loveless elder brother. In varying proportions, also, these are the ingredients of all ill temper.

Ill temper is not in what it is alone, but in what it reveals. It is a test for love, a symptom, a revelation of an unloving nature. It is not enough to deal with the temper. We must go to the source and change the inmost nature. Souls are made sweet not by taking the acid fluids out but by putting something in—a great love. The spirit of Christ penetrating our spirits, sweetens, purifies, and transforms all.

HENRY DRUMMOND

What Would Jesus Do
The Businessman

You must have accurate and honest weights and measures,
so that you may live long in the land
the LORD your God is giving you.

DEUTERONOMY 25:15 NIV

What would Jesus do in Milton Wright's place as a businessman?

He would engage in the business first of all for the purpose of glorifying God, and not for the primary purpose of making money. All money that might be made He would never regard as His own, but as trust funds to be used for the good of humanity. His relations with all the persons in His employ would be the most loving and helpful. He could not help but think of all of them in the light of souls to be saved. This thought would always be greater than His thought of making money in the business. He would never do a single dishonest or questionable thing or try in any remotest way to get the advantage of anyone else in the same business.

The principle of unselfishness and helpfulness in the business would direct all its details. He would shape the entire plan of His relations to His employees, to the people who were His customers, and to the general business world with which He was connected.

Milton Wright said, "Intelligent unselfishness ought to be wiser than intelligent selfishness. I am absolutely convinced that Jesus in my place would be absolutely unselfish. He would love all these men in His employ. He would consider the main purpose of all the business to be a mutual helpfulness and would conduct it all so that God's kingdom would be evidently the first object sought."

CHARLES SHELDON

Halfhearted Love

*My purpose is that they may be encouraged in heart
and united in love,
so that they may have the full riches of
complete understanding.*

COLOSSIANS 2:2 NIV

I have learned that when anyone becomes in earnest about his
soul's salvation, and he begins to seek God, it does not take long
for an anxious sinner to meet an anxious Savior. Those who seek
for Him with all their hearts, find Christ.

I am tired and sick of halfheartedness. I don't like a half-
hearted man. I don't care for anyone to love me halfheartedly.
And the Lord won't have it. If we are going to seek for Him and
find Him, we must do it with all our hearts.

I believe the reason why so few find Christ is that they do
not search for Him with all their hearts. Everything God has
done proves that He is in earnest about the salvation of men's
souls. And the Lord wants us to be in earnest when it comes to
this great question of the soul's salvation. I never saw men seeking Him with all their hearts but they soon found Him.

It was quite refreshing one night to find a young man who
thought he was not worth saving, he was so vile and wicked.
There was hope for him because he was so desperately in earnest
about his soul. He had a sight of himself in God's looking glass
and had a very poor opinion of himself. But the moment he sees
God by the eye of faith, he is down on his knees, and, like Job,
he cries, "Behold, I am vile."

DWIGHT LYMAN MOODY

God Is Life

You have granted me life and steadfast love,
and your care has preserved my spirit.

Now, nothing wills and works with God but the spirit of love, because nothing else works in God Himself. The Almighty brought forth all nature for this only end that boundless love might have its infinity of height and depth to dwell and work in. All the striving and working properties of nature are only to give essence and substance, life and strength to the invisible hidden spirit of love, that it may come forth into outward activity and manifest its blessed powers, that creatures born in the strength and out of the powers of nature might communicate the spirit of love and goodness, give and receive mutual delight and joy to and from one another.

All below this state of love is a fall from the one life of God, and the only life in which the God of love can dwell. Partiality, self, mine, yours, etc., are traits that can only belong to creatures that have lost the power, presence, and spirit of the universal good. They can have no place in heaven. Think not therefore that the spirit of pure, universal love, which is the one purity and perfection of heaven, has been or can be carried too high, or its absolute necessity too much asserted. For it admits of no degrees of higher or lower, and is not in existence until it is absolutely pure and unmixed, no more than a line can be straight until it is absolutely free from all crookedness.

WILLIAM LAW

Loving Thoughts

I hate vain thoughts: but thy law do I love.
PSALM 119:113 KJV

A blessed sign of love is to entertain good thoughts of God. He who loves his friend construes what his friend does in the best sense. Malice interprets all in the worst sense; love interprets all in the best sense. Love is an excellent commentator upon divine guidance; it thinks no evil. He who loves God has a good opinion of God.

This is the language of a gracious spirit: "My God sees what a hard heart I have; therefore, He drives in one wedge of trial after another to break my heart. He knows how I am full of bad temper, how sick of a disease; therefore, He cleanses by blood to save my life. This severe action is either to restrain some vice or to exercise some grace. How good is God who will not let me alone in my sins, but smites my body to save my soul!" In this way, he who loves God takes everything with a good attitude.

Love puts a glowing interpretation upon all God's actions. You who are prone to murmur at God, as if He had dealt ill with you, be humbled for this. Say to yourself, "If I loved God more, I should have better thoughts of God." It is Satan who makes us have good thoughts of ourselves and hard thoughts of God. Love takes all in the fairest sense; it thinks no evil.

THOMAS WATSON

The Greatest Thing

> "Who is like you, O LORD, among the gods
>   Who is like you, majestic in holiness
>   awesome in splendor, doing wonders?
>
> EXODUS 15:11 NRSV

Love is the greatest thing that God can give us, and it is the greatest thing we can give to God. It is the old; it is the new; it is the great commandment; it is all the commandments. The consideration of God's goodness and bounty are most commonly the first motive of our love. But when we are once entered and have tasted the goodness of God, we love the source for its own excellence.

Perfection and admiration create love. For perfection and admiration, there is in God an infinite nature, unchanging, eternal, all-powerful, holy, merciful, filled with justice, and perfect. The consideration of which may be heightened, if we consider our distance from all these glories: our smallness, limited nature, inconstancy, weakness, ignorance, poverty, harsh natures, and unmerciful inclinations.

Love does all things that may please the beloved person. Love is obedient. Love gives away all things to advance the interest of the beloved person. Love is always liberal and expressive. It suffers all things that are imposed by its beloved. Love is patient and content with anything, provided it can be with its beloved. Love is also impatient of anything that may displease the beloved person. Love is not divided between God and God's enemy. We must love God with all our heart; that is, give Him a whole and undivided affection, having love for nothing else but such things which He allows, and which He commands or loves Himself.

JEREMY TAYLOR

Gracious Love

The LORD is compassionate and gracious,
slow to anger, abounding in love.
PSALM 103:8 NIV

Had God told us that He was not gracious, that He took no interest in our welfare, and that He had no intention of pardoning us, we could have no peace and no hope. In that case, our knowing God would only make us miserable. For how fearful a thing must it be to have the great God who made us, the great Father of Spirits, against us and not for us!

Strange to say, this is the very state of anxiety in which we may find many who profess to believe in God! With the Bible in their hands and the cross before their eyes, they wander on in a state of darkness and fear, such as would have arisen had God revealed Himself in hatred, not in love. They seem to believe the very opposite of what the Bible teaches us concerning God. They seem to attach a meaning to the cross that is the very opposite of what the gospel declares. Had God been all frowns and the Bible all terrors and Christ all sternness, these people could not have been in a more troubled and uncertain state than that in which they are. How is this? Have they misunderstood the Bible? Have they mistaken the character of God, looking on Him as an austere man and a hard master?

But God has declared Himself gracious. God is love. The more, then, that we know of this God and of His grace, the more will His peace fill us.

HORATIUS BONAR

Embrace His Love

Steadfast love and faithfulness will meet;
righteousness and peace will kiss each other.

PSALM 85:10 NRSV

The lovely will of God only means loving-kindness, tender mercies, and blessings to our souls. I wish I could show to everyone the unfathomable sweetness of the will of God. Heaven is a place of infinite bliss because His will is perfectly done there. Our lives share in this bliss just in proportion as His will is perfectly done in us. He loves us with more than the love of friendship. As a bridegroom rejoices over his bride, so does He rejoice over us.

He loves us and the will of love is always a blessing for its loved one. Some of us know what it is to love, and we know that if we could only have our way, our beloved ones would be overwhelmed with blessings. All that is good and sweet and lovely in life would be poured out upon them from our lavish hands, had we but the power to carry out our will for them. And if this is the way of love with us, how much more must it be so with our God, who is love itself. If we could but get a glimpse into the mighty depths of His love, our hearts would spring out to meet His will and embrace it as our richest treasure. We would abandon ourselves to it with an enthusiasm of gratitude and joy that such a wondrous privilege could be ours.

HANNAH WHITALL SMITH

Cheerful Love

Each of you must give as you have made up your mind,
not reluctantly or under compulsion,
for God loves a cheerful giver.
2 CORINTHIANS 9:7 NRSV

If you know the love of Jesus as the deer thirsts for the brooks, so will you desire greater portions of His love. If you do not desire to know Him better, then you do not love Him because love always cries, "Nearer, nearer." Only be content with an increasing acquaintance with Jesus. Seek to know more of Him in His divine nature, in His human relationship, in His finished work, in His death, in His resurrection, in His present glorious intercession, and in His future royal appearance. An increase of love to Jesus and a better understanding of His love to us is one of the best tests of growth in grace.

Our God requires no slaves to adorn His throne. He is the Lord of the empire of love and would have His servants dressed in the uniform of joy. If He sees that we serve Him from force and not because we love Him, He will reject our offering. Take away joyful willingness from the Christian, and you have removed the test of his sincerity. In the joy of the Lord, we are strong.

Cheerfulness is to our service what oil is to the wheels of a railway car. Without oil, the axle soon grows hot and accidents occur. If there be not a cheerfulness to oil our wheels, our spirits will be clogged with weariness. Let us show to the people of the world that our religion is to us a delight and a joy!

CHARLES HADDON SPURGEON

Continue your love to those who know you,
your righteousness to the upright in heart.

PSALM 36:10 NIV

Jesus says, "As the Father has loved Me, so have I loved You: Continue in My love." There is much more to this statement than is commonly believed. It was Christ's purpose to deposit in our laps a sure pledge of God's love toward us. The love in question here has to do with us because it is as the head of the church that Christ testifies to God's love for Him. Let us fix our eyes on Christ because in Him we see the pledge of God's love clearly exhibited. God poured His love upon Him so that it might flow from Him to the members of His body. This is also the significance of the title "the beloved Son, in whom the will of the Father is satisfied." We must consider the purpose of this love, which is that God in Christ may be well pleased with us. Christ was loved by the Father not in and for Himself alone, but that He might with Himself unite us with the Father.

Some explain the words "Continue ye in My love" to mean that Christ decreed for His disciples to love one another. He in fact bids us live always in the joy of the love with which He once and for all loved us, warning us not to deprive ourselves of it. Many reject the grace offered them. Once we are beneficiaries of the grace of Christ, let us see to it that we do not fall away from it through our own fault.

JOHN CALVIN

Live in Love

"If you obey my commands, you will remain in my love."
JOHN 15:10 NIV

The home of our soul is to be the love of Christ. We are to live our life there. This is what Christ means for our life to be and what He really can make it. Our continuous living in the vine is to be living in His love.

The love of the Father to the Son is not a sentiment—it is a divine life, an infinite energy, an irresistible power. It carried Christ through life, death, and the grave. The Father loved Him, dwelt in Him, and did all for Him. So the love of Christ to us, too, is an infinite living power that will work in us. The feebleness of our Christian life is that we do not take time to believe that this divine love does really delight in us, and will possess and work all in us.

It is possible so to live moment by moment and to believe that everything that makes it difficult or impossible will be overcome by Christ Himself. This is the secret of the true Christian life.

Turn away from the visible if you would see and possess the invisible. Turn away from yourself and your efforts if you would have your heart filled with Him and the certainty of His love. Come away from all else, and set your heart on Jesus and His love. Occupy yourself with that love, worship it, and wait for it. You may be sure it will reach out to you and by its power take you up into itself as your home.

ANDREW MURRAY

Love in Lights

> *And so we know and rely on*
> *the love God has for us. God is love*
> *Whoever lives in love lives in God*
> *and God in him*
>
> 1 JOHN 4:16 NIV

When Mr. Moody organized the church in Chicago, he was eager that everybody should always hear this one truth that God is love. He had it put on the gas jets right above the pulpit. The first thing you would see when you went in there on an evening was that text shining out in letters of fire.

One stormy night, before the time of the meeting, the door stood ajar. A man partly intoxicated saw it open and thought he might go in and get warm. When he pushed the door open, he saw the text blazing out, "God is love."

He pulled the door closed and walked away muttering to himself. He said, "God is not love. If God were love, He would love me. God does not love a wretch like me." But it kept on burning down into his soul, "God is love! God is love! God is love!" After a while he retraced his steps and took a seat in a corner.

When Mr. Moody walked down after the meeting, he found the man weeping like a child. "What is the trouble?" Mr. Moody asked. "What was it in the sermon that touched you?"

"I didn't hear a word of your sermon," the man said. "It i the text up there."

Mr. Moody sat down and from his Bible showed him the way of life, and he was saved.

REUBEN ARCHER TORREY

Love through Rose-Colored Glasses

Saul and Jonathan were lovely and pleasant in their lives.
2 SAMUEL 1:23 KJV

It was very lovely and pleasant of David to speak favorably of Saul and Jonathan. David had no hesitation, of course, in saying this of his beloved Jonathan, every memory of whom was very pleasant, like a sweet strain of music or the scent of the spring breeze. But he might have been excused for omitting Saul from the graceful and generous description he heaped on the kindred soul of his friend. But death had obliterated the sad, dark memories of recent days. Time had transported the psalmist across the dream of years to Saul as he was when David was first introduced to him.

This is the love of God, which He breathes into the hearts of His children. They become perfect in love, as He is. It is Godlike for His children to love their enemies, bless those who curse them, and pray for all who despitefully use and persecute them. Is such love ours? Do we forbear from thinking evil? Do we look on the virtues more often than the failures of our friends? Do we cast the mantle of forgiveness over the injuries done to us and dwell tenderly on the excellencies of our foes? Such is the love that never fails but endures when faith has turned to fruition, and hope has realized its dreams.

We need most of all a baptism of love. A piece of clay will become fragrant if placed near the fragrance of roses. Let us lie where John did, on the bosom of incarnate love, until we begin to love as he did.

F. B. MEYER

Stepping-Stones of Love

"Indeed, you love the people;
all your holy ones are in your hands.
They follow in your steps
and accept your instruction."

DEUTERONOMY 33:3 NLT

The facts in the Bible are like stepping-stones across a brook. Before you reach the shallows where they lie, you wonder how you will get over. But on stepping down to the edge of the water, you see that they span the space from bank to bank. You must come down to them, see how strongly fixed they are in the oozy bed, and notice how easily the villagers cross. Then you will be able to trust them. Finally, with a light heart and great sense of relief, you step from one to another.

It is a fact that God loves each of us with the tenderest and most special love. You may not believe or feel it. The warm summer sun may be shining against your shuttered and curtained window without making itself seen or felt within. Your failure to realize and appreciate the fact of God's love toward you cannot alter it being so.

After the peace was signed between the North and the South in the great American Civil War, there were soldiers hiding in the woods and starving on berries, who might have returned to their homes. They either did not know or did not credit the Good News. They went on starving long after their comrades had been welcomed by their wives and children. Theirs was the loss, but their failure in knowledge or belief did not alter the fact that peace was proclaimed and that the door was wide open for their return.

F. B. MEYER

Charity and the Wealthy

And the King shall answer and say unto them,
Verily I say unto you,
Inasmuch as ye did it unto one of these my brethren,
even these least, ye did it unto me.
MATTHEW 25:40 ASV

We were created to be a help to each other. God has made no one so independent as not to need the assistance of another. The richest and most powerful man upon the face of this earth needs the help and assistance of those who are around him. Though he may be great today, a thousand accidents may make him as low tomorrow. He who is rolling in plenty today may be in as much scarcity tomorrow.

What difference is there between the king on the throne and the beggar on the dunghill when God demands their breaths? There is no difference, my brethren, in the grave, nor will there be any at the Day of Judgment. You will not be excused because you have had a great estate, a fine house, and lived in all the pleasures that earth could afford you. Neither will you be judged according to the largeness of your estate but according to the use you have made of it.

Let me beseech you, my rich brethren, to consider the poor of the world, and how commendable and praiseworthy it is to relieve those who are distressed. Consider how pleasing this is to God, how delightful it is to man, and how many prayers you will have put up for your welfare by those persons whom you relieve. God has blessed you for the relief of His poor.

GEORGE WHITEFIELD

Charity among the Poor

*Pure religion and undefiled before God and the Father is this,
to visit the fatherless and widows in their affliction,
and to keep himself unspotted from the world.*

JAMES 1:27 KJV

I exhort you who are poor to be charitable to one another. You may not have money or the things of this life to bestow upon one another. Yet you may assist them, by comforting and advising them not to be discouraged though they are low in the world. In sickness you may help them according as you have time or ability. Do not be unkind to one another. Do not grieve or vex or be angry with each other for this is giving the world an advantage over you.

And if God stirs up any to relieve you, do not make an ill use of what His providence by the hands of some Christian hath bestowed upon you. Be always humble and wait on God. Do not murmur or brood if you see any relieved and you are not. Wait on the Lord, and help one another according to your abilities from time to time.

Consider how easy it is for many of you by putting your small contribution together to help one who is in distress. The little you give may be the means of bringing one from distress into flourishing circumstances. And then if there is a true spirit of a Christian in them, they can never be sufficiently thankful to God the author and to you as the instrument in being so great a friend to them in their melancholy circumstances. Consider also what peace of conscience you will enjoy. How satisfactory must be the thought of having relieved the widow and the fatherless?

GEORGE WHITEFIELD

Obligation to Love

"Since you are precious and honored in my sight,
and because I love you,
I will give men in exchange for you,
and people in exchange for your life."
ISAIAH 43:4 NIV

Our obligation to love, honor, and obey any being is in proportion to his loveliness, honorableness, and authority. When we say anyone is very lovely, it is the same as saying that he is one who is very much to be loved. Or, if we say such a one is more honorable than another, the meaning of the words is that he is one that we are more obliged to honor.

But God is a being infinitely lovely. He has infinite excellency and beauty. He is a being of infinite greatness, majesty, and glory; therefore, He is infinitely honorable. He is infinitely exalted above the greatest kings of the earth, and therefore He is infinitely more honorable than they. He is infinitely worthy to be obeyed Himself, and we have an absolute, universal, and infinite dependence upon Him.

You lived such a wicked life; it would have been most just with God to cast you off. But He has had mercy upon you. He made His glorious grace appear for your everlasting salvation. You had no love for God; yet He exercised unspeakable love to you. So great a value has God's grace set on you that you have been redeemed at the price of the blood of His own Son. God hath made you a joint heir with Christ of His glory. You were ungrateful for past mercies; yet God not only continued those mercies but bestowed unspeakably greater mercies upon you.

JONATHAN EDWARDS

Paths of Love

*"With unfailing love you will lead this people
whom you have ransomed.
You will guide them in your strength
to the place where your holiness dwells."*

EXODUS 15:13 NLT

You must remember that our God has all knowledge and all wisdom. He may guide you into paths wherein He knows great blessings are awaiting you. But to the shortsighted human eyes around you, the paths may seem sure to result in loss. You must recognize that He knows the end of things from the beginning. He alone can judge what the results of any course of action may be. You must realize that His very love for you may lead you to run counter to the loving wishes of even your dearest friends.

You may be called upon to turn your back on father or mother or husband or wife. The child of God who enters upon this life of obedience is sooner or later led into paths which meet with the disapproval of those he best loves. Unless he is prepared for this and can trust the Lord through it all, he will scarcely know what to do.

The nearer we are to Christ, the more shall we be enabled to show by example the meekness and gentleness of our Lord. The more tender will be our consideration for those who are our natural guardians and counselors. If in obedience to Him we are led to act contrary to the wishes of our friends, we shall prove that His will is our motive by the love and patience that marks our conduct toward them.

HANNAH WHITALL SMITH

Polished with Love

Listen, my child. . .
Don't neglect your mother's teaching.
PROVERBS 1:8 NLT

You know a mother has to love her babe before it is born. Like God, she has to go into the shadows of the valley of death to bring it into the world, and she will love her child and suffer for it. I think, women, that one of the awful things in hell will be that there will be no mother's love there. Nothing but black, bottomless, endless, eternal hate in hell—no mother's love.

I thank God for what mother's love has done for the world. Surely as Moses was put in his mother's arms by the Egyptian princess, so God has put the babes in your arms as a charge by Him to raise and care for. Every child is put in a mother's arms as a responsibility from God. She has to answer to God for the way she deals with that child. That babe is put in your arms to train for the Lord. No mother has any more right to raise her children for materialism than I have to pick your pockets. She has no more right to do that than a bank cashier has to take the savings of the people.

One of the worst sins you can commit is to be unfaithful to your trust. That child is a jewel that belongs to God, and He gives it to you to polish for Him. Will you promise that from now on you will try, with God's help, to do better than you ever have done to raise your children for God?

BILLY SUNDAY

Love in Action

Place me like a seal over your heart,
like a seal on your arm;
for love is as strong as death,
its jealousy unyielding as the grave.
It burns like blazing fire, like a mighty flame.

SONG OF SONGS 8:6 NIV

Love to God must be active. Love is no idle ornament. It sets the head studying for God and the feet running in the ways of His commandments. Pretenses of love are insufficient. Love has not only a smooth tongue but also a kind heart. He will be eyes to the blind and feet to the lame. The bellies of the poor shall be where he sows the golden seeds of liberality. Some say they love God, but their love is lame because they give nothing to good uses. Indeed, faith deals with invisibles, but God hates that love which is invisible. Love vents itself in good works.

He who is a lover of God gives Him such a love as he bestows upon none else. Love to God is permanent. Love is like the pulse of the body, always beating. It is not a desert but a spring flood. Nothing can hinder a Christian's love to God. Nothing can conquer love, not any difficulties or oppositions. Neither the sweet waters of pleasure nor the bitter waters of persecution can quench love. Love to God abides firm to death. Light things, such as chaff and feathers, are quickly blown away, but a tree that is rooted survives the storm. He who is rooted in love, endures. True love never ends.

THOMAS WATSON

Two Labor in Love

For God is not unjust to forget your work
and labor of love which you have shown toward His name,
in that you have ministered to the saints,
and do minister.
HEBREWS 6:10 NKJV

I consider it one of the especial mercies that this day I have as much desire as ever, yes, more than ever, to live for Him who has done so much for me. My greatest grief is that I love Him so little. I desire many things concerning myself, but I desire nothing so much as to have a heart filled with love to the Lord. I long for a warm, personal attachment to Him.

I consider it further an exceedingly great mercy that I have been kept in uninterrupted love and union with my brother, friend, and fellow-laborer Henry Craik. Very few of the blessings that the Lord has bestowed on him, on me, and on the two churches, whose servants we are, are of greater importance. There is not one point of importance as it regards the truth on which we differ. In judgment as to matters connected with the welfare of the saints among whom we labor, we have been almost invariably at once of one mind.

We have had much joy on account of the scriptural conduct of many of the children of God among whom we labor. The two churches have shown, in some measure, that even in our day there can be love among the brethren. We have had much more joy than sorrow during the last five years.

GEORGE MÜLLER

Linger in the Gallery of Love

Incline your ear, and come to me;
listen, so that you may live.
I will make with you an everlasting covenant,
my steadfast, sure love for David.

ISAIAH 55:3 NRSV

Seek feeling and you will miss it. Be content to live without it, and you will have all you require. If you are always noticing your heartbeats, you will bring on heart disease. If you are ever muffling against cold, you will become very subject to chills. If you are perpetually thinking about your health, you will induce disease. If you are always consulting your feelings, you will live in a dry and thirsty land.

Be indifferent to emotion. If it is there, be thankful. If it is absent, go on doing the will of God, counting on Him, and speaking well of Him. It is impossible to rush into God's presence, catch up anything we fancy, and run off with it. To attempt this will end in mere delusion and disappointment. Nature will not unveil her rarest beauty to the chance tourist. Pictures that are the result of a life of work do not disclose their secret loveliness to those who stroll down a gallery. And God's best cannot be ours apart from patient waiting in His holy presence.

It is as if a girl should spend an hour in her room wondering in what dress to meet her lover, who is waiting impatiently below. Let her go to him, and if she desires it, he will soon enough tell her clearly his preference. Get into the presence of Jesus, and you will be told clearly and unmistakably His will.

F. B. MEYER

Love Like Christ

For the love of Christ urges us on,
because we are convinced that one has died for all;
therefore all have died.
2 CORINTHIANS 5:14 NRSV

Seeing God in everything will make us loving and patient with those who annoy and trouble us. They will be to us then only the means for accomplishing His tender and wise purposes toward us. We shall even find ourselves at last inwardly thanking them for the blessings they bring us.

If our Father permits a trial to come, it must be because that trial is the best thing that could happen to us. We must accept it with thanks from His dear hand. The trial itself may be hard upon us, and I do not mean that we can enjoy the suffering of it. But we can and must love the will of God in the trial because His will is always sweet, whether it be in joy or in sorrow.

If you are really one with Christ, you will be sweet to those who are cross to you. You will bear everything and make no complaints. When you are reviled, you will not revile again and feel nothing but love in return. You will seek the honor of others rather than your own. You will take the lowest place and be the servant of all, as Christ was. You will literally and truly love your enemies and do good to them who despitefully use you. You will, in short, live a Christlike life and show outwardly—as well as feel inwardly—a Christlike spirit. This is what it is to be one with Christ.

HANNAH WHITALL SMITH

Love and Good Temper

[Love] is not easily provoked.

1 CORINTHIANS 13:5 KJV

Good temper is a remarkable ingredient in love. We are inclined to look upon bad temper as a very harmless weakness. We speak of it as a mere infirmity of nature, a family failing, a matter of temperament, not a thing to take into very serious account in estimating a person's character. And yet right in the heart of Paul's analysis of love in 1 Corinthians 13:5, it finds a place: Love is not easily provoked.

The Bible again and again returns to condemn anger as one of the most destructive elements in human nature. The peculiarity of ill temper is that it is the vice of the virtuous. It is often the one blot on an otherwise noble character. You know men who are all but perfect and women who would be entirely perfect but for an easily ruffled, quick-tempered, or touchy disposition. This compatibility of ill temper with high moral character is a strange and sad problem.

The truth is there are two great classes of sins—sins of the body and sins of the disposition. The prodigal son may be taken as a type of the first, his elder brother of the second. Now society has no doubt whatever as to which of these is the worse. Its brand falls, without a challenge, upon the prodigal. But are we right? We have no balance to weigh one another's sins, and coarser and finer are but human words; faults in the higher nature may be less excusable than those in the lower, and to the eye of Him who is love, a sin against love may seem a hundred times more dishonorable.

HENRY DRUMMOND

Love and the Faithful Father

Know therefore that the LORD your God is God,
the faithful God who maintains
covenant loyalty with those who love him
and keep his commandments,
to a thousand generations.

DEUTERONOMY 7:9 NRSV

Unquestionably, obedience is a high virtue. To obey belongs, pre-eminently, to the soldier. It is his first and last lesson, and he must learn how to practice it all the time without question and uncomplainingly. Obedience is faith in action, and it is the very test of love. The Son of God is held in the heart of the Father's love by virtue of His obedience! The factor that enables the Son of God to reside in His Father's love is revealed in His own statement. Jesus said, "For I do, always, those things that please Him."

What is obedience? It is doing God's will. It is keeping His commandments. Does God give commandments that we cannot obey? Is He so arbitrary, so severe, and so unloving as to issue commandments that cannot be obeyed? The answer is that in all of holy scripture not a single instance is recorded of God having commanded any person to do a thing that was beyond that person's power. Is God so inconsiderate as to require of us that which we are unable to render? Surely not.

Let us ponder this thought a moment: Do earthly parents require of their children duties that they cannot perform? Where is the father who would think of being so unjust and so tyrannical? Is God less kind and less just than faulty, earthly parents? Are they better and more just than a perfect God? How utterly foolish and untenable a thought!

EDWARD MCKENDREE BOUNDS

Singular Love

> *But I will sing of your strength,*
> *in the morning I will sing of your love;*
> *for you are my fortress,*
> *my refuge in times of trouble.*
>
> PSALM 59:16 NIV

Singular love has no equal. It is when all warmth and comfort is closed out of the heart, except the love of Jesus alone. Other delights fail to please because the sweetness of Him is so comforting and lasting. His love is so burning and gladdening that he who has singular love may feel with joy the fire of love burning in his soul. That fire is so pleasant that no man can speak of it except he who feels it.

With singular love, the soul is Jesus loving, Jesus thinking, and Jesus desiring. It is burning in longing only for Him, singing in Him, resting on Him. Then the thought turns to song and melody. The soul that is in this degree may boldly say, "I mourn for love! I languish to come to my loved Jesus."

He who most withdraws his love from the world and from unreasonable lusts shall be most able and shall most speedily increase in love. Those who have a liking to things other than Jesus and in the sweetness of His law do not come to singular love. He who has singular love desires to be unbound from the bond of his body and to be in full joy with Jesus, whom he loves. In this manner shall a lover of Jesus Christ be. He shall so burn in love that he shall be wholly turned into the fire of love.

JOHN WYCLIFFE

The Nature of Christ's Love

*For I am not ashamed of the gospel;
it is the power of God for salvation
to everyone who has faith, to the Jew first
and also to the Greek.*

ROMANS 1:16 NRSV

I will present these things as helps to the knowledge of the nature of the love of Christ, and helps to retain it. First, you cannot know the love of Christ before you know the badness of your nature. He who sees but little of his sinful nature will hardly know much of the love of Christ. He who sees of himself nothing at all will hardly ever see anything of the love of Christ. But he who sees most of what a miserable character he is, he is likely to see most of what is the love of Christ. So then if a man would be kept sure and steadfast, let him labor before all things to know his own wretchedness.

Labor to see the emptiness, shortness, and pollution that clings to a man's own righteousness. This also must in some measure be known before a man can know the nature of the love of Christ.

To know the nature of Christ's love, be much in acquainting yourself with the nature of the law and the nature of the gospel. The law is a servant, both first and last, to the gospel. For here is nothing that Satan more desires than that the law may take the place of Christ and faith.

JOHN BUNYAN

United in Love

But whoever continually keeps his word is the kind of person
in whom God's love has truly been perfected.
This is how we can be sure that we are in union with him.

1 JOHN 2:5 IS

There are many relations in life that require from the different parties only very moderate degrees of devotion. We may have pleasant friendships with one another and yet spend a large part of our lives in separate interests and widely differing pursuits. There is not enough love between us to give us the desire to share one another's most private affairs.

But there are other relations in life where all this is changed. The friendship becomes love. The two hearts give themselves to one another. A union of souls takes place, which makes all that belong to one the property of the other. Separate interests and separate paths in life are no longer possible. The reserve and distance suitable to mere friendship gives way to love. The wishes of one become binding obligations to the other. The deepest desire of each heart is that it may know every secret wish or longing of the other so that it may fly on the wings of the wind to gratify it.

Do such as these chafe under this yoke which love imposes? Do they envy the cool, calm, reasonable friendships they see around them, and regret the nearness into which their souls are brought to their beloved one because of the obligations it creates? No, they glory in these very obligations. All the tender longing love of your heavenly master makes love a blessing and longed-for privilege.

HANNAH WHITALL SMITH

Love and the New Covenant

"O LORD, God of Israel,
there is no God like you in heaven above or on earth beneath,
keeping covenant and steadfast love for your servants
who walk before you with all their heart."

KINGS 8:23 NRSV

If anyone thinks he believes in Christ and has not the law written in his heart to love his brother as Christ loved him, the faith of that person is vain. It is built upon sand of his own imagination and not upon the rock of God's word. True faith makes a man to love his brother.

In the sacrifices of the Old Testament, Moses offered half the blood to God and sprinkled the people with the other half to confirm the covenant. The new covenant of Christ is confirmed with a better blood to make people see love and to love again. For if God gave us His Son, what will He deny us? If God so loved us when we were sinners and knew Him not, how much more does He love us now that we love again?

Our service to Christ is only to believe in Him for the remission of sin, to call upon Him and give Him thanks, and to love our neighbors for His sake. Now they who believe in Christ for the remission of their sins and for His sake love their foes are not Christ's enemies. Sin is forgiven only for Christ's sake; and again, that our duty is to love our neighbors no less than Christ loved us. Let us exhort each other to trust in Christ and to love each other as Christ did.

WILLIAM TYNDALE

The Holy Spirit's Love

And this expectation will not disappoint us
For we know how dearly God loves us
because he has given us
the Holy Spirit to fill our hearts with his love

ROMANS 5:5 NL

We have considered the bountiful overflow of the Father's love and our hearts have burned within us as we dwelt upon and felt the glow of the love of the Son. Now as we think of the blessing of the Spirit, may He reveal Himself to us through these holy words. They were written by His inspiration and can never be fully understood save by His own illumination. The Bible is a supernatural book, a divine revelation. To all those, whether learned or unlearned, in whom the Holy Ghost has wrought the childlike spirit, it is an open book. They love it, feast upon it and grow thereby.

It is very important to have clear thoughts about the third Person of the Trinity. Many Christians fail in this respect, and lose much in consequence. He has as distinct a personality as the Son of God. We must not think or speak of Him vaguely, as though He were an influence merely and not a Person. Our Savior teaches us that we should know Him, "for He abideth with you, and shall be in you."

It is the purpose of God that the presence and the love of the Spirit should be made known to those in whom He dwells. Many a believer to whom Christ has left peace knows little of it, but those who are filled with the Spirit are filled with peace. The fruit of the Spirit is love, joy, peace.

HUDSON TAYLOR

Joy and Happiness

Satisfy us in the morning with your unfailing love,
that we may sing for joy and be glad all our days.
PSALM 90:14 NIV

If anyone asks the question, "How can I be a happy Christian?" our Lord's answer is very simple: "I have spoken to you, that My joy may be in you, and that your joy may be fulfilled." To many Christians the thought of a life wholly dwelling in Christ is one of strain and painful effort. They cannot see that the strain and effort only come when we do not yield ourselves unreservedly to the life of Christ in us.

We are to have Christ's own joy in us. And what is Christ's own joy? There is no joy like love. There is no joy but love. Christ had spoken of the Father's love and His own residing in joy, and of His having loved us with that same love. His joy is nothing but the joy of love, of being loved and of loving. He wants us to share the joy of being loved of the Father by our loving and living for those around us. This is just the joy of being truly branches—living in His love and then giving up ourselves in love to bear fruit for others.

Religion is meant to be in everyday life a thing of unspeakable joy. And why do so many complain that it is not so? They do so because they do not believe there is joy like the joy of living in Christ and in His love.

ANDREW MURRAY

Devoted to Missionary Work

*We ought always to thank God for you,
brothers, and rightly so,
because your faith is growing more and more,
and the love every one of you has for each other
is increasing.*

2 THESSALONIANS 1:3 NIV

Wherever a missionary lives, traders are sure to come. They are mutually dependent, and each aids in the work of the other. But experience shows that the two employments cannot very well be combined in the same person. No missionary with whom I ever came in contact traded. While the traders, whom we introduced and rendered secure in the country, waxed rich, the missionaries have invariably remained poor and have died so.

We have sent out missionaries with a bare subsistence only and are unsparing in our applause of some for not being worldly-minded whom our stinginess made to live as did the prodigal son. I do not speak of myself, nor need I to do so, but for that very reason I feel at liberty to interpose a word in behalf of others.

The command to "go into all the world and preach the gospel to every creature" must be obeyed by Christians either personally or by substitute. Now it is quite possible to find people whose love for the heathen and devotion to the work will make them ready to go forth on the terms "bare subsistence." But what can be thought of the justice of Christians and churches who not only work their substitutes at the lowest terms but regard what they give as charity! The matter is the more grave in respect to the missionary who may have a wife and family.

DAVID LIVINGSTONE

Do It for Love

Act on the principles of love and justice,
and always live in confident dependence on your God.
HOSEA 12:6 NLT

The man who does his business with all his heart is sure to prosper. It is a great thing to love our lifework and to have an aim that kindles us to action whenever we think of it. Those who are happy in their circumstances cannot be sufficiently thankful. But what of those who are bound to a work that they did not choose and do not like, who find their daily toil irksome and distasteful—is there any help for them? Can they possibly learn to do such work from their hearts? Certainly: because of Him who set it and for whom it may be done.

Love performs the most onerous duties with all its heart if they advance the comfort and help of those whom it loves more than itself. A mother or wife performs tasks from which the hired person would shrink. She does them with all her heart, not considering for a moment the disagreeableness and hardness of the demand. So if we look at our lifework as appointed by God, if we can hear the voice of Jesus saying, "Do this for Me," there is no further thought of hardship or distaste. Remember to do all your lifework for Jesus. Do all in His name and for His glory. Ask Him to fill your heart with submissive, loyal obedience. You will find that when you introduce the personal element of service to Christ into the most ordinary acts, they will glisten like a piece of gold tapestry.

F. B. MEYER

Love, Envy, and Kindness

Love is not envious or boastful or arrogant.

1 CORINTHIANS 13:4 NRSV

Love does not envy. This indeed is implied when it is said, "Love is kind." For kindness and envy are inconsistent: They can no more reside together than light and darkness. If we earnestly desire happiness to all, we cannot be grieved at the happiness of any. The fulfilling of our desire will be sweet to our soul. So we will not be pained at their happiness. If we are always doing what good we can for our neighbor and wishing we could do more, it is impossible that we should brood at a good he receives. Instead it will be the very joy of our heart. No matter how we may flatter ourselves or one another, he who envies has not love.

It follows that love is not rash or hasty in judging. As many as love their neighbor for God's sake will not easily listen to an ill opinion of anyone to whom they wish all good, spiritual as well as secular. They cannot condemn him even in their heart without evidence nor upon slight evidence. Indeed, upon any evidence, if it is possible, have him and his accuser brought face-to-face. Or, at the least inform him of the accusation and let him speak for himself. Every one of you feels that he cannot but act like this with regard to one whom he tenderly loves. He who does not act this way has not love.

JOHN WESLEY

Loving Trust

Many are the woes of the wicked,
but the LORD's unfailing love
surrounds the man who trusts in him.
PSALM 32:10 NIV

Dear Mr. Partridge,

Nearly every time the newspapers come that you send, I feel so ashamed of my not having written sooner. What a world of unrest, doubt, and pessimism you seem to live in at home. There seems to be no solid foundation for mankind to rest on. Does it point to our Lord's near approach in the Second Coming? I think so, and I hope so! My only drawback is that I fear my children [twins and other children who were abandoned and outcast by natives at Calabar, West Africa] are not all ready. But they are His, and He surely has infinitely more interest and love in and for them than I have, so He will do all things well for us all. He will not throw back the children given to Him in loving trust.

I have had a rebuke this morning from 1 John 4:18, the last clause: "He that feareth is not made perfect in love." How dishonoring to our Father to keep misunderstanding Him and imputing anything unworthy to Him.

Things here go on smoothly. We thank God for a willing people and for the adherence of the young. It is a hard fight with heathenism. They all want their children educated, but they don't want them to serve Christ. Whenever the Christian and heathen practices clash, they are fiercely on the heathen side. Few of the women are moving Christward, although they are friendly and kind to us personally.

MARY SLESSOR

Love and Giving

He defends the cause of the fatherless and the widow,
and loves the alien, giving him food and clothing.

DEUTERONOMY 10:18 NIV

The difficult thing is not to seek things for ourselves at all. After we have sought them, bought them, won them, and deserved them, we have taken the cream off them for ourselves already. It takes little sacrifice then, perhaps, to give them up. But not to seek them—that is the greater work. There is no greatness in things. Things cannot be great. The only greatness is unselfish love. Even self-denial in itself is nothing; it is almost a mistake. It is more difficult not to seek our own at all than, having sought it, to give it up. I must take that back. It is only true of a partly selfish heart. Nothing is a hardship to love.

I believe that Christ's yoke is easy. And I believe it is an easier way than any other. I believe it is a happier way than any other. The most obvious lesson in Christ's teaching is that there is no happiness in having and getting anything, but only in giving. And half the world is on the wrong scent in the pursuit of happiness. They think it consists in having and getting, and in being served by others. It consists in giving and in serving others. He who would be great among you, said Christ, let him serve. He who would be happy, let him remember that there is but one way—it is more blessed, it is more happy to give than to receive.

HENRY DRUMMOND

Love Your Enemies

But I say unto you which hear, Love your enemies,
do good to them which hate you.

LUKE 6:27 KJV

It is a smaller thing to wish well or even to do well to one who has done you no evil. It is far greater—a sort of magnificent goodness—to love your enemy and always to wish him well, and do well to him who wishes you ill and who does you harm when he can.

Such recommendations are for the perfect sons of God. Although all the faithful should strive toward them and through prayer to God and earnest endeavor bring their souls up to this level, still so high a degree of goodness is not possible. In prayer, we say, "Forgive us our debts, as we forgive our debtors." For this means, "Forgive us our debts when we ask for forgiveness, as we also forgive our debtors when they ask for forgiveness."

If one seeks forgiveness, he should no longer be regarded as an enemy, and it should not now be as difficult to love him as it was when he was actively hostile. Now a man who does not forgive from the heart one who asks forgiveness and is repentant of his sins can in no way suppose that his own sins are forgiven by the Lord. The One who, when He was teaching the prayer, strongly emphasized this sentence, saying: "For if you forgive men their trespasses, your heavenly Father will also forgive your trespasses. But if you will not forgive men, neither will your Father forgive your offenses."

AUGUSTINE

Love and Tenderness

> *He ransoms me from death and surrounds me*
> *with love and tender mercies.*
>
> PSALM 103:4 NLT

Discomfort and unrest are impossible to the souls who come to know that God is their real and actual Father. I must make it plain that it is a father, such as our highest instincts tell us a good father ought to be, of whom I am speaking. Sometimes earthly fathers are unkind or tyrannical or selfish or even cruel—or they are merely indifferent and neglectful—but none of these can be called good fathers. But God, who is good, must be a good father or not a father at all. We must all of us have known good fathers in this world or at least can imagine them. I knew one, and he filled my childhood with sunshine by his most lovely fatherhood. I have learned to know a little about the perfect fatherhood of God because of my experience with this lovely earthly father.

But God is not only a father, He is a mother as well, and we have all of us known mothers whose love and tenderness have been without bound or limit. And it is very certain that God could never have created earthly fathers and mothers who were more tender and more loving than He is Himself. We must heap together all the best of all the fathers and mothers we have ever known or can imagine, and we must tell ourselves that this is only a faint image of God, our Father in Heaven. What a good father ought to do, God, who is our Father, is absolutely sure to do.

HANNAH WHITALL SMITH

Noble Love

These were more noble than those in Thessalonica,
in that they received the word with all readiness of mind,
and searched the scriptures daily,
whether those things were so.
ACTS 17:11 KJV

Ah, Lord God, my holy lover, when You come into my heart, all that is within me will rejoice. You are my glory and the exultation of my heart. You are my hope and refuge in the day of my tribulation. But because my love is as yet weak and my virtue imperfect, I must be strengthened and comforted by You. Visit me often, therefore, and teach me Your holy discipline. Free me from evil passions and cleanse my heart of all disorderly affection so that, healed and purified within, I may be fit to love, strong to suffer, and firm to persevere.

Love is an excellent thing, a very great blessing indeed. It makes every difficulty easy and bears all wrongs with composure. For it bears a burden without being weighted and renders sweet all that is bitter. The noble love of Jesus spurs to great deeds and excites longing for that which is more perfect. Love tends upward; it will not be held down by anything low. Love wishes to be free and estranged from all worldly affections lest its inward sight be obstructed, lest it be entangled in any transitory interest and overcome by adversity.

Nothing is sweeter than love, nothing stronger or higher or wider; nothing is more pleasant, nothing fuller, and nothing better in heaven or on earth, for love is born of God and cannot rest except in God who is above all created things.

THOMAS À KEMPIS

Forsaken Love

Can a woman forget her nursing child,
or show no compassion
for the child of her womb?
Even these may forget,
yet I will not forget you.
ISAIAH 49:15 NRSV

Love of your children should move you to serve the Lord. Most people express a great fondness for their children. Very often their own lives are wrapped up in those of their offspring. "Can a woman forget her sucking child?" asks God by His prophet Isaiah. He speaks of it as a monstrous thing and scarcely credible, but the words immediately following affirm it to be possible: "Yes, they may forget." Experience also assures us they may. Father and mother may both forsake their children, for what greater degree of forgetfulness can they express toward them than to neglect bringing them up in the knowledge and fear of God?

It is true indeed that parents seldom forget to provide for their children's bodies, but then how often do they forget to secure the salvation of their immortal souls? But is this their way of expressing their fondness for the fruit of their bodies? Is this the best testimony they can give of their affection to the darlings of their hearts?

How can it be expected they should learn their duty, except those set over them take care to teach it to them? The more they are taught their duty to God, the better they will perform their duties to you. To neglect the improvement of their souls, out of a dread of spending too much time in religious duties, is acting quite contrary to your own interest as well as duty.

GEORGE WHITEFIELD

Special Love

This is how God showed his love among us:
He sent his one and only Son into the world
that we might live through him.
1 JOHN 4:9 NIV

More is evidently implied in the expression "God so loved the world" than simply its greatness. It is most exceptional in its character. Unless we understand this, we shall be in danger of falling into the strange mistake of some people who are forever talking about God's love for sinners, but whose notions of the nature of this love never lead to repentance or to holiness. Some people seem to think of this love as simply good nature. They conceive of God only as a very good-natured being, whom nobody needs to fear. Such notions have not the least influence toward holiness but the very opposite. It is only when we come to understand what this love is in its nature that we feel its moral power promoting holiness.

It may be reasonably asked, "If God so loved the world with a love characterized by only greatness, why did He not save all the world without sacrificing His Son?" This question suffices to show us that there is deep meaning in this word. It was not a mere emotion or feeling. It was not a blind impulse. God had emotion but not emotion only. Indeed the Bible everywhere teaches us that God's love for man, lost in his sins, was paternal—the love of a father for his offspring—in this case, for a rebellious, disobedient, prodigal offspring. In this love there must of course blend the deepest compassion.

CHARLES FINNEY

Cry for Help

Above all, love each other deeply,
because love covers over a multitude of sins.

1 PETER 4:8 NIV

Those who will turn truly to Christ must flee situations, sights, and deeds that tempt them to sin. When one among a hundred withstands evil enticings and turns to God, following the steps of Christ, despising the joys of his present life, and seeking to love everlasting heavenly things, the devil finds a thousand deceits to ensnare and trouble him. The devil finds a thousand kinds of temptations to cast him down from God's love to the love of the world. And he begins with the smallest, that by foul thoughts he may make him to be foul toward God.

He who is truly fed with the bread that came down from heaven bows not his love to those things to which the evil one entices. Temptations are overcome by patience and meek suffering. What is patience? It is a glad and willing suffering of troubles. He who is patient murmurs not at adversity but rather at all times praises God.

He who truly loves his maker refuses to desire any things that are in the world. It is sweetness for him to speak of Him and be with Him. To think upon his maker is refreshing to him. The fiery darts of the enemy are put out with the meekness and sweetness of the love of Christ. Therefore when we are tempted, let us cry for the help of our Father, as a child cries after the comfort of its mother.

JOHN WYCLIFFE

Love to Teach Children

He will love you, he will bless you, he will increase you.
He will bless the babies from your womb.
DEUTERONOMY 7:13 TM

I found a teacher at our services when she ought to have been attending to her class. Upon my asking why she was at our meeting, she said: "I have a very small class—only five little boys."

"What?" said I. "You have come here and neglected these little ones! Why, in that little head may be the seeds of a reformation. There may be a Luther, a Wheaton, a Wesley, or a Bunyan among them. You may be neglecting a chance for them, the effects of which will follow them through life."

Look what a kind teacher did in Southern Illinois. She had taught a little girl to love the Savior, and the teacher asked her, "Can you get your father to come to the Sunday school?" This father was a swearing, drinking man, and the love of God was not in his heart. But under the training of that teacher, the little girl went to her father, told him of Jesus' love, and led him to that Sunday school. What was the result? I heard before leaving for Europe that her father had been instrumental in founding over 780 Sunday schools in Southern Illinois.

What a privilege a teacher has—a privilege of leading souls to Christ. Let every Sunday school teacher say, "By the help of God I will try to lead my scholars to Christ."

DWIGHT LYMAN MOODY

Increase in Love

> The LORD passed before him,
> and proclaimed, "The LORD, the LORD,
> a God merciful and gracious, slow to anger,
> and abounding in steadfast love and faithfulness,
> keeping steadfast love for the thousandth generation,
> forgiving iniquity and transgression and sin."
>
> EXODUS 34:6–7 NRSV

We may the better stir up and increase our love to God if we cut off every degree of undue affection to the things of this world. Restrain our imagination because it is usually pleased with the entertainment of shadows and gaudiness.

Every act of love to a sin is a perfect enemy to the love of God. It is a great shame to take any part of our affection from the eternal God and bestow it upon his creature in defiance of the Creator. Remove worldly cares and multitudes of secular businesses because if these take up the intention and actual application of our thoughts, they will also possess our passions. If we dwell in the affairs of the world, we shall also grow in love with them, and all our love shall be spent upon trifles and vanities.

Talk with God by frequent prayer. In particular, ask that your desires may be right—and love to have your affections with Him regular and holy. Call to Him for health, run to Him for counsel, and beg of Him for pardon. It is as natural to love Him to whom we make such addresses and on whom we have such dependencies, as it is for children to love their parents. For it is not my governor, my employer, or my friend who supports me or provides my needs, but God.

JEREMY TAYLOR

Copy God's Love

"Whoever has my commands and obeys them,
he is the one who loves me.
He who loves me will be loved by my Father,
and I too will love him and show myself to him."
JOHN 14:21 NIV

It is a vain thing to say we love Christ if we slight His commands. Does that child love his father who refuses to obey him? If we love God, we shall obey Him in things difficult and things dangerous.

Forgiving our enemies is hard. We are apt to forget kindnesses and remember injuries, but if we love God, we shall leave behind offences. When we seriously consider how many affronts and provocations He has put up with at our hands, this makes us copy Him and endeavor to bury an injury than to retaliate it.

Love made Christ suffer for us. Love was the chain that fastened Him to the cross. If we love God, we shall be willing to suffer for Him. Love is the most suffering grace. It will suffer reproaches, bonds, and imprisonments for Christ's sake. Love will carry men out above their own strength. How did divine affection carry the early saints above the love of life and the fear of death! These divine heroes were willing to suffer rather than by their cowardice to make the name of God suffer. They refused to come out of prison on sinful terms.

Many will not forego the least comfort or undergo the least cross for His sake. May not Christ suspect us when we pretend to love Him and yet will endure nothing for Him?

THOMAS WATSON

Encourage Love

May our Lord Jesus Christ himself and God our Father,
who loved us and by his grace gave us
eternal encouragement and good hope,
encourage your hearts and strengthen you
in every good deed and word.

2 THESSALONIANS 2:16–17 NIV

Surely man's relationship to God may be held as settled now. It is time to take up the other problem, man's relationship to man. With a former theology, man as man as a human being was of no account. He was a mere theological unit, an unknown quantity. He was taught to believe, therefore not to love. Now we are learning slowly that to believe is to love: that the first commandment is to love God, and the second like unto it—another version of it—is to love man. Not only the happiness but also the efficiency of love as a power and as a practical success in the world is coming to be recognized.

The fact that Christ led no army, He wrote no book, spent no money, but that He loved and so conquered, this is beginning to strike men. And Paul's argument is gaining adherents that when all prophecies are fulfilled, and all our knowledge becomes obsolete, and all tongues grow unintelligible, this thing, love, will abide and see them all out one by one into the oblivious past. This is the hope for the world: that we shall learn to love, and in learning that, unlearn all anger and wrath and evil speaking and malice and bitterness.

HENRY DRUMMOND

Love Everlasting

But the steadfast love of the LORD is
from everlasting to everlasting
on those who fear him.
PSALM 103:17 NRSV

Jesus will not let His people forget His love. If all the love they have enjoyed should be forgotten, He will visit them with fresh love. "Do you forget My cross?" says He. "I will cause you to remember it. At My table I will manifest Myself once more to you."

Mothers do not let their children forget them. If the boy has gone to Australia and does not write home, his mother writes, "Has John forgotten his mother?" Then there comes back a sweet letter, which proves that the gentle reminder was not in vain. So is it with Jesus. He says to us, "Remember Me." Our response is, "We will remember Your love."

Your love is ancient as the glory that You had with the Father before the world was. We remember Your eternal love when You embraced us. We remember the love that suggested the sacrifice of Yourself. We remember Your love as it was manifest to us in Your holy life, from the manger of Bethlehem to the garden of Gethsemane. We track You from the cradle to the grave—for every word and deed of Yours was love. We rejoice in Your love that death did not exhaust Your love that shone resplendent in Your resurrection. We remember that burning fire of love that will never let You hold Your peace until Your chosen ones are all safely housed, until Zion is glorified, and Jerusalem settled on her everlasting foundations of light and love in heaven.

CHARLES HADDON SPURGEON

Love for the Multitudes

> *But when he saw the multitudes,*
> *he was moved with compassion on them,*
> *because they fainted, and were scattered abroad,*
> *as sheep having no shepherd.*
>
> MATTHEW 9:36 KJV

Maxwell rose to speak to a crowd in the tent. This time he felt calmer. What would Jesus do? He spoke as he thought once he never could speak. Who were these people? They were immortal souls. What was Christianity? A calling of sinners, not the righteous, to repentance. How would Jesus speak? What would He say? He could not tell all that His message would include, but he felt sure of a part of it. And in that certainty he spoke on.

Never before had he felt "compassion for the multitude." What had the multitude been to him during his ten years in the First Church but a vague, dangerous, dirty, troublesome factor in society, outside of the church and of his reach, an element that caused him occasionally an unpleasant twinge of conscience, a factor in the slum district of Raymond that was talked about as the "masses," in papers written by the brethren in attempts to show why the "masses" were not being reached. But tonight as he faced the masses, he asked himself whether after all this was not just about such a multitude as Jesus faced most often, and he felt the genuine emotion of love for a crowd which is one of the best indications a preacher ever has that he is living close to the heart of the world's eternal Life. It is easy to love an individual sinner, especially if he is personally picturesque or interesting. To love a multitude of sinners is distinctively a Christlike quality.

CHARLES SHELDON

Love One Another

"My command is this:
Love each other as I have loved you."
JOHN 15:12 NIV

Christ is the Son of God's love—the bearer, revealer, and communicator of that love. His life and death were all love. Love is His life and the life He gives. He only lives to love, to live out His life of love in us, to give Himself in all who will receive Him. The Holy Spirit is the Spirit of love. He cannot impart Christ's life without imparting His love. Salvation is nothing but love conquering and entering us.

Nothing can be more natural than that Christians should love one another, even as Christ loved them. The life they received from their heavenly vine is nothing but love. This is the one thing He asks above all others: "Hereby shall all men know that you are My disciples: Love one another." As the special sort of vine is known by the fruit it bears, the nature of the heavenly vine is to be judged by the love His disciples have to one another.

Love your fellow Christians as the way to stay in the love of your Lord. Let your interaction with the Christians in your own family be holy, tender, Christlike love. Let your thoughts of the Christians around you be in the spirit of Christ's love. Let your life and conduct be the sacrifice of love—give yourself up to think of their needs to help and to serve them. The life Christ lives in you is love. As you live out your life, let it be all love.

ANDREW MURRAY

Love as an Emotion

Your love has given me great joy and encouragement,
because you, brother,
have refreshed the hearts of the saints.

PHILEMON 7 NIV

Love as a feeling, the source of Christian joy, is incapable of a scientific definition. It must be experienced in order to be known. It is not originated by conscious choice, but it arises in the believer's sensibilities through the agency of the Holy Spirit by the inward revelation of Christ as altogether lovely. It is not constant but variable in its presence and intensity.

The most spiritual person may at times be without any consciousness of this sensibility and of the joy which accompanies it. At other times he may realize a love divine burning in his heart like a furnace glowing with sevenfold intensity. These spiritual phenomena do not seem to be regulated by any law other than this: that they occur only in those who have the most intimate knowledge of Christ and are the most surrendered to His will.

The purpose of love as a feeling is to awakening joy and not only to cheer and encourage the believer amid his conflicts, but also to strengthen love as a principle, which is absolutely essential to Christian character. Christian love as a principle seems to be a composite embracing an intellectual agreement to the truth of Christ's claims, an admiration of the stainless purity of His character, and an irreversible self-surrender of the will to His authority as a sovereign, to His infallibility as a teacher, and to His sufficiency as the only Savior from the guilt of sin and the love of sin.

DANIEL STEELE

The Loving Heart

So now, O Israel,
what does the LORD your God require of you?
Only to fear the LORD your God,
to walk in all his ways, to love him,
to serve the LORD your God with all your heart
and with all your soul.
DEUTERONOMY 10:12 NRSV

When I have seen the amazing strength of love for souls that has been felt by Christians, I have been wonderfully impressed with the amazing love of God and His desires for their salvation.

We naturally credit right motives to those whom we love, and put the best allowable interpretation upon their words and deeds. A lack of this is evidence conclusive of an unloving heart in regard to professed converts. Charity, or love, is very ready to judge kindly and favorably of those who profess to be converted to Christ, and will naturally watch over them with interest, pray for them, instruct them, and have as much confidence in them as it is reasonable to have.

We always enjoy the saying and doing of those things that please those whom we most love. If we do not enjoy the service of God, it is because we do not truly serve Him. If we love Him supremely, it is impossible that we should not enjoy His service at every step. Always remember that whenever you lose your enjoyment of serving God, you may know that you are not serving Him right.

While the heart is full of the love of God, God is feared and not man. A desire for the applause of men is kept down, and it is enough to please God, whether men are pleased or displeased.

CHARLES FINNEY

Love and Easy Burdens

For the love of God is this
that we obey his commandments
And his commandments are not burdensome

1 JOHN 5:3 NRSV

I never knew anyone to come to Christ yet who did not have to give up something. But the only things God asks you to give up are the things that are doing you harm. God has given to each one of us a guarantee that He will never ask us to give up anything that is for our good, and that guarantee is His own Son. do not think if God has given His Son to die for us, He is going to ask us to give up anything that is good for us.

I remember when once I was talking to a young lady about coming to Christ. She said, "Well, I would like to be a Christian. But there is too much to give up."

I said, "Do you think God loves you?"

"I know He does," she replied.

"How much do you think God loves you?"

"God loved me enough to give His Son to die for me," she said.

I said, "Do you think that God, if He loved you enough to give His Son to die for you, will ask you to give up anything that is good for you to keep?"

She said, "No, He will not."

I said, "Do you want to keep anything that is not for your highest good?"

She replied, "No."

"Then do you not think you would better come to Christ right now?"

She said, "I will," and she did.

REUBEN ARCHER TORREY

Ideal Love

*"How often I have longed to gather your children together,
as a hen gathers her chicks under her wings,
but you were not willing!"*
LUKE 13:34 NIV

God combines both father and mother in one, in our highest
ideals of both. He comprises all the love, tenderness, and self-
sacrifice that we cannot but recognize to be the essence of par-
enting. Although we know perfectly well that He says He does
care for us in just this tender and loving way, yet we say, "If I
could only believe that, of course I should be comforted." Now
here is just where our wills must come in. We must believe it.
We must say to ourselves, "God says it, and it is true, and I am
going to believe it no matter how it looks." Then we must never
suffer ourselves to doubt or question it again.

The all-sufficiency of God ought to be as complete to the
child of God as the all-sufficiency of a good mother is to a child.
We all know the utter rest of the little child in the mother's love.
That the child's mother is there is enough to make all fears and
all troubles disappear.

My own experience as a child taught me this beyond any
possibility of question. My mother was the remedy for all my
own ills and, I fully believed, for the ills of the whole world, if
only they could be brought to her. When anyone expressed
doubts as to her capacity to remedy everything, I remembered
with what fine scorn I used to annihilate them by saying, "Ah,
but you don't know my mother!"

HANNAH WHITALL SMITH

Heart Full of Love

> "But be very careful to keep the commandment
> and the law that Mose.
> the servant of the LORD gave you.
> to love the LORD your God,
> to walk in all his ways, to obey his commands,
> to hold fast to him and to serve him
> with all your heart and all your soul."
>
> JOSHUA 22:5 NIV

We must all admit that our soul is too narrow. It holds too little, knows too little, and is deficient in willpower and, above all in capacity of love. When we are called to run in the way o God's commandments, we break down in despair and cry, "If I am to be a runner, You must first enlarge my heart."

"There is," remarks one of the old Puritans, "a straitness, slavery, and narrowness in all sin. Sin crumples up our souls, which i they were freely spread abroad would be as large and wide as the whole universe. Any man who has his will enlarged to the exten of God's will, by loving whatever God loves and nothing else enjoys boundless liberty and a boundless sweetness."

God's love embraces the universe. We who have partaken o the divine nature must also love as He does. Thomas à Kempi says, "He who desires glory in things outside of God, or to take pleasure in some private good, shall many ways be encumbered and confined. But if heavenly grace enters in and true charity there will be no envy or narrowness of heart; neither will self love busy itself because divine charity overcomes all things and enlarges all the powers of the soul." Give unto us, God, thi largeness of heart!

F. B. MEYER

Amazing Love

The amazing grace of the Master, Jesus Christ,
the extravagant love of God,
the intimate friendship of the Holy Spirit,
be with all of you.
2 CORINTHIANS 13:14 TM

How do you and I wish we had known Jesus sooner, and that we had more of His love? It is amazing love, it is forgiving love, it is dying love, it is exalted and interceding love, and it is glorified love. I am talking of the love of Jesus Christ who loved me before I loved Him. He saw me polluted in blood, full of sores, a slave to sin, death, and hell, running to destruction. Then He said unto my soul, "Live." He snatched me as a brand plucked from the burning. It was love that saved me. It was all of the free grace of God and that only.

My brethren, the kingdom of God is within me, and this fills me so full of love that I would not be in my natural state again, not for millions of millions of worlds. Eternity itself will be too short to set forth the love of the Lord Jesus Christ.

If there are any here who are strangers to this love of the Lord Jesus Christ, do not despair. Come, come unto Christ, and He will have mercy upon you. He will pardon all your sins. He will love you freely and take you to be with Himself. You need not fear, you need not despair when God has had mercy upon such a wretch as I. And He will save you also if you will come unto Him by faith.

GEORGE WHITEFIELD

Love and Courtesy

[Love] doth not behave itself unseemly.

1 CORINTHIANS 13:5 KJV

Courtesy is love in society. It is love in relation to etiquette. Politeness has been defined as love in trifles. Courtesy is said to be love in little things. And the one secret of politeness is to love. Love cannot behave itself unseemly. You can put the most untutored persons into the highest society, and if they have a reservoir of love in their hearts, they will not behave themselves unseemly. They simply cannot do it.

Carlyle said of Robert Burns that there was no truer gentleman in Europe than this plowman-poet. It was because he loved everything—the mouse, the daisy, and all the things, great and small, that God had made. So with this simple passport he could mingle with any society and enter courts and palaces from his little cottage on the banks of the Ayr River.

You know the meaning of the word "gentleman." It means a gentle man—a man who does things gently and with love. And that is the whole art and mystery of it. The gentleman cannot in the nature of things do an ungentle, an ungentlemanly thing. The ungentle soul, the inconsiderate, unsympathetic nature cannot do anything else.

People are devoted, and rightly, to their rights. But there come times when people may exercise even the higher right of giving up their rights. Love strikes much deeper. It would have us not seek them at all, ignore them, and eliminate the personal element altogether from our calculations. It is not hard to give up our rights. They are often external.

HENRY DRUMMOND

Love in the Heart

"For the LORD does not see as man sees;
for man looks at the outward appearance,
but the LORD looks at the heart."
1 SAMUEL 16:7 NKJV

Ask yourself whether you have ever in your lives brought forth any fruit to God. Have you ever done anything from a gracious respect to God or out of love to God? By only seeking your worldly interest, you do not bring forth fruit to God. To be sober, moral, and religious only to be seen of men or out of respect to your own credit and honor does not bring forth fruit to God. How is doing that for God, which is only for the sake of custom or to be esteemed of men?

For men to pray, read, hear, and to be strict and diligent in religious and moral duties merely from the fear of hell does not bring fruit to God. What thanks are due to you for being willing to take some pains to escape burning in hell to all eternity? There is never a devil in hell but would gladly do the same.

There is no fruit brought forth to God where there is nothing done from love to God or from any true respect to Him. God looks at the heart. He does not stand in need of our services, neither is He benefited by anything that we can do. He does not receive anything of us because it benefits Him, but only as a suitable testimony of our love and respect to Him. This is the fruit that He seeks.

JONATHAN EDWARDS

Colored with Love

My child, keep your father's commandment,
and do not forsake your mother's teaching.
PROVERBS 6:20 NRSV

Commanding an army is little more than sweeping a street or pounding an anvil compared with the training of a boy or girl. To teach a child to love truth and hate a lie, to love purity and hate vice is greater than inventing a rocket that will take you to the moon before breakfast. Unconsciously you set in motion influences that will condemn or bless the old universe.

A man sent a friend of mine some crystals from the *Scientific American* and said: "One of these crystals as small as a pinpoint will give a noticeable green hue to 7,000 gallons of water." Think of it! Power enough in an atom to color 7,000 gallons of water. There is power in a word or act to adversely influence a boy and through him afflict a community. There is power enough in a word to color the life of that child so it will become a power to lift the world to Jesus Christ. The mother will put in motion influences that will either touch heaven or hell. Talk about greatness!

There is power in a mother's love. A mother's love must be like God's love. How God could ever tell the world that He loved it without a mother's example has often puzzled me. If the devils in hell ever turned pale, it was the day mother's love flamed up for the first time in a woman's heart.

BILLY SUNDAY

Love That Makes Us Better

*For the LORD is good; his mercy is everlasting;
and his truth endureth to all generations.*
PSALM 100:5 KJV

The love of Christ is not accompanied with those unruly or uncertain motions that ours is attended with. His love has no ebbing, no flowing, no going beyond, no coming short, and so nothing of uncertainty. True, there is a way of showing of this love, which is suited to our capacities as human beings, and by that we see it sometimes more, sometimes less. It is exhibited to us as we do or do not walk with God in this world. I speak now of saints.

Love in Christ does not lean toward undue or unlawful objects. It always acts according to God, and at anytime there is not the least shadow of swerving. Love in Christ requires no beauty in the object to be beloved. Because we fully do not know love, He comes down to our capacities and speaks about His love to us according as we find love to work in ourselves. He describes His love by borrowing from us instances of our love to wife and children.

Love in Christ decays not. It cannot be tempted to do so by anything that happens. This love continues to act until all things that are imperfections are completely and everlastingly subdued. The reason is that Christ loves to make us pleasing and wholesome, not because we are so.

JOHN BUNYAN

Measuring Love

Whom have I in heaven but you?
And there is nothing on earth
that I desire other than you.

PSALM 73:25 NRSV

The measure of our love to God must be to love Him without measure. God, who is the chief of our happiness, must have the chief of our affections. Others may have the milk of our love, but God must have the cream. Love to God must be above all other things, such as the oil that swims above the water. Relations may lie on the bosom, but Christ must lie in the heart.

If the world were placed in one scale and Christ in the other, He must weigh heaviest. If one had a friend who supplied him continually with money and gave him all his allowance, were not he worse than a barbarian who did not respect and honor that friend? Such a friend is God. He gives you breath, and He bestows a livelihood upon you. Will you not love Him?

When the body is cold and has no heat, it is a sign of death. That man is dead who has no heat of love in his soul to God. This reproof falls heavy upon the infidels of this age who are so far from loving God that they do all they can to show their hatred of Him. Oh, how far are they from being lovers of God, who scarcely ever think of God! A sinner crowds God out of his thoughts. He never thinks of God unless with horror, as the prisoner thinks of the judge.

THOMAS WATSON

Teaching Love

The earth, O LORD,
is full of your steadfast love;
teach me your statutes.
PSALM 119:64 NRSV

The master of one of the schools in Bristol reports: "I am thankful to say that there is a spirit of inquiry among the boys, and I hope one or two have accepted the Lord Jesus as their Savior."

Another teacher reports: "I feel thankful that I have again the privilege of bearing testimony to the goodness and mercy of God through the past year. My heart has been greatly cheered and encouraged by seeing the work of the Holy Spirit among my dear scholars. From personal conversation with them, I found several were earnestly seeking Jesus. One dear girl was rejoicing that He loved her. Another little girl wrote me a little letter in which she expressed her hope that God would bless her. She also added, 'I would like to love Jesus with my whole heart because I know He loves me and has died to save me.' Another dear child was melted to tears by the simple story of Christ's love.

"The earnest attention which the dear children give to the Word of God is also a cause of much thankfulness. Many have given evidence that they have been impressed by the truth of God. There is an eagerness amongst the children to know the truth of God."

The child of God should make it his particular business to encourage sinners to seek after the Lord, and to increase the faith and love of the brethren through speaking well of the name of the Lord.

GEORGE MÜLLER

Love for the Church

*No one hates his own body but lovingly cares for it,
just as Christ cares for his body, which is the church.*

EPHESIANS 5:29 NLT

God loves the church with a love too deep for human imagination. He loves her with all His infinite heart. Therefore let the church be of good courage. The Lord says, "I am jealous for Jerusalem and for Zion with a great jealousy." The Lord loves His church so much that He cannot bear that she should go astray to others. When she has done so, He cannot endure that she should suffer too much or too heavily. He will not have His enemies afflict her. He is displeased with them because they increase her misery. When God seems most to leave His church, His heart is warm toward her.

History shows that whenever God uses a rod to chasten His servants, He always breaks it afterward as if He loathed the rod that gave His children pain. Like as a father pities his children, so the Lord pities them who fear Him.

If this is true of His church collectively, it is also true of each individual member. You may fear that the Lord has passed you by, but it is not so. He who counts the stars and calls them by their names is in no danger of forgetting His own children. He knows your case as thoroughly as if you were the only creature He ever made or the only saint He ever loved. Approach Him and be at peace.

CHARLES HADDON SPURGEON

Standing on the Promises of Love

*Has not God chosen those who are poor
in the eyes of the world to be rich in faith
and to inherit the kingdom he promised
those who love him?*
JAMES 2:5 NIV

In earlier life I used to seek after greater faith by considering how great God was, how rich and how strong. Why should He not give me money for His work, since He was so rich? Why not carry the entire burden of my responsibilities, since He was so mighty? These considerations helped me less, however, than my now certain conviction that He is absolutely faithful. He is faithful to His promises and faithful to the soul that at His clear call has stepped out into any enterprise for Him.

We may lose heart and hope, our head may turn dizzy, our heart faint, and the mocking voices of our foes suggest that God has forgotten or forsaken us. But He remains faithful. He cannot deny Himself. He cannot throw aside responsibilities that He has assumed. Often I have gone to God in desperate need, aggravated by nervous depression and heart sickness, and said, "My faith is flickering out. Its hand seems paralyzed, its eye blinded, its old glad song silenced forever. But You are faithful, and I am counting on You!"

The soul loves to stand upon the promises of God. We find no difficulty in trusting our friends because we open our hearts, like south windows, to their love. Where would be our difficulty about faith if we ceased worrying about it and were occupied with the object of faith—Jesus Christ our Lord?

F. B. MEYER

Badge of Love

Jesus resplendent with light
from God the Father as the voice
of Majestic Glory spoke:
"This is my Son, marked by my love,
focus of all my delight."
2 PETER 1:17 TM

When man sinned, selfishness triumphed. Adam at once begins to accuse the woman of having led him astray. Love to God had gone; love to man was lost. Of the first two children of Adam, one becomes a murderer of his brother. Sin had robbed the world of love. Yes, there may have been beautiful examples of love even among the heathen but only as a little remnant of what was lost. One of the worst things sin did for mankind was to make people selfish, for selfishness cannot love.

The Lord Jesus Christ came down from heaven as the Son of God's love. He lived a life of love in fellowship with His disciples, in compassion over the poor and miserable, in love even to His enemies, and He died the death of love. Now Jesus calls us to walk in love. He demands that though a man hate you, still you love him. True love cannot be conquered by anything in heaven or upon the earth. The more hatred there is, the more love triumphs and shows its true nature. This is the love that Christ commanded His disciples to exercise.

You all know what it is to wear a badge. And Christ said to His disciples in effect: "I give you a badge, and that badge is love. That is to be your mark. It is the only thing in heaven or on earth by which men can know Me."

ANDREW MURRAY

Scene of Love from Paul's Journeys

After saying good-by to each other,
we went aboard the ship,
and they returned home.
ACTS 21:6 NIV

Following his visit to Ephesus, Paul arrived at Tyre, where he stopped a few days. Here he found some disciples who begged Paul not to go to Jerusalem, saying through the Spirit that he should not go up to that city. But Paul adhered to his original purpose to go to Jerusalem. The account says: "But when our time was up, we left and continued on our way. All the disciples and their wives and children accompanied us out of the city, and there on the beach we knelt to pray."

What a sight to observe on that seashore! Here is a family picture of love and devotion, where husbands, wives, and even children are present, and prayer is made out in the open air. What an impression it must have made upon those children! The vessel was ready to depart, but prayer must cement their affections and bless wives and children, and bless their parting—a parting which was to be final so far as this world was concerned. The scene is beautiful and does honor to the head and heart of Paul, to his person and his piety, and shows the tender affection in which he was held. Never did a seashore see a grander picture or witness a lovelier sight—Paul on his knees on the sands of that shore, invoking God's blessing upon these men, women, and children.

EDWARD McKENDREE BOUNDS

Love and the Name of Jesus

And this is his commandment,
That we should believe on the name
of his son Jesus Christ, and love one another,
as he gave us commandment.

1 JOHN 3:23 KJV

Whosoever desires to love God, if you will neither be deceived nor deceive, if you will be saved and not fail, if you will stand and not fall, study to have this name—Jesus—constantly in mind. If you do this, the enemy shall fall and you shall stand, and the enemy shall be enfeebled and you shall be strengthened.

The name, Jesus, truly held in mind, roots up vices, plants virtues, brings love to people, gives people a taste of heavenly things, removes discord, produces peace, gives everlasting rest, and does away with fleshly desires. It fills those who love it with spiritual joy. The righteous man desires to be blessed because he has truly loved this name, Jesus. He is called righteous because he seeks earnestly to love Jesus.

The more we love, the more we yearn to love. The love of Jesus by self is delightful and desirable. Therefore no joy shall be lacking for those who seek earnestly to love Him whom angels desire to behold. Therefore many people wish to have joy with Christ, but as they love not His name, Jesus, they shall have sorrow without end, whatever they do. If they give all things that they have to poor people, unless they love this name, Jesus, they shall labor in vain.

I sought to love Jesus, and the more I grew complete in His love, so much the sweeter His name became to me.

JOHN WYCLIFFE

Love and Death

Whoever does not love abides in death.
1 JOHN 3:14 NRSV

Without love, nothing can make death comfortable. By comfortable I do not mean lacking consciousness. I would not say that he died comfortably who died by the shot of a cannon, any more than he who having his conscience seared died as unconcerned as the beasts that perish. But by a comfortable death, I mean a calm passage out of life, full of rational peace and joy. Such a death the world cannot give without love.

One man who died with love called all who were near him by their names and said, "Think of heaven, talk of heaven. All the time is lost when we are not thinking of heaven." Now this was the voice of love.

Another good soldier of Jesus Christ was grappling with his last enemy—death. Some of his last breath was spent in a psalm of praise to Him who was then giving him the victory. He was asked, "Have you the love of God in your heart?" He lifted up his eyes and hands, and answered with the whole strength he had left, "Yes, yes!" To one who asked if he was afraid of the devil, he replied, "No, no. My loving Savior has conquered every enemy: He is with me. I fear nothing." Soon afterward, he fell into a sort of slumber, and his soul sweetly returned to God who gave it.

Perfect love casts out whatever might have caused torment. And whoever you are who has the like measure of love, your end shall be like his.

JOHN WESLEY

Love Endures Forever

> *"Give thanks to the LORD of hosts, for the Lord is good,*
> *for his steadfast love endures forever!"*
>
> JEREMIAH 33:11 NRSV

If it is better to love God than the world, surely also it is better to love God than sin. What is there in sin that any should love it? Sin is a debt. Does any man love to be in debt? Sin is a disease. Will any man hug a disease? Will he love his plague sores? Sin is compared to leprosy. Sin is a misshapen monster: Lust makes a man brutish; malice makes him devilish. What is in sin to be loved? Sin is an enemy. It is compared to a serpent. It has four stings— shame, guilt, horror, death. Will a man love that which seeks his death? Surely then it is better to love God than sin.

Love is the most abiding grace. This will stay with us when other graces take their farewell. In heaven we shall need no repentance because we shall have no sin. In heaven we shall not need patience because there will be no hardship. In heaven we shall need no faith because faith looks at things unseen. But then we shall see God face-to-face, and where there is vision, there is no need of faith.

But when the other graces are out-of-date, love continues. In this sense love is greater than faith because it abides the longest. Faith is the staff we walk with in this life. But we shall leave this staff at heaven's door, and only love shall enter.

THOMAS WATSON

The Law of Love

If you really keep the royal law found in Scripture,
"Love your neighbor as yourself," you are doing right.
JAMES 2:8 NIV

The law was given by Moses, but grace was given by Jesus Christ. The law was given to bring us unto the knowledge of ourselves that we might thereby feel and perceive that we are of a sinful nature. The law condemned all our deeds and us. It required that which is impossible for our nature to do. It required perfect love. The law condemned us to death.

We have grace in Christ, that is, promises of life by His merits. In the gospel, when we believe the promise, we receive the spirit of life. We are justified in the blood of Christ from all the things that the law condemned us. And we receive love unto the law, power to fulfill it, and grow in it daily. Christ brings the love of God unto us.

You see two ways that people are badly deceived. First are those who justify themselves with outward deeds. They abstain from what the law forbids and do what the law commands. They set themselves above other sinners and condemn them. They do not see how the law requires love from the bottom of their hearts. Those also are deceived who without all fear of God give themselves unto all manner of vices, having no respect for the law of God.

By grace we know God as our most merciful Father and consent to the law, love it, desire to fulfill it, and sorrow because we cannot. But the blood of Christ has made satisfaction for the rest.

WILLIAM TYNDALE

Blessings of Love

You bestow on him blessings forever;
you make him glad with the joy of your presence.

PSALM 21:6 NRSV

We frequently use the word "blessing" so vaguely as to overlook the primary meaning. For instance, we use it frequently as a synonym of praise. In speaking of blessing God, we think of praising Him. Blessing does not merely mean praise. Blessing is the moving of the heart toward an object of affection.

Blessing is always accompanied with joy. It is a joy, and it gives joy both to the giver and the receiver. A little child playing with his toys may be both happy and satisfied. But the little one hears the mother's footsteps, sees the mother open the door, and instantly the toys are dropped and forgotten. The little arms are stretched out and the little feet are running to meet the welcome mother. The motherly arms are as quickly stretched forth toward the child, and with longer steps the mother hastens to meet the little one and clasps the child to her bosom.

But whose heart is the more glad? The little one's heart is full. The mother's heart is also full; but her capacity is greater, and so her joy is deeper. And is not this true of our heavenly Father? When His heart blesses ours, and ours blesses Him, we are full of joy. But His heart is infinitely greater than ours, and His joy in His people far exceeds all their joy in Him as the infinite exceeds the finite.

HUDSON TAYLOR

Zeal and Love

But just as you excel in everything—
in faith, in speech, in knowledge,
in complete earnestness and in your love for us—
see that you also excel in this grace of giving.

CORINTHIANS 8:7 NIV

Love must be obedient, pure, simple, and communicative; that is, it must be expressive. However, zeal must come after a long growth of a temperate and well-regulated love. That zeal only is good which in a fervent love has temperate expressions. For let the affection boil as high as it can, yet if it boil over into irregular and strange actions, it will need many excuses. Moses broke the tablets of the law by being passionately zealous against them who broke the first commandment.

Zeal must spend its greatest heat principally in those things that concern ourselves, but with great care and restraint in those that concern others. Remember that zeal must in no sense contradict any action of love. Love to God includes love to our neighbor, and therefore no pretence of zeal for God's glory must make us uncharitable to our brother. Doing so is as pleasing to God as hatred is an act of love. Zeal directed to others can spend itself in nothing but charitable actions for their good.

Let loose zeal in matters of internal, personal, and spiritual actions that are matters of direct duty such as prayers and thanksgiving. Zeal is only acceptable and safe when it advances the love of God and our neighbors. In brief, let your zeal (if it must be expressed in anger) be always more severe against yourself than against others.

JEREMY TAYLOR

I Love the Word of God

> "The one who sowed the good seed
> is the Son of Man."
> MATTHEW 13:37 NIV

In the hope that others would be induced to join him in Christianity, Chief Sechele asked me to begin family worship with him in his house. I did so and was surprised to hear how well he conducted the prayer in his own simple and beautiful style, for he was quite a master of his own African language. At this time we were suffering from the effects of a drought, and none except his family, whom he ordered to attend, came near his meeting.

"In former times," said he, "when a chief was fond of hunting, all his people got dogs and became fond of hunting, too. If he was fond of dancing or music, all showed a liking to these amusements, too. If the chief loved beer, they all rejoiced in strong drink. But in this case it is different. I love the Word of God, and not one of my kinsmen will join me."

His friends seemed to think that I [David Livingstone] had thrown a charm over him and that he had become mine. They all treated us still with respectful kindness, but to Sechele himself they said things which, as he often remarked, had they ventured on in former times would have cost them their lives. It was trying, after all we had done, to see our labors so little appreciated. But we had sown the good seed and have no doubt but it will yet spring up, though we may not live to see the fruits.

DAVID LIVINGSTONE

Marvelous Love

To thank GOD for his marvelous love,
for his miracle mercy to the children he loves.
PSALM 107:21 TM

Great and marvelous are Your works, God, that our soul knows quite well. You have showed marvelous loving-kindness. We must sing to You because You have done marvelous things. It is marvelous that You have set Your love upon us, that You have watched over our interests with unwearied care, that our sins or unbelief have never diverted Your love from us.

"Marvelous" is the only word we can use as we think of the well-beloved Son who descended to the bed in a manger, of the agony and bloody sweat of the cross and passion—and all for us who were His enemies. But it is most marvelous of all that You made us children and joint heirs with Christ. To think that we shall shine as the sun in Your kingdom and be included in that circle of love and life of which the throne of God and the Lamb is the center! Surely the marvels of Your grace will only seem the greater when eternity with its boundless ages gives us time to explore them.

The danger, however, is that we should become strong in our own conceit and credit ourselves with the position which is due to the grace of God alone. We need the truly humble spirit of the little child that we may never boast of ourselves! God cannot trust some of us with prosperity and success because our nature could not stand them.

F. B. MEYER

Love and Happiness

Create in me a clean heart, O God,
and renew a right spirit within me
PSALM 51:10 KJV

Without love, nothing can so benefit us as to make our lives happy. By happiness I mean not a slight, trilling pleasure that perhaps begins and ends in the same hour, but such a state of well-being that gives the soul a steady, lasting satisfaction. The fact that nothing without love can benefit us as to our present happiness will appear from this single consideration: You cannot lack love in any one single instance without pain. The more you depart from love, the greater is the pain. Are you lacking in long-suffering? Then as far as you fall short, you fall short of happiness. The more the opposite tempers—anger, fretfulness, revenge—prevail, the more unhappy you are.

The storm cannot be eased or peace ever returned to your soul unless meekness, gentleness, patience, or, in one word, love, take possession of it. If any man find in himself ill will, malice, envy, or any other temper opposite to kindness, then misery is there. The stronger the temper, the more miserable he is. The soul of the malicious or envious person is the very type of hell—full of torment as well as wickedness. He has already the worm that never dies, and he is hastening to the fire that never can be quenched. The great gulf is not yet fixed between him and heaven. There is a Spirit still willing to renew his heart in the love of God and so lead him up to eternal happiness.

JOHN WESLEY

An Individual Savior

For their sake he remembered his covenant,
and showed compassion
according to the abundance of his steadfast love.
PSALM 106:45 NRSV

Toward whom is this love of God exercised? Toward us—toward all beings of our lost race. To each one of us He manifests this love.

How does He commend this love? By giving His Son to die for us. By giving one who was a Son and a Son well-beloved. It is written that God "gave Him a ransom for all" and that "He tasted death for every man." We are not to suppose that He died for the sum total of mankind in such a sense that His death is not truly for each one in particular. It is a great mistake into which some fall, to suppose that Christ died for the human race in general and not for each one in particular. By this mistake the gospel is likely to lose much of its practical power on our hearts. So we are to regard Jesus as having loved us personally and individually.

He would also commend the great strength of this love. We should think we gave evidence of a strong love if we were to give our friend a great sum of money. But what is any sum of money compared with giving up a dear Son to die? Oh, surely it is surpassing love, beyond measure wonderful, that Jesus should not only labor and suffer but should really die! Was ever love like this?

CHARLES FINNEY

Learning Love

From him the whole body,
joined and held together by every supporting ligament,
grows and builds itself up in love, as each part does its work.

EPHESIANS 4:16 NIV

To learn love is the supreme work to which we need to address ourselves in this world. Is life not full of opportunities for learning love? Every man and woman every day has a thousand of them. The world is not a playground; it is a schoolroom. Life is not a holiday but an education. The one eternal lesson for us all is how better we can love. What makes a person a good ball player? Practice. What makes a person a good artist, a good sculptor, a good musician? Practice. What makes a person a good person? Practice. Nothing else.

If a man does not exercise his arm, he develops no biceps muscle; and if a man does not exercise his soul, he acquires no muscle in his soul, no strength of character, no vigor of moral fiber, nor beauty of spiritual growth. Love is a rich, strong, and vigorous expression of the whole round Christian character—the Christlike nature in its fullest development. And the components of this great character are only to be built up by ceaseless practice. What was Christ doing in the carpenter's shop? Practicing. Though perfect, we read that He learned obedience, and He increased in wisdom and in favor with God and man.

Talent develops itself in solitude—the talent of prayer, of faith, of meditation, of seeing the unseen. Character grows in the stream of the world's life. That chiefly is where we are to learn love.

HENRY DRUMMOND

Love and the Gospel in Brief

Remembering without ceasing your work of faith,
and labour of love,
and patience of hope in our Lord Jesus Christ,
in the sight of God and our Father.

1 THESSALONIANS 1:3 KJV

When you ask me to be brief, if I should answer, "God should be worshiped in faith, hope, love," you would doubtless reply that this was shorter than you wished, and might then ask for a brief explanation of what each of these three means. What should be believed, what should be hoped for, and what should be loved?

You would have the answers to all these questions if you really understood what a man should believe, what he should hope for, and what he ought to love. For these are the chief things—indeed, the only things—to seek for in religion.

You have asked for something you could carry around, not just baggage for your bookshelf. Therefore we may return to these three ways in which, as we said, God should be served: faith, hope, love.

What, then, shall I say of love, without which faith can do nothing? There can be no true hope without love. Indeed, as the apostle James says, "Even the demons believe and tremble." However, they neither hope nor love. Instead, they tremble because they believe as we do that what we hope for is coming to pass. The apostle Paul approves and commends the faith that works by love and that cannot exist without hope. Consequently, it is that love is not without hope, hope is not without love, and neither hope nor love is without faith.

AUGUSTINE

Love and Joy

"Rejoice in that day and leap for joy!
For indeed your reward is great in heaven."

LUKE 6:23 NKJV

Infinite love must be a mystery to our finite capacity. The saints' everlasting rest must consist in the enjoyment of God by love. Joy has a share in this attainment of the inconceivable comfort that the blessed feel in seeing, knowing, loving, and being beloved of God. All Christ's ways of mercy tend to end in the saints' joys. He wept, sorrowed, and suffered that they might rejoice. He sends the Spirit to be our comforter. He multiplies promises and makes known our future happiness that our joy may be full.

He never brings us into so low a condition that He does not leave us more cause of joy than sorrow. The Lord cares for our comfort here. What that joy will be where the soul has been perfectly prepared for joy! It shall be our work, our business, eternally to rejoice!

Poor, humble, drooping soul, how would it fill you with joy now, if a voice from heaven should tell you of the love of God, the pardon of your sins, and assure you of your part in these heavenly joys? What then will your joy be when your actual possession shall convince you of your title, and you shall be in heaven before you are well aware! It is not your joy only. It is a mutual joy as well as a mutual love. There is joy in heaven at your conversion, and there will be joy at your glorification. The angels will welcome you to heaven and congratulate your safe arrival.

RICHARD BAXTER

Love Does Not Grow Tired

For I desire steadfast love and not sacrifice,
the knowledge of God rather than burnt offerings.
HOSEA 6:6 NRSV

One who is in love flies, runs, and rejoices. He is free, not bound. He gives all for all and has all in all. Love often knows no limits but overflows all bounds. Love feels no burden, thinks nothing of troubles, attempts more than it is able, and does not plead impossibility because it believes that it may and can do all things. For this reason the one with love is able to do all, performing and effecting much, but he who does not love falls and fails.

Love is watchful. Sleeping, it does not slumber. Wearied, it is not tired. Pressed, it is not restricted. Alarmed, it is not confused. Love is swift, sincere, kind, pleasant, and delightful. Love is strong, patient and faithful, prudent, and long-suffering. Love is never self-seeking because in whatever a person seeks for himself, there he falls from love. Love is circumspect, humble, and upright. It is not intent upon vain things. It is sober and chaste, firm and quiet, guarded in all the senses.

He who is not ready to suffer all things and to stand resigned to the will of the Beloved is not worthy to be called a lover. A lover must embrace willingly all that is difficult and bitter for the sake of the Beloved, and he should not turn away from Him because of adversities.

THOMAS À KEMPIS

Compromised Love

"Quick! Catch all the little foxes
before they ruin the vineyard of your love,
for the grapevines are all in blossom."

SONG OF SONGS 2:15 NLT

True love cannot be stationary. It must either decline or grow. Despite all the unworthy fears of our poor hearts, divine love is destined to conquer.

Are we not all too apt to seek Him rather because of our need than for His joy and pleasure? This should not be. We do not admire selfish children who only think of what they can get from their parents and are unmindful of the pleasure that they may give or the service that they may render. But are not we in danger of forgetting that pleasing God means giving Him pleasure? Some of us look back to the time when the words "to please God" meant no more than not to sin against Him and not to grieve Him. However, would the love of earthly parents be satisfied with the mere absence of disobedience? Or would a bridegroom be satisfied if his bride only sought him for the supply of her own need?

Ah, how often the enemy succeeds by one device or another in tempting the believer away from that position of entire consecration to Christ in which alone the fullness of His power and of His love can be experienced. Little compromises with the world—disobedience to the still small voice in little things, little indulgences of the flesh to the neglect of duty—the enemies may be small, but the mischief done is great.

HUDSON TAYLOR

Dwell in Love and Peace

My people will live in peaceful dwelling places,
in secure homes,
in undisturbed places of rest.
ISAIAH 32:18 NIV

When we move into a new house, we not only move in ourselves, but we take with us all our belongings, and above all, we take our family. No one would be so foolish as to leave outside anything he cared for or anyone he loved. But I am afraid there are some of God's children who move into the dwelling place of God themselves, but who by their lack of faith leave outside those they love best. More often than not, it is their children who are so abandoned. We would be horrified at a father who in a time of danger should flee into a fortress for safety but should leave his children outside. Yet hundreds of Christians do this very thing. Every anxious thought in which we indulge about our children proves that we have not really taken them with us into the dwelling place of God.

If we trust for ourselves, we must trust for our loved ones also, and especially for our children. God is more their Father than their earthly fathers are, and if they are dear to us, they are far dearer to Him. We cannot do anything better for them than to trust them to His care and hardly anything worse than to try to keep them as our own. We must make up our minds to move into our dwelling place in God and to take there with us all our possessions—above all, those we love.

HANNAH WHITALL SMITH

What Would Jesus Do—The Newspaper Editor

Entirely out of place is obscene, silly, and vulgar talk;
but instead, let there be thanksgiving.

EPHESIANS 5:4 NRSV

What would Jesus do as editor of a daily newspaper?

He would never allow a sentence or a picture in His paper that could be called bad, coarse, or impure in any way. He would probably conduct the political part of the paper from the standpoint of nonpartisan patriotism, always looking upon all political questions in the light of their relation to the kingdom of God and advocating measures from the standpoint of their relation to the welfare of the people, always on the basis of "What is right?" never on the basis of "What is for the best interests of this or that party?"

The end and aim of a daily paper conducted by Jesus would be to do the will of God. That is, His main purpose in carrying on a newspaper would not be to make money or gain political influence. But His first and ruling purpose would be to so conduct His paper that it would be evident to all His subscribers that He was trying to seek first the kingdom of God by means of His paper. This purpose would be as distinct and unquestioned as the purpose of a minister, missionary, or any unselfish martyr in Christian work anywhere.

All questionable advertisements would be impossible.

As editor of a daily paper today, Jesus would give large space to the work of the Christian world. He would devote a page possibly to the facts of reform, of sociological problems, of institutional church work and similar movements.

CHARLES SHELDON

Heaven's Loved Inhabitants

Blessed the guest at home in your place!
We expect our fill of good things in your house,
your heavenly manse.
PSALM 65:4 TM

If there is anything that ought to make heaven near to Christians, it is knowing that God and all their loved ones will be there. What is it that makes home so attractive? Is it because we have a beautiful home? Is it because we have beautiful lawns? Is it because we have beautiful trees around that home? Is it because we have beautiful paintings upon the walls inside? Is it because we have beautiful furniture? Is that all that makes home so attractive and so beautiful? No, it is the loved ones there.

I remember when after being away from home some time I went back to see my honored mother. I thought in going back I would take her by surprise and come in unexpectedly upon her. I went into one room and then into another, and I went all through the house, but I could not find that loved mother. When I was told she had gone away, the old place didn't seem like home at all. Home had lost its charm to me. It was my mother who made home so sweet to me. It is the loved ones who make home so sweet to everyone. It is the loved ones who are going to make heaven so sweet to all of us. Christ is there, God the Father is there, and many, many who were dear to us who lived on earth are there—and we shall be with them by and by.

DWIGHT LYMAN MOODY

Love the Word

> Jesus answered him,
> "Those who love me will keep my word,
> and my Father will love them,
> and we will come to them
> and make our home with them.
> Whoever does not love me does not keep my words;
> and the word that you hear is not mine,
> but is from the Father who sent me."
>
> JOHN 14:23–24 NRSV

You women, if you found that your husband was giving his love and attention to some other woman, and if you saw that some other woman was encroaching on his mind and heart and was usurping your place and was pushing you out of the place, wouldn't you grieve? Don't you think that God grieves when you push Him out of your life? You don't treat God square. You businessmen don't treat God fair. You let a thousand things come in and take the place that God Almighty had. You blame God for things you have no right to blame Him for. He is not to blame for anything.

You judge God. The spirit loves the Bible; the devil loves the flesh. You never think of going out on the street without dressing. You would be arrested before you went a block. You never think of going without breakfast, do you? I bet there are multitudes who have come here without reading the Bible or praying for this meeting. You can measure your desire for salvation by means of the amount of self-denial that you are willing to practice for Jesus Christ.

BILLY SUNDAY

The Luster of Love

Love the LORD, all you his saints.
The LORD preserves the faithful,
but abundantly repays the one who acts haughtily.
PSALM 31:23 NRSV

There are but few who love God. Many give Him hypocritical kisses, but few love Him. The wicked would flee from God; they would neither be under His rules nor within His reach. They fear God but do not love Him. All the strength in men or angels cannot make the heart love God.

Without love, all our religion is vain. It is not how much we do but how much we love. If a servant does not do his work willingly and out of love, it is not acceptable. Duties not mingled with love are as burdensome to God as they are to us. David therefore counsels his son Solomon to serve God with a willing mind. To do duty without love is not sacrifice but penance.

Love is a pure flame kindled from heaven. By it we resemble God, who is love. Believing and obeying do not make us to be like God, but by love we grow to be like Him. Love is a grace which most delights in God and is most delightful to Him. Love puts a flourishing and luster upon all the graces. The graces seem to be eclipsed, unless love shine and sparkle in them. Faith is not true, unless it works by love. The waters of repentance are not pure, unless they flow from the spring of love. Love is the incense that makes all our services fragrant and acceptable to God.

THOMAS WATSON

Ingredients of Life

> By day the LORD directs his love,
> at night his song is with me—
> a prayer to the God of my life.
>
> PSALM 42:8 NIV

I have seen a picture of a young man and a young woman standing in a field. If the young man or the young woman had been standing in the field alone, it would have been incomplete. No life is complete unless it has the element of love in it.

Love is the divine element in life, because God is love and because he who loves is born of God; therefore, let us keep our friendships in repair. They are worth spending time over because they constitute so large a part of our lives. Let us cultivate this spirit of friendship that it may grow into a great love, not only for our friends but also for all humanity.

Those of you who are going to the mission field must remember that your mission will be a failure unless you cultivate this element of love. Two years ago I came to a remote island in the South Pacific. At one end of the island were a missionary and his wife. At the other end were another missionary and his wife. You would suppose they would see each other every day, but they were not on loving terms. They were on war terms. What was the trouble about? It was a quarrel over a word in the native language that they should use for "God" in their translation of the New Testament.

HENRY DRUMMOND

The Father's Powerful Love

The LORD loves those who hate evil;
he guards the lives of his faithful;
he rescues them from the hand of the wicked.
PSALM 97:10 NRSV

We have often walked in the field in the early morning and have noticed how the rising sun has turned each dewdrop into a glittering gem. One ray of its own bright light makes a little sun of each of the million drops that hang from the pendent leaflets and sparkle everywhere. But it is helpful to remember that the glorious orb itself contains infinitely more light than all the dewdrops ever did or ever will reflect.

And so of our heavenly Father. He Himself is the great source of all that is noble and true and of all that ever has been loving and trustworthy. Each beautiful trait of each beautiful character is but the dim reflection of some ray of His own great perfection. And the sum total of all human goodness and tenderness and love is but as the dewdrops to the sun. How blessed then to confide in the infinite and changeless love of such a father as our Father in heaven!

How safe, too! Oft times the love of earthly parents has not failed, yet they have been powerless to bless and to keep. In the presence of human want or suffering, how inadequate has the strongest human love oft proved to be! Not so the love of our heavenly Father. His resources and His power are as inexhaustible as His love.

HUDSON TAYLOR

The Tender Advocate

In love a throne will be established;
in faithfulness a man will sit on it. . .
one who in judging seeks justice.

ISAIAH 16:5 NIV

Christ is altogether lovely as an advocate. He appears in the presence of God to prevent any new alienation and to continue the state of friendship and peace between God and us. He makes our cause His own and acts for us in heaven. He is touched with a most tender understanding of our troubles and dangers. He is not only one with us by way of representation but also one with us in respect of sympathy and affection.

Christ our advocate tracks our cause and business in heaven as His great and primary design and business. It is as if our concerns were so attended to by Him there that all the glory and honor which is paid Him in heaven would not divert Him one moment from our business. He pleads the cause of believers by His blood. Unlike other advocates, it is not enough for Him to lay out only words, which is a cheaper way of pleading, but He pleads for us by the voice of His own blood. Every wound He received for us on earth is a mouth opened to plead with God on our behalf in heaven. No friend in the world is so generous and bountiful to this as Jesus Christ is to believers.

No friend in the world loves his friend with as impassioned and strong affection as Jesus Christ loves believers. There is no end of the account of Christ's love.

JOHN FLAVEL

Love and Trust

"Do not let your hearts be troubled.
Trust in God; trust also in me."
JOHN 14:1 NIV

Unbelief is the mother of disobedience and of all my sins and shortcomings—my temper, my pride, my unlovingness, my worldliness, and my sins of every kind. Though these differ in nature and form, yet they all come from the one root, namely, that we do not believe in the freedom and fullness of the divine gift of the Holy Spirit to dwell in us, strengthen us, and fill us with the life and grace of God all the day long.

If people really believed in the infinite love of God, what a change it would bring about! What is love? It is a desire to communicate oneself for the good of the object loved—the opposite to selfishness. The mother is willing to sacrifice herself for the good of her child. So God in His love is ever willing to impart blessing, and He is omnipotent in His love. This is true, my friends: God is omnipotent in love. He is doing His utmost to fill every heart. "But if God is really anxious to do that, and if He is Almighty, why does He not do it now?" You must remember that God has given you a will, and by the exercise of that will, you can hinder God and remain content with the low life of unbelief. Come now, and let us see the cause of the difference between God's high, blessed provision for His children and the low, sad experience of many of us in the unbelief that distrusts and grieves Him.

ANDREW MURRAY

God's Love Is Enough

O Israel, hope in the LORD;
for with the LORD there is unfailing love
and an overflowing supply of salvation.

PSALM 130:7 NLT

Paul could say triumphantly in the midst of many and grievous trials that nothing could separate us from the love of God, which is in Christ Jesus our Lord. In the face of all we know about the God of all comfort, you can realize with Job, David, Paul, and the saints of all ages that nothing else is needed to quiet all your fears but just this: that God is. Nothing can separate you from His love, absolutely nothing—neither death nor life, nor angels, nor principalities, nor powers, nor things present, nor things to come, nor height, nor depth, nor any other creature. Every possible contingency is provided for here. Not one of them can separate you from the love of God, which is in Christ Jesus our Lord.

After such a declaration as this, how can any of us dare to question or doubt God's love? Since He loves us, He cannot exist and fail to help us. We know by our own experience what a necessity it is for love to pour itself out in blessing on the ones it loves. Can we not understand that God who is love, who is, if I may say so, made out of love, simply cannot help blessing us? We do not need to beg Him to bless us; He simply cannot help it.

Therefore God is enough! God is enough for time. God is enough for eternity. God is enough!

HANNAH WHITALL SMITH

Listen to Love

Then a cloud appeared and enveloped them,
and a voice came from the cloud:
"This is my Son, whom I love. Listen to him!"
MARK 9:7 NIV

If we will but listen, God's created works will teach us precious lessons of obedience and trust. From the stars in their trackless courses through space down to the minutest atom, the things of nature obey the Creator's will. And God cares for everything and sustains everything that He has created. He who upholds the unnumbered worlds at the same time cares for the wants of the little brown sparrow that sings its humble song.

When the rich man feasts in his palace or when the poor man gathers his children about the scanty table, each is tenderly watched by the heavenly Father. No tears are shed that God does not notice. If we would but fully believe this, all undue anxieties would be dismissed. Our lives would not be so filled with disappointment as now. Everything, whether great or small, would be left in the hands of God, who is not perplexed by the multiplicity of cares or overwhelmed by their weight. We should then enjoy a rest of soul to which many have long been strangers.

As your senses delight in the attractive loveliness of the earth, think of the world that is to come that shall never know the blight of sin and death, where the face of nature will no more wear the shadow of the curse. Let your imagination picture the home of the saved, and remember that it will be more glorious than your brightest imagination can portray.

ELLEN G. WHITE

Genuine Love

> *Above all, clothe yourselves with love, which binds everything together in perfect harmony.*
>
> COLOSSIANS 3:14 NRSV

You cannot find a Christian who will not tell you that what he gave up for Christ was nothing compared to what he got. Suppose there was some young woman who, being poor and unable to buy real jewelry, bought imitation. She had a brass ring which she thought people would think was gold, but no one ever thought so. She had a string of white beads and thought people believed they were real pearls, but no one ever dreamed it. She had a pair of earrings with bits of glass and wished people to believe that they were real diamonds. Nobody ever thought such a thing.

After a while a young fellow falls in love with her. One night he says to her, "Mary, I wish you would throw away that brass ring and that white bead necklace and those pieces of brass and glass in your ears."

But she says, "Well, John, I love you, but I really cannot do it."

A few nights after, John comes again with a big leather box. Inside it are a real gold ring with two beautiful emeralds and a beautiful diamond, a necklace of real pearls, and genuine diamond earrings. "They are for you if you will throw away that brass and glass of yours."

How long do you think it would take Mary to throw away her imitation jewels? Men and women, cast all the baubles of this world's pleasures into the fire and receive the gold and emeralds and rubies and diamonds and pearls of heaven.

REUBEN ARCHER TORREY

He Loves People

*"Because the LORD loves his people,
he has made you their king."*

2 CHRONICLES 2:11 NIV

You have heard of Helen Keller who was born deaf, unable to speak, and blind. Until she was seven years of age, her life was an absolute blank. Nothing could go into that mind because the ears and eyes were closed to the outer world. Then they began to put in little bits of knowledge and bit by bit to educate her.

But they reserved the religious instruction for Phillips Brooks. When she was twelve years old, they took her to him, and he talked to her through the young lady who had been the means of opening her senses and who could communicate with her by the exceedingly delicate process of touch. Phillips Brooks began to tell her about God and what He had done and how He loves people and what He is to us.

The child listened very intelligently and finally said, "Mr. Brooks, I knew all of that before, but I did not know His name." Have you not often felt something within you that was not you, some mysterious pressure, some impulse, some guidance, something lifting you and impelling you to do that which you would not yourself ever have conceived of? Perhaps you did not know His name—it is God who works in you. If we can really build our life upon that great, simple fact, the first principle of religion which we are so prone to forget—that God is with us and in us—we will have no difficulty or fear about our future life.

HENRY DRUMMOND

To Live Is to Love

And the grace of our Lord was exceeding abundant
with faith and love which is in Christ Jesus.

1 TIMOTHY 1:14 KJV

Let the first great object of our lives be to achieve the character that is built around love. Never offer people a thimbleful of gospel. Do not offer them merely joy, merely peace, merely rest, or merely safety. Tell them how Christ came to give men a more abundant life than they have, a life abundant in love. Many of the current religious teachings are addressed only to a part of a person's nature. They offer peace, not life; faith, not love; justification, not regeneration. And people slip back again from such religion because it has never really held them.

To love abundantly is to live abundantly, and to love forever is to live forever. Therefore, eternal life is inextricably bound up with love. We want to live forever for the same reason that we want to live tomorrow. Why do you want to live tomorrow? It is because there is someone who loves you, and whom you want to see tomorrow, be with, and love back. There is no other reason why we should live on than that we love and are beloved. No worse fate can befall a man in this world than to live and grow old alone, unloving, and unloved. So long as he has friends—those who love him and whom he loves—he will live, because to live is to love. Love must be eternal. It is what God is. Love is life. Love never fails, and life never fails so long as there is love.

HENRY DRUMMOND

First Love

We love him, because he first loved us.
JOHN 4:19 KJV

Under our first love, what promises did we make to Him? But how disobediently have we behaved ourselves in this covenant? How little have we reverenced Him? How little have we lived to His glory? Have we not been a shame and reproach to His gospel? Have we not crucified Him afresh, and has He not been sorely wounded in the house of His friends?

When commanded by Him to go work in His vineyard, we have often said, "We go, Lord." But we went not. Or if we did go, with what reluctance has it been? How unwilling to watch with our dear Lord and Master only one hour? And when His time of love was come, He entered into a covenant with us, and we became His. He washed us also with water and thoroughly washed us by His precious blood from the guilt of all our sins. In short, we were made exceedingly beautiful, and the kingdom of God was constructed in our hearts. We were renowned among our neighbors for our love to God, and all who know us took knowledge of us that we had been with Jesus.

But how we have fallen, who were once sons of the morning! How we have trusted in our own beauty, have grown spiritually proud, and provoked our patient and unspeakably long-suffering Lord to anger. Where is that ardent love we spoke of when we told Him that though we should die for Him, we would not deny Him in any wise?

GEORGE WHITEFIELD

Old Love

The LORD has appeared of old to me, saying
"Yes, I have loved you with an everlasting love;
Therefore with lovingkindness I have drawn you."

JEREMIAH 31:3 NKJV

All of you know that old love is the best love. When we have an old acquaintance, a friend, who has loved us for many years, indeed that love is sweet. Though we may love new friends, yet when an old friend and a new friend meet together, we may say that the old is better. Now this should endear God to us. From all the ages of eternity, God had thoughts of you. God intended the Lord Jesus Christ to save your souls and mine. God, to endear Jeremiah to Him, tells him, "I have loved you with an everlasting love." Lord Jesus, when He calls His elect people up to heaven, says, "Come, you blessed of My Father." What follows? "Receive the kingdom prepared for you." How long? "From the foundation of the world."

The righteousness of Jesus Christ may properly be called an everlasting righteousness. Christianity, in one sense, is as old as the creation. All the saints who have been saved or who ever will be saved are all saved by the righteousness of Christ. It was through faith in Him that Abel was saved. It was through the sacrifice of Jesus Christ that Abraham was accepted and that all the prophets of old were accepted. Persons under the law and under the gospel are to be saved only through Christ; therefore Christ's righteousness may properly be called an everlasting righteousness.

GEORGE WHITEFIELD

Love Freely Given

I will heal their backsliding, I will love them freely:
for mine anger is turned away from him.
HOSEA 14:4 KJV

There is a great deal of difference between a willingness not to be condemned and a willingness to receive Christ for your Savior. Nobody loves misery, so they would not choose an eternity of it. Doubtless you are willing to be saved from eternal misery. That is a very different thing from being willing to come to Christ. People very commonly mistake the one for the other, but they are quite two different things.

You may love deliverance but hate the deliverer. You tell of a willingness for deliverance, but what is the object of that willingness? It does not respect Christ. The inclination of your will goes no further than self; it never reaches Christ. You are willing not to be miserable; that is, you love yourself, and there your will and choice come to an end. It is but a vain pretense and delusion to say or think that you are willing to accept Christ.

There is certainly a great deal of difference between a forced compliance and a free willingness. Force and freedom cannot consist together. Now if that willingness whereby you think you are willing to have Christ for a Savior is merely a forced thing, then your heart does not go out after Christ of itself. Instead you are forced and driven to seek an interest in Him. This forced compliance is not what Christ seeks of you. He seeks a free and willing acceptance. He seeks not that you should receive Him against your will but with a free will.

JONATHAN EDWARDS

Soar with Love

GOD *loves the pure-hearted and well-spoken;*
good leaders also delight in their friendship.
PROVERBS 22:11 TM

It is too much familiarity with unprofitable companions from which I would dissuade you. Not only the enemies of godliness will prove hurtful companions to us—though these indeed are chiefly to be avoided—but too frequent company with persons whose conversations are empty and unedifying may divert our thoughts from heaven.

We need the most constant and powerful help for our spirits to soar. A stone is as likely to rise and fly in the air as our hearts are naturally to move toward heaven. You need not hinder the rocks from flying up to the sky. It is sufficient that you do not help them; and surely if our spirits have not great assistance, they may easily be kept from soaring upward. Think of this in the choice of your company! When your spirits are so predisposed for heaven that you need no help to lift them up, you may be less careful of your company. But until then, as you love the delights of a heavenly life, be careful.

How will it advantage you in a divine life to hear how the market goes or what news is stirring? What will it assist to the raising of your heart to hear some unimportant controversy? No, if you had been newly warming your heart in the contemplation of the blessed joys above, this discussion would benumb your affections and quickly freeze your heart again. People cannot well talk of one thing and mind another, especially things of such different natures.

RICHARD BAXTER

Brave Love

But let us, who are of the day, be sober,
putting on the breastplate of faith and love;
and for an helmet, the hope of salvation.
1 THESSALONIANS 5:8 KJV

The brave lover stands firm in temptations and pays no heed to the crafty persuasions of the enemy. As Jesus pleases him in prosperity, so in adversity Jesus is not displeasing to him. The wise lover regards not so much the gift of Him who loves as the love of Him who gives. He regards the affection of the giver rather than the value of the gift and sets his beloved above all gifts. The noble lover does not rest in the gift but in Jesus who is above every gift.

All is not lost, then, if you sometimes feel less devout than you wish toward Jesus. That good and sweet feeling which you sometimes have is the effect of present grace and a certain foretaste of your heavenly home. It is not an illusion that you are sometimes engrossed in intense joy and then quickly returned to the usual follies of your heart. For these are evils that you suffer rather than commit. So long as they displease you and you struggle against them, it is a matter of merit and not a loss.

You must know that the old enemy tries by all means in his power to hinder your desire for good and to turn you from every devotional practice. He suggests many evil thoughts that he may cause you weariness and horror, and draw you away from prayer and holy reading.

Fight like a good soldier, and if you sometimes fall through weakness, rise again with greater strength than before, trusting in Christ's most abundant grace.

THOMAS À KEMPIS

Tests of Love

The LORD your God is testing you to
find out whether you love him
with all your heart and with all your soul.

DEUTERONOMY 13:3 NIV

Let us test ourselves impartially whether we are in the number of those who love God. Our love will be best seen by the fruits of it. It concerns us to search carefully whether any of these fruits grow in our garden.

He who is in love, his thoughts are ever upon the object. He who loves God is transported with the contemplation of God. The thoughts are as travelers in the mind. God is the treasure, and where the treasure is, there is the heart. By this we may test our love to God. What are our thoughts most upon? Can we say we are filled with delight when we think on God?

Love desires familiarity and conversation. If we love God, we prize His ordinances because there we meet with God. He speaks to us in His Word, and we speak to Him in prayer. Let us examine our love to God. Do we desire intimacy of communion with God? Lovers cannot be long away from each other. Those who love God know not how to be away from Him. They can bear the want of anything but God's presence. They can do without health and friends, they can be happy without a full table, but they cannot be happy without God. What shall we say to those who can be all their lives long without God? Does that woman love her husband who cannot endure to be in his presence?

THOMAS WATSON

Honored and Beloved

Honor everyone.
Love the family of believers.
1 PETER 2:17 NRSV

I received a small sum of money with the following letter from one of the former orphans: "Beloved sir, once more it is the privilege of one of your former orphans to write you a few lines and ask your acceptance of this small offering of thanksgiving to God for all His loving-kindness to me and mine. I need hardly say that, as each year passes away, my respect for you and love for the dear place where I spent the best part of my childhood increases. I express my gratitude to the Father of the fatherless, who put it in the heart of you, His honored and beloved servant, to carry out such a noble scheme to the glory of God.

"How often, when tempted to indulge in the sin of unbelief, has the thought of my six years at the orphanage come across my mind like a gleam of sunshine. There the clothes I wore, the food I ate, the bed I slept on, and the walls around me were all in answer to believing prayer. What better prescription for any infidel than to go to the orphanage and inquire into its working!

"I pray that none of us orphans who have been sheltered there will be found wanting in that great day when we shall all stand around the throne of God. You, dear sir, will receive the reward of all your labors of love. May we all be there to thank you."

GEORGE MÜLLER

Know the Love of Christ

I led them with cords of human kindness,
with bands of love.
I was to them like those who lift infants to their cheeks.
I bent down to them and fed them.

HOSEA 11:4 NRSV

We see the love of Christ in that the human nature, the nature of man, is taken into union with God. By this very act of the heavenly wisdom, we have an inconceivable pledge of the love of Christ to man. He took into union with Himself our nature. What did it signify but that He intended to take into union with Himself our person. For this very purpose, He assumed our nature. In that flesh He died for us, the just for the unjust, that He might bring us to God.

We may yet see more of His love in that He is gone into heaven, there to make ready and to prepare for us our mansions as if we were the lords and He the servant! This is love!

Also, we may see another degree of His love. Now in His absence, He has sent the third Person in the Trinity to supply in His place another comforter of us, that we may not think He forgot us. Yes, He has sent the Holy Spirit to fortify our spirits, and to strengthen us under all adversity.

He is now and has been ever since His ascension into glory laying out Himself as high priest for us. We also see yet more of His love by the fact that He will have us where He is, that we may see and be partakers of His glory.

JOHN BUNYAN

Advancing Love

> *"If you love those who love you,*
> *what credit is that to you?*
> *Even 'sinners' love those who love them."*
> LUKE 6:32 NIV

Do you find divine love advancing in your soul? Do you feel yourself more and more sensible of the presence of God? Can you, even when your natural spirits are weak and low, and you are not in any frame of mind for devotion, nevertheless find a pleasing rest in the thought that God is near you and that He sees the secret sentiments of your soul?

How does your mind stand affected toward those who differ from you in their religious sentiments and practices? I do not say that Christian love will require you to think every error harmless. But to hate persons because we think they are mistaken, and to aggravate every difference in judgment or practice into a fatal error that destroys all Christian communion and love, is a symptom generally much worse than the evil it condemns.

Do you love the image of Christ in a person who thinks himself obliged in conscience to profess and worship in a manner different from yourself? Further, can you love and honor that which is truly amiable and excellent in those in whom much is defective, in those in whom there is narrowness of spirit, which may lead them perhaps to slight you? Can you love them as the disciples and servants of Christ who through a mistaken zeal may be ready to cast out your name as evil and to warn others against you as a dangerous person? Does your love show itself solid and sincere?

PHILIP DODDRIDGE

What Would Jesus Do
The Rich Heiress

"What do you want me to do for you?"
Jesus asked him.

MARK 10:51 NIV

Virginia Page said, "I find it specially difficult to answer that question on account of my money. Our Lord never owned any property. What I am trying to discover is a principle that will enable me to come to the nearest possible to His action as it ought to influence the entire course of my life so far as my wealth and its use are concerned.

"I have been educated in one of the most expensive schools in America and launched into society as an heiress. I can do as I please. I can gratify almost any want or desire; and yet when I honestly try to imagine Jesus living the life I have lived and am expected to live, I am under condemnation for being one of the most wicked, selfish, useless creatures in all the world.

"Dear friends, I do not want any of you to credit me with an act of great generosity. I have come to know lately that the money which I have called my own is not mine, but God's. If I, as steward of His, see some wise way to invest His money, it is not an occasion for vainglory or thanks from anyone simply because I have proved in my administration of the funds He has asked me to use for His glory."

Virginia Page, one of the city's leading society heiresses, dedicated her entire fortune to the Christian daily paper and the work of reform in the slum district known as the Rectangle.

CHARLES SHELDON

Love and the Unbelieving Son

For you, O Lord, are good and forgiving,
abounding in steadfast love to all who call on you.
PSALM 86:5 NRSV

A mother asked a minister of the gospel to visit her son to win him to Christ. The preacher found the young man's mind full of skeptical notions and impervious to argument. Finally the young man was asked to pray, just once, for light. He replied: "I do not know anything perfect to whom or to which I could pray."

"How about your mother's love?" said the preacher. "Isn't that perfect? Hasn't she always stood by you, been ready to take you in and care for you when even your father had really kicked you out?"

The young man choked with emotion and said, "Y–e–s, sir, that is so."

"Then pray to love—it will help you. Will you promise?" He promised.

That night the young man prayed in the privacy of his room. He kneeled down, closed his eyes, and struggling a moment uttered the words: "O love." Instantly as by a flash of lightning, the Bible text came to him: "God is love." He said brokenly, "O God!" Then another flash of divine truth, and a voice said, "God so loved the world that He gave His only begotten Son." Then instantly he exclaimed, "O Christ, You are divine love; show me light and truth." It was all over. He was in the light of the most perfect peace. He ran downstairs and told his mother.

That young man is today an eloquent minister of Jesus Christ.

EDWARD MCKENDREE BOUNDS

Love's Plan for Your Life

*The LORD will work out his plans for my life—
for your faithful love, O LORD, endures forever.*

PSALM 138:8 NLT

There is an experience that becomes more and more familiar to everyone who is trying to follow Christ—a feeling of the growing loneliness of his Christian life. It comes from a sense of the personal interest that Christ takes in him. It sometimes seems so strong, as if an unseen arm linked in his were taking him aside for a nearer intimacy and a deeper and more private fellowship. It is a humbling realization that God makes Himself as real to each poor unit as if he were the whole. Christ has died for others but in a particular sense for the individual. God has a love for all the world but a particular love for each person.

But if there is one thing more than another which is more personal to the Christian—one thing which is a finer symbol of God's love and interest—it is the private knowledge of God's will. And this is more personal, just as it is more private. My private portion of God's love is only a private share in God's love—only a part—the same in quality and kind as all the rest of God's love, which all the others get from God. But God's will for me is a thing for myself. There is a will of God for me that is willed for no one else.

If I have God's will in my character, my life may become great and good. It may be useful and honorable. God has a life plan for every human life.

HENRY DRUMMOND

Love in Harmony

Dear friends, since God so loved us,
we also ought to love one another.
1 JOHN 4:11 NIV

There are two errors against which the children of God—particularly those who have just come to trust in His grace—especially need to guard. The first is that of looking to their own works, trusting to anything they can do, to bring themselves into harmony with God. Those who are trying to become holy by their own works in keeping the law are attempting an impossibility. All that people can do without Christ is polluted with selfishness and sin. It is the grace of Christ alone, through faith, that can make us holy.

The opposite and no less dangerous error is that belief in Christ releases people from keeping the law of God; that since by faith alone we become partakers of the grace of Christ, our works have nothing to do with our redemption. But obedience is not a mere outward compliance but the service of love. The law of God is an expression of His very nature. It is an embodiment of the great principle of love. If our hearts are renewed in the likeness of God, if the divine love is implanted in the soul, will not the law of God be carried out in the life?

We do not earn salvation by our obedience because salvation is the free gift of God, to be received by faith. But obedience is the fruit of faith. If we stay in Christ, if the love of God dwells in us, our feelings, our thoughts, our purposes, our actions will be in harmony with the will of God as expressed in the precepts of His holy law.

ELLEN G. WHITE

Suitable Friend

A friend loves at all times,
and kinsfolk are born to share adversity.
PROVERBS 17:17 NRSV

Can you love a little shining earth, a walking piece of clay? More so, can you love that God, that Christ, that glory, which are so truly and unmeasurably lovely? You can love your friend because he loves you. But is the love of friends like the love of Christ? Their weeping or bleeding for you do not ease your pain or stop the course of your tears or blood. But the tears and blood that fell from your Lord have an effective and healing quality. If love should foster love, what incomprehensible love is here before you! Pour out all the reserve of your affections here, although all is too little.

Ahead is the region of light; this is the land of darkness. The twinkling stars, shining moon, and radiant sun are all but lanterns hung out of your Father's house to light you while you walk in this dark world. Blessed forever be that love that has rescued me from this bewitching darkness!

Who is more suitable for our love than Christ? His Godhead and humanity, His fullness and freeness, His willingness and constancy, all proclaim Him your most suitable friend. Although your eyes have never seen your Lord, yet you have heard His voice, received His benefits, and lived close to His heart. He taught you to know yourself and Him. He opened that first window through which you saw into heaven.

RICHARD BAXTER

Love of God's Laws

> "Woe to you Pharisees,
> because you give God a tenth of your mint,
> rue and all other kinds of garden herbs,
> but you neglect justice and the love of God."
>
> LUKE 11:42 NIV

God judges after the content of the heart and the thoughts of the mind. His law is not content with the outward work only but rebukes those works that spring not of love, although they appear outward honest and good. Christ rebuked the Pharisees above all others who were open sinners and called them hypocrites. Yet no people lived as pure as the Pharisees in keeping the outward deeds of the law. Paul himself confessed as keeping the law he was such a one as no man could complain about, but he persecuted Christians and tormented them to compel them to blaspheme Christ.

If you act as a Pharisee, you live outwardly the works of the law and judge them who fail to do so. Inwardly, in your heart, you wish that there were no law nor God to enforce the law if it were possible, so painful it is unto you to have your sinful appetites kept down. You teach another man not to steal when you are a thief in your heart and would steal if you could. You understand not the law right. It cannot be satisfied but with an unfeigned love.

The law is spiritual, and no person fulfills it except that by doing it through love from the bottom of the heart. The law is spiritual and will be both loved and fulfilled by a spiritual heart.

WILLIAM TYNDALE

Supported by Love

When I thought, "My foot is slipping,"
your steadfast love, O LORD, held me up.
PSALM 94:18 NRSV

It is always helpful to fix our attention on the Godward aspect of Christian work. The work of God does not mean so much man's work for God as God's own work through man. Furthermore, in our privileged position of fellow workers with Him—while fully recognizing all the benefits and blessings to be bestowed on a sin-stricken world through the proclamation of the gospel and the spreading of the Truth—we should never lose sight of the higher aspect of our work: that of obedience to God, of bringing glory to His name, of gladdening the heart of our God and Father by living and serving as His beloved children.

Many circumstances connected with my own early life and service presented this aspect of work vividly to me. As I think of some of them, I am reminded of how much the cause of missions is indebted to many who are never themselves permitted to see the mission field. Many, it may be, who are unable to give largely of their substance and who will be not a little surprised in the Great Day to see how much the work has been advanced by their love, their sympathy, and their prayers.

For myself and for the work that I have been permitted to do for God, I owe an unspeakable debt of gratitude to my beloved and honored parents, who have passed away and entered into rest but the influence of whose lives will never pass away.

HUDSON TAYLOR

Redeem Time for Love

*So he [Paul] reasoned in the synagogue with the Jews
and the God-fearing Greeks, as well as in the marketplace
day by day with those who happened to be there.*
ACTS 17:17 NIV

Monday, August 22, 1743 (London)—After a few of us had
joined in prayer, about four o'clock I set out and rode easily to
Snow Hill; where, the saddle slipping quite upon my mare's neck,
I fell over her head, and she ran back into Smithfield. Some boys
caught her and brought her to me again, cursing and swearing all
the way. I spoke plainly to them, and they promised to amend
their ways.

I was setting forward when a man cried, "Sir, you have lost
your saddlecloth." Two or three more came to help me put it on,
but these, too, swore at almost every word. I turned to one and
another and spoke in love. They all took it well and thanked me
much. I gave them two or three little books which they promised to read over carefully.

Before I reached Kensington, I found my mare had lost a
shoe. This gave me an opportunity of talking closely for nearly
half an hour both to the blacksmith and his assistant. I mention
these little circumstances to show how easy it is to redeem every
fragment of time (if I may so speak) when we feel any love to
those souls for which Christ died.

JOHN WESLEY

Love Is God's Gift

*Bear with each other and forgive
whatever grievances you may have
against one another.
Forgive as the Lord forgave you.*

COLOSSIANS 3:13 NIV

Think for a moment of a clock and of what its hands mean. The hands tell me what is within the clock. If I see that the hands stand still or that the clock is slow or fast, I say that something inside the clock is not working properly. Temper is just like the revelation that the clock gives of what is within. Temper is a proof whether the love of Christ is filling the heart or not. How many find it easier in church, prayer meeting, or in work for the Lord to be holy and happy than in the daily life with spouse and children. Some find it easier to be holy and happy outside the home than in it!

Think what liberty many Christians give to their tongues. They say, "I have a right to think what I like." When they speak about each other, when they speak about their neighbors, when they speak about other Christians, how often there are sharp remarks! God shut my mouth if I am not to speak in tender love. How often there are found among Christians who are banded together in work sharp criticism, sharp judgment, hasty opinion, unloving words, secret contempt of each other, and secret condemnation of each other! Just as a parent's love covers her children and delights in them and has the tenderest compassion with their foibles or failures, so there ought to be in the heart of every believer a tender love toward every brother and sister in Christ.

ANDREW MURRAY

Friend of My Heart

*"If you belonged to the world,
the world would love you as its own."*
JOHN 15:19 NRSV

Friend of my heart's love and of all the confidence of my heart,
am Sechele," Livingstone's first Christian wrote. "I am undone
by the Boers who attacked me, though I had no guilt with them.
They demanded that I should be in their kingdom, and I
refused. They demanded that I should prevent the English from
passing northward. I replied, 'These are my friends, and I can
prevent not one of them.'

"They came on Saturday, and I asked them not to fight on
Sunday, and they assented. They began on Monday morning at
dawn and fired with all their might and burned the town with
fire and scattered us. They killed sixty of my people, and cap-
tured women and children and men. Two hundred children
were carried away as slaves."

Added by Livingstone: "My house, which had stood perfectly
secure for years under the protection of the natives, was plundered.
The books of a good library—my solace in our solitude—were
not taken away, but handfuls of the leaves were torn out and
scattered over the place. My stock of medicines was smashed,
and all our furniture and clothing carried off.

"I do not mention these things by way of making a pitiful
wail over my losses, though I do feel sorry for the loss of lexi-
cons, dictionaries, and other books which had been the companions of my boyhood. The plundering only set me entirely
free for my expedition to the north. I have never since had a
moment's concern for anything I left behind."

DAVID LIVINGSTONE

Love That Does Not Fade

> *Give thanks to the LORD, for he is good*
> *his love endures forever*

The fairest pictures must have their shadows. The rarest and mos brilliant gems must have dark backgrounds to set off their beauty. If there is something pleasing, there is also something sour. If person has every ability to delight us, there is also some natura corruption intermixed with it to put us off. But it is not so in ou altogether lovely Christ; His excellencies are pure and unmixed. He is a sea of sweetness without one drop of bitterness.

Survey the human race. You will observe strength in one person, beauty in a second, faithfulness in a third, wisdom in fourth. But you shall find none excelling in them all as Chris does. Bread has one quality, water another, raiment another, an medicine another. But none has them all in itself as Christ does. He is bread to the hungry, water to the thirsty, a garment to th naked, and healing to the wounded.

Take away Christ, and where is the loveliness of any enjoy ment? The best creature comfort apart from Christ is but a bro ken and empty well. It cannot hold one drop of true comfort. I is as a beautiful image in the mirror: turn away the face, an where is the image? Riches, honors, and comfortable relation are sweet when the face of Christ smiles upon us through them but without Him, they are empty trifles.

The beauty and loveliness of all other things are fading and perishing, but the loveliness of Christ is fresh for all eternity.

JOHN FLAVE

Affection Rejected

"But while he was still far off, his father saw him and was filled with compassion; he ran and put his arms around him and kissed him."
LUKE 15:20 NRSV

Suppose a son has gone far away from the paths of obedience and virtue. He has had one of the best of fathers, but he would not hear his counsels. He had a wise and affectionate mother, but he sternly resisted all the appeals of her tenderness and tears. Despite the most watchful care of parents and friends, he would go astray. As one madly bent on self-ruin, he pushed on, reckless of the sorrow and grief he brought upon those he should have honored and loved.

At last the youth finds himself ruined in constitution, in fortune, and in good name. He has sunk far too low to retain even self-respect. Nothing remains for him but agonizing reflections on past folly and guilt.

"Alas," he cries, "I have almost killed my venerable father, and long ago I had quite broken my mother's heart. All that folly and crime a son could do, I have done to bring down their gray hairs with sorrow to the grave. I have plucked down a double ruin on my own head. No sinner ever more richly deserved to be doubly condemned than myself."

Truth flashes upon his soul, his heart quails, and his conscience thunders condemnation. So it must be with every sinner when all his sins against God shall stand revealed before his eyes, and there shall be nothing left for him but intense and unqualified self-condemnation.

CHARLES FINNEY

What Would Jesus Do—
The Beautiful Singer

Because Christ also suffered for us,
leaving us an example,
that ye should follow his steps.

1 PETER 2:21 KJV

Of what Christian use was Rachel Winslow's talent of song? Was the best she could do to sell her talent for so much a month, go on a concert company's tour, dress beautifully, enjoy the excitement of public applause, and gain a reputation as a great singer? Was that what Jesus would do?

She said, "I have made up my mind to use my voice in some way so as to satisfy my own soul that I am doing something better than pleasing fashionable audiences or making money or even gratifying my own love of singing. I am going to do something that will satisfy me when I ask: 'What would Jesus do?' I am not satisfied and cannot be when I think of myself as singing myself into the career of a concert company performer.

"During the week I am going to sing at the White Cross meetings down in the Rectangle, the slum district. They use a tent. It is in a part of the city where Christian work is most needed. What have we done all our lives for the suffering, sinning side of the city of Raymond? How much have we denied ourselves or given of our personal ease and pleasure to bless the place in which we live or imitate the life of the Savior?"

Miss Winslow has chosen to give her great talent to the poor of the city. Her plans include a musical institute where choruses and classes in vocal music shall be a feature. She is enthusiastic over her lifework.

CHARLES SHELDON

Let Love Shine

He is my loving God and my fortress,
my stronghold and my deliverer,
my shield, in whom I take refuge,
who subdues peoples under me.
PSALM 144:2 NIV

God is the most adequate and complete object of our love. He is wisdom, beauty, love, and the very essence of goodness. There is nothing in God that can cause a loathing. The more we enjoy of Him, the more we are filled with delight. There is nothing in God to deaden our affections or quench our love. Surely, then, here is enough to induce us to love God—we cannot spend our love upon a better object.

Love makes duty a pleasure. He who loves God is never weary of serving Him. He is sure to dwell with God in heaven if he has God dwelling in his heart. So that to love God is the truest self-love. He who does not love God does not love himself.

Love to God evidences sincerity. To love God is a better sign of sincerity than to fear Him. Repentance is no better than flattery when it arises only from fear of God's judgments and has no love mixed with it. Loving God evidences that God has the heart.

Do you love God? Then you may be sure of God's love to you. As it is with burning glasses, if the magnifying glass can set a fire, it is because the sun has first shined upon it. So if our hearts burn in love to God, it is because God's love has first shined upon us.

THOMAS WATSON

Love Will Last

"Though the mountains be shaken
and the hills be removed,
yet my unfailing love for you will not be shaken."

ISAIAH 54:10 NIV

Why did Paul single out love as the supreme possession? It is a very remarkable reason. In a single word, it is this: It lasts. "Love," urges Paul, "never fails." He runs through the things that people thought were going to last and shows that they are all fleeting, temporary, passing away.

Then Paul with even greater boldness adds, "Whether there be knowledge, it shall vanish away." The wisdom of the ancients, where is it? It is wholly gone. You put yesterday's newspaper in the fire. Its knowledge has vanished away. In every branch of science, it is the same. "Now we know in part. We see through a glass darkly."

Can you tell me anything that is going to last? Many things Paul did not choose to name. He did not mention money, fortune, and fame. Instead he picked out the great things of his time, the things the best people thought had something in them, and brushed them firmly aside. There is a great deal in the world that is delightful and beautiful; there is a great deal in it that is great and engrossing; but it will not last. All that is in the world—the lust of the eye, the lust of the flesh, and the pride of life—are but for a little while. The immortal soul must give itself to something that is immortal. And the only immortal things are these: Now abides faith, hope, love, but the greatest of these is love.

HENRY DRUMMOND

God's Gift of Love

Jesus said to them,
"If God were your Father, you would love me,
for I came from God and now I am here.
I did not come
on my own, but he sent me."

JOHN 8:42 NRSV

This is the love of God, not that He gives us something, but that He gives us someone in whom is all life and blessing—Jesus Himself. It is the will of the Father that we should have Jesus as ours, even as He has Him. God has given His Son, given Him wholly to become ours.

How I do wish that all Christians may understand this. The one great work of God's love for us is that He gives us His Son. In Him, we have all. The one great work of our heart must be to receive Jesus who has been given to us and to consider Him and use Him as ours. I must begin every day anew with the thought, *I have Jesus to do all for me.* In all weakness, darkness, or danger, and in the case of every desire or need, let your first thought always be, *I have Jesus to make everything right for me because God has given Him to me.* Let this always be your first thought: *The Father has given me Jesus to care for me.*

For this purpose, consider this gift of God every day as yours. Take Him new every day. Through faith, you have the Son. The love of God has given the Son. Take Him and hold Him fast in the love of your heart.

ANDREW MURRAY

Memorial Gifts of Love

"Truly I tell you,
wherever the gospel is proclaimed
in the whole world,
what she has done will also be told
as a memorial to her."

MARK 14:9 ISV

In the days of our Lord's life on earth, when the shadow of the cross was already upon Him, one only amongst all His followers, a woman—Mary—had understood and really taken in His repeated declaration of the sufferings that awaited Him. When she came to anoint Him beforehand for the burial and broke the precious alabaster box she had reserved for this very purpose, the thief who kept the bag had only angry words of criticism and reproach. How sweet to her wounded spirit was her Master's commendation, "She hath done what she could!"

On an earlier occasion, as He sat over against the treasury, many who were rich cast in large sums of silver and of gold, but He turned from them and their gifts to draw attention to a certain poor widow who brought two mites (small copper coins) and cast them in. She had gladdened the heart of Him who was the Creator of all wealth and the real owner of it all. She, said He, had given more than they all because she of her want had given all that she had! And of her, as of Mary, in whatsoever language the Word of God is translated, in whatsoever region of earth it is read, the Master's commendation is made known.

There is a day coming in which before assembled worlds He will make manifest the loving gifts and the secret service of His redeemed ones.

HUDSON TAYLOR

Comforting Love

Finally, brethren, farewell. Become complete.
Be of good comfort, be of one mind, live in peace;
and the God of love and peace will be with you.

2 CORINTHIANS 13:11 NKJV

God sent His Son to be the comforter of a mourning world. All through His life, the Lord Jesus Christ fulfilled His divine mission. For this is the glory of a religion of love. When His disciples asked Him to call down fire from heaven to consume some people who refused to receive Him, He turned and rebuked them. He came to save sinners. He had no other mission.

Two little girls were talking about God, and one said, "I know God does not love me. He could not care for such a teeny, tiny little girl as I am."

"Dear me, sis," said the other little girl, "don't you know that is just what God is for—to take care of teeny, tiny little girls who can't take care of themselves, just like us?"

"Is He?" said the first little girl. "I did not know that. Then I don't need to worry anymore, do I?"

If any troubled, doubting heart should read these lines, then let me tell you again in trumpet tones that this is just what the Lord Jesus Christ is for—to care for and comfort all who mourn. All who mourn, all who are cast down—I love to think of such a mission of comfort in a world of mourning like ours; and I long to see every cast down and sorrowing heart comforted with this comforting of God.

HANNAH WHITALL SMITH

Tender Lov

"For the Lord disciplines those whom he loves
and chastises every child whom he accepts."

HEBREWS 12:6 NRSV

Sometimes everything seems so firmly established in prosperity that no dream of disaster disturbs us. Our reputation is assured our efforts have all been successful beyond our hopes, and ou soul is at ease. The need for God is in danger of becoming far of and vague. Then the Lord is obliged to put an end to it all, and our prosperity crumbles around us like a house built on sand.

We are tempted to think He is angry with us. But in truth it is not anger but tender love. His very love compels Him to take away the outward prosperity that is keeping our souls from entering the interior spiritual kingdom for which we long. When the fig tree ceases to blossom and there is no fruit in the vines, when the flock shall be cut off from the fold and there shall be no herd in the stalls, then, and often not until then, will our souls learn to rejoice in the Lord only and to joy in the God of our salvation.

It might look as far as the outward seeing goes as though i was God's wrath that did this. Many a frightened Christian thinks it is. But His wrath is not against us. His love could do no less than destroy these refuges in order that we may be delivered. Paul declared that he counted all things but loss that he might win Christ. When we learn to say the same, the peace and joy that the gospel promises become our permanent possession

HANNAH WHITALL SMITH

Love from a Height

He will send from heaven and save me,
he will put to shame those who trample on me.
God will send forth his steadfast love and his faithfulness.

PSALM 57:3 NRSV

God shows His love by the sacrifice He has made for us. Sacrifice is the great test of love. People tell you that they love you, but you cannot tell whether they really love you until the opportunity comes for them to make a sacrifice for you.

You and I sometimes dwell upon the love of Christ to give up heaven for us. We look at Him in the courtyard of Pilate, fastened to the whipping post with His bare back exposed to the lash of the Roman soldier. We look at Him as the lash cuts into His back again, again, and again until it is all torn and bleeding. Oh, how He loves us!

But looking down from the throne in heaven was God, and every lash that cut the back of Christ cut the heart of God. We see the soldiers with the crown of thorns, pressing it on His brow, and we see the blood flowing down. Oh, how He loved us! But every thorn that pierces His brow pierced also the heart of God. Through that awful day we see Him on the cross. We hear the last cry. We see how He loved us. But looking down from the throne of light and glory was God, and every nail that pierced His hands and feet pierced the heart of God.

What are you going to do about this love?

REUBEN ARCHER TORREY

Love's Evil Opposite

*For I knew that thou art a gracious God,
and merciful, slow to anger, and of great kindness.*

JONAH 4:2 KJV

Bad temper! Abuse your wife, and abuse your children; abuse your husband; turn your old machine-gun tongue loose. A lady came to me and said, "Mr. Sunday, I know I have a bad temper, but I am over with it in a minute." So is the shotgun, but it blows everything to pieces.

You abuse the receptionist because she doesn't connect you in a minute. Bad temper! I say you abuse your wife; you go cussing around if supper isn't ready on time, cussing because the coffee isn't hot. You dig your fork into a hunk of beefsteak and put it on your plate, and then you say: "Where did you get this, in the harness shop? Take it out and make a hinge for the door."

Then you go to your store or office and smile, and everybody thinks you are an angel about to sprout wings and fly to the imperial realm above. Bad temper! You growl at your children. You snap and snarl around the house until they have to go to the neighbors to see a smile. They never get a kind word—no wonder so many of them go to the devil quickly.

You say, "Mr. Sunday, the church is full of hypocrites." So's hell. I say to you: If you don't want to go to hell and live with that whole bunch forever, come into the church where you won't have to associate with them very long. There are no hypocrites in heaven.

BILLY SUNDAY

Love Grown Dark

When Jesus therefore saw his mother,
and the disciple standing by,
whom he loved, he saith unto his mother,
Woman, behold thy son!
JOHN 19:26 KJV

A poor man sent his son to school in the city. The young man was walking down the street with two of his school friends. His father, who was hauling wood, saw him and went to the sidewalk to speak to him. But the boy was ashamed of his father and said, "I don't know you." Will such a young man ever amount to anything? Never!

I remember a very promising young man whom I had in Sunday school in Chicago. His mother took in washing to educate her four children. This was her eldest son, and I thought that he was going to redeem the whole family. One day he stood with his mother at the cottage door—it was a poor house because she could not pay for their schooling, feed and clothe her children, and rent a very good house, too. When they were talking, a young man from the high school came up the street. This boy walked away from his mother. The next day the young man asked, "Who was that I saw you talking to yesterday?"

He replied, "That was my washerwoman."

I thought, *Poor fellow! He will never amount to anything.* That was a good many years ago. He has gone down, down, down, and now he is just a miserable wreck. Of course he would go down. Ashamed of his mother who loved him and toiled for him and bore so much hardship for him!

DWIGHT LYMAN MOODY

*And [Jesus] went down with [His parents],
and came to Nazareth, and was subject unto them.*

LUKE 2:51 KJV

Some years ago I heard of a poor woman who sent her boy to school and college. When he was to graduate, he wrote his mother to come, but she wrote back that she could not because she was so shabby that she was afraid he would be ashamed of her. He wrote back that he didn't care how she was dressed and urged her so strongly that she came.

He met her at the station and took her to a nice place to stay. The day came for his graduation, and he walked down the broad aisle with that poor mother dressed very shabbily and put her into one of the best seats in the house. To her great surprise, he was the valedictorian of the class. He won a prize, and when it was given to him, he stepped down, kissed his mother, and said, "Here, Mother, here is the prize. It is yours. I would not have had it if it had not been for you." Thank God for such a man!

I have read of one heathen custom in China which would do us credit in this so-called Christian country. On every New Year's morning each man and boy, from the emperor to the lowest peasant, is said to pay a visit to his mother, carrying her a present varying in value according to his station in life. He thanks her for all she has done for him and asks a continuance of her favor another year.

DWIGHT LYMAN MOODY

Seek Love for One Another

Wondrously show your steadfast love,
O savior of those who seek refuge
from their adversaries at your right hand.
PSALM 17:7 NRSV

I would now write a few lines than appear unmindful of you. You are dear to me. Yes, so dear that I desire to live and die with you if our Lord permit. Why should I not tell you so by letter? I will write then as a token of brotherly remembrance and of love toward you. May it quicken you to prayer on my behalf.

In looking back upon my past life, I know not where to begin or where to end in making mention of the Lord's mercies. His long-suffering toward me in the days of my unrepentant life cannot be described. If, however, I have much reason to praise God for His mercies toward me in those days, I have more abundant reason to admire His gentleness, long-suffering, and faithfulness toward me since I have known Him. How can I sufficiently praise Him for this long-suffering? He has been always the same gracious, kind, loving father, friend, supporter, teacher, and comforter to me.

Let us seek to be faithful in the Lord and toward each other! Let us seek to love each other in the truth and for the truth's sake. It is comparatively easy to begin to love, but it requires much watchfulness not to grow weary in love when little or no love is returned. But as our gracious, faithful God, notwithstanding all our wavering, loves us without change, so should we, His children, love each other. Lord, help us to do so!

GEORGE MÜLLER

Jesus Loves My Soul

"Because he loves me," says the LORD,
"I will rescue him; I will protect him."

PSALM 91:14 NIV

Two Americans, who were crossing the Atlantic, met on Sunday to sing hymns. As they sang "Jesus, Lover of My Soul," one of them heard an exceedingly rich and beautiful voice behind him. He looked around, and although he did not know the face, he thought that he knew the voice. When the music ceased, the man asked if he had not been in the Civil War. The man replied that he had been a Confederate soldier.

"Were you at such a place on such a night?" asked the first.

"Yes," he replied, "and a curious thing happened that night. I was posted on sentry duty in the edge of a wood. About midnight when everything was very still and I was feeling homesick and miserable and weary, I thought that I would comfort myself by praying and singing 'Jesus, Lover of My Soul.' A peace came down upon me, and through the long night I remember having felt no more fear."

"Now," said the other, "listen to my story. I was a Union soldier and was in the wood that night with a party of scouts. I saw you standing, although I did not see your face. My men had their rifles focused upon you waiting the word to fire, but when you sang the words 'Cover my defenseless head with the shadow of Thy wing,' I said, 'Boys, lower your rifles; we will go home.' "

God was working in each of them. By just such means, God keeps His people and guides them.

HENRY DRUMMOND

Our Love Shows God's Power

I declare that your steadfast love is established forever;
your faithfulness is as firm as the heavens.
PSALM 89:2 NRSV

During the three years the disciples had walked with Christ, all of His teaching could not make them of one heart and one soul. But the Holy Spirit came from heaven and shed the love of God in their hearts, and they were of one heart and one soul. The same Holy Spirit who brought the love of heaven into their hearts must fill us, too. Nothing less will do. Even as Christ did, one might preach love for three years with the tongue of an angel, but that would not teach people to love unless the power of the Holy Spirit should come upon them to bring the love of heaven into their hearts.

Think of the church at large. What divisions! Think of the different bodies. That there are differences of opinion does not trouble me. We do not have the same constitution, temperament, and mind. But how often hate, bitterness, contempt, separation, and unlovingness are caused by the truths of God's Word! Our doctrines have been more important than love. We often think we are valiant for the truth, and we forget God's command to speak the truth in love. The very dearest truths of God have become mountains that have separated us.

If we want to pray in power, and if we want to expect the Holy Spirit to come down in power, then we must enter into a covenant with God that we love one another with a heavenly love. Are you ready for that?

ANDREW MURRAY

The One Who Hates Love

*"He has blinded their eyes and hardened their heart,
so that they might not look with their eyes,
and understand with their heart and turn—
and I would heal them."*

JOHN 12:40 NRSV

We may know the love of Christ by the nature of it. His love is free, divine, heavenly, everlasting, and incorruptible. All other love is either corruptible, transient, mixed, or earthly. His love is divine, for it is the love of the holy nature of God.

I confess that it is hard in time of temptation to hold fast the soul to all these things. But this love of Christ must be such because love is essential to His nature. There is nothing that Satan sets himself more against than breaking the love of Christ in its own proper inborn luster. For he knows that the love of Christ destroys his kingdom, which stands in profaneness, errors, and delusions.

Satan has an aptitude to alter all things. He can make God seem to be to us a most fierce and terrible destroyer. He can make Christ appear to be a terrible exactor of obedience. And most amazingly, Satan can steal His love. He can make supposed sins unpardonable, and unpardonable ones appear as virtues. He can make the law to be received for gospel and cause that the gospel shall be thrown away as a fable. He can persuade that faith is fancy, and that fancy is the best faith in the world. It is for this purpose that Christ bids us to continue in His love because the right knowledge and faith drives away all such confusion.

JOHN BUNYAN

What Would Jesus Do—
The College President

Jesus answered. . . "You must follow me."
JOHN 21:22 NIV

Donald Marsh, president of Lincoln College, said, "What would Jesus do in my place? I have tried to satisfy myself by thinking that He would simply go on as I have done, attending to the duties of my college work, teaching the classes in ethics and philosophy. But I have not been able to avoid the feeling that He would do something more.

"I belong to a class of professional men who have always avoided the duties of citizenship. We have lived in a little world of literature and scholarly seclusion. I understand that our city officials are a corrupt, unprincipled set of men, and thoroughly selfish so far as the affairs of city government are concerned. Yet all these years I have been satisfied to let other men run the municipality and have lived in a little world of my own, out of touch and sympathy with the real world of the people.

"What would Jesus do? My plain duty is to take a personal part in this coming election, go to the primaries, throw the weight of my influence, whatever it is, toward the nomination and election of good men, and plunge into the very depths of the entire horrible whirlpool of deceit, bribery, political trickery, and saloonism as it exists in the city of Raymond today.

"I would sooner walk up to the mouth of a cannon anytime than do this. I would so much prefer to remain quietly in my scholastic life with my classes. But this is my cross; I must take it up or deny my Lord."

CHARLES SHELDON

Love Without Delay

It is good to. . .
declare your steadfast love in the morning,
and your faithfulness by night.

PSALM 92:1–2 NRSV

Enter upon saving souls with the right intentions. Aim at the glory of God in the person's salvation. Do it not to get a name for yourself or to bring people to depend upon you. Do it in obedience to Christ and in imitation of Him. Extend His tender love to people's souls.

Do not delay. While you are making ready to teach a person, sin is taking root, and temptations to sin multiply. Conscience grows seared, and the heart becomes hardened. Christ is shut out. Time runs on. Death and judgment are at the door. What if the person dies while you are getting ready! A physician is no better than a murderer who negligently delays until his patient is dead or past cure.

Let your appeal proceed from compassion and love. To jeer, scoff, and vilify are not likely ways to reform people or convert them to God. Go to poor sinners with tears in your eyes so they may see that you have earnest compassion for their case. Let them perceive it is the desire of your heart to do them good and that it is your love for their souls that forces you to speak. Say to them, "Friend, love will not permit me to see you perish. I seek nothing but your own happiness. You will have the gain and comfort if you come to Christ." If we were to go to every neighbor like this, what blessed fruit should we quickly see!

RICHARD BAXTER

Love of Money

For the love of money is a root of all kinds of evil,
and in their eagerness to be rich some have wandered away
from the faith and pierced themselves with many pains.
1 TIMOTHY 6:10 NRSV

The love of money keeps many men from coming to Christ. Many a man knows that if he came to Christ he would lose money by it. There are things in his business that would need to be given up. But he is not willing to sacrifice the profits he gets in crooked ways. He is deliberately choosing a larger income and eternal death instead of Jesus Christ and eternal life.

How many a young fellow has come to me, and when I have urged him to come to Christ, he has said, "I believe it is a good thing, but I should have to give up my employment if I did."

Two young ladies said to Mrs. Torrey, when they seemed to be very near a decision, "We cannot come to Christ. We are employed in a large shop, and our employer requires us to misrepresent the goods. We cannot do that and be Christians, can we?"

"No, you cannot," Mrs. Torrey replied, and the young ladies said, "If we don't, then we lose our positions." God pity the man or the merchant who requires his employees to lie! How sad it is that those young women were ready to choose their position and small salary in the place of Jesus Christ and life eternal!

REUBEN ARCHER TORREY

Love Secured in the Heart

*Let no debt remain outstanding,
except the continuing debt to love one another,
for he who loves his fellowman has fulfilled the law.*

ROMANS 13:8 NIV

Our Lord speaks of His relationship to us as the rule of our love to others: "Love one another, as I have loved you." But is it a vain thing to imagine that we can keep His commandments and love others, even as He kept His Father's and loved us? Would the attempt end in failure and discouragement? Undoubtedly, if we seek to carry out the injunction in our strength, or without a full understanding of the truth of Jesus as the vine and us as its branches.

It is not the question of what we feel able to accomplish but of what Christ is able to work in us. We need to be brought to an entirely new mode of life. With the surrender to be cleansed from all that is of self and detached from all that is in the world, to live only and wholly as Christ lived for the glory of the Father.

Christ showed us that His love was the same love with which the Father had loved Him. Christ and His love are inseparable; they are identical. God is love, and Christ is love. God and Christ and the divine love can only be known by having them, by their life and power working within us. Our Lord gave His life for us as proof of His friendship. He gave His life to secure a place for His love in our hearts to rule us.

ANDREW MURRAY

The Gospel Feast

And the angel said to me,
"Write this: Blessed are those who are
invited to the marriage supper of the Lamb."
REVELATION 19:9 NRSV

Many of you, perhaps, are not hungry. What say you, my dear friends? I would put the question to you once more, "Will you taste of Christ's supper, or will you not?" You shall all be welcome. There is milk at this feast for babes as well as meat for strong people and for persons of riper years. There is room and provision for high and low, rich and poor, one with another. Our Savior will thank you for coming. Astonishing love! The thought of it quite overcomes me. Help me, help me, believers, to bless and praise Him.

And that this love may excite us to come afresh to Him as we had never come before! For though we have been often feasted, yet our souls will starve unless we renew our acts of faith and throw ourselves as lost, undone sinners continually at the feet of Christ. Feeding upon past experiences will not satisfy our souls any more than what we did eat yesterday will sustain our bodies today. No, believers must look for fresh influences of divine grace and beg of the Lord to water them every moment. Come you to the marriage feast. You are as welcome now as ever. And may God set your souls longing for that time when we shall sit down and eat bread in the kingdom of heaven! There we shall have full measure of divine love and enjoy the glorious Emmanuel forevermore.

GEORGE WHITEFIELD

Love Sees the Bright Side

[Love] always hopes.
1 CORINTHIANS 13:7 NIV

You will find, if you think for a moment, that the people who influence you are people who believe in you. In an atmosphere of suspicion, people shrivel up. But in an atmosphere of encouragement, they expand and find instructive fellowship. It is a wonderful thing that here and there in this hard, uncharitable world there should still be left a few rare souls who think no evil. Love imputes no motive, sees the bright side, and puts the best construction on every action. What a delightful state of mind to live in! What a blessing even to meet with it for a day! If we try to influence others, we shall soon see that success is in proportion to their belief of our belief in them. The respect of another is the first restoration of the self-respect that a man has lost. Our ideal of what he is becomes to him the hope and pattern of what he may become.

He who loves will rejoice in the truth. He will rejoice not in what he has been taught to believe, not in this church's doctrine or in that, not in this ism or in that ism, but in the truth. He will strive to get at facts. He will search for truth with a humble and unbiased mind and cherish whatever he finds. Love for truth includes the self-restraint which refuses to take advantage of others' faults, the charity which delights not in exposing the weakness of others, the sincerity of purpose that endeavors to see things as they are and rejoices to find them better than suspicion feared.

HENRY DRUMMOND

Triumph of Love

For in Christ Jesus. . .
the only thing that counts is
faith working through love.
GALATIANS 5:6 NRSV

If we love God, we have all winds blowing for us, and everything in the world shall conspire for our good. We know not what trials we may meet with, but to them who love God, all things shall work for good. Every wind shall blow us to the heavenly port. Our cross shall make way for a crown.

The lack of love to God is the cause of desertion. The seed in the parable which had no root fell away. A person who has not the love of God rooted in his heart will fall away in time of temptation. He who loves God will cling to Him. That soldier who has no love to his commander will leave him when he sees an opportunity and run over to the enemy's side.

What shall we do to love God? Study God. If we would study Him more, we will love Him more. Take a view of His superlative excellencies, His holiness, His incomprehensible goodness. Labor for an interest in God. The more we believe, the more we love. Faith is the root, and love is the flower that grows upon it. Make it your earnest request to God that He will give you a heart to love Him. This is an acceptable request; surely God will not deny it. He will pour of His Spirit upon you, whose golden oil shall make the lamp of your love burn bright.

THOMAS WATSON

Love in Heaven

*The faith and love that spring from the hope
that is stored up for you in heaven
and that you have already heard about
in the word of truth,
the gospel that has come to you.*

COLOSSIANS 1:5–6 NIV

I enjoy my parents and my near and beloved friends with some delight. When I have given my whole heart to my friend, how sweet was that exercise of my love! What will it then be to live in the perpetual love of God! To see a family live in love with husband and wife, parents and children doing all in love to one another, and to see a town live together in love without any envyings, brawlings, contentions, lawsuits, or divisions; but every man loving his neighbor as himself, thinking they can never do too much for one another but striving to go beyond each other in love—how happy, how delightful a sight is this!

What blessed fellowship will the family of heaven be where there is no division nor differing judgments, no resentment, no deceitful friendship, no, not one unkind expression, not an angry look or thought; but all are one in Christ who is one with the Father, and all live in the love of Him who is love Himself! How near then will my soul be united to God! I shall so heartily, strongly, and incessantly love Him! Ah, my wretched heart can think of such a day and work and life with such joy! But my future enjoyments will be even livelier.

RICHARD BAXTER

The Loving Servant

For ye, brethren, were called for freedom;
only use not your freedom for an occasion to the flesh,
but through love be servants one to another.
GALATIANS 5:13 ASV

Do not be ashamed to serve others for the love of Jesus Christ and to seem poor in this world. Do not be self-sufficient, but place your trust in God. Do what lies in your power, and God will aid your good will. Put no trust in your own learning nor in the cunning of any man, but rather in the grace of God who helps the humble and humbles the proud.

If you have wealth, do not glory in it, nor in friends because they are powerful, but instead glory in God who gives all things, and who desires above all to give Himself. Do not boast of personal stature or of physical beauty, qualities that are marred and destroyed by a little sickness. Do not take pride in your talent or ability, for fear that you will displease God to whom belongs all the natural gifts that you have.

Do not think yourself better than others lest, perhaps, you be accounted worse before God who knows what is in man. Do not take pride in your good deeds, for God's judgments differ from those of men, and what pleases them often displeases Him. If there is good in you, see more good in others so that you may remain humble. It is very harmful to think yourself better than even one. The humble live in continuous peace, while in the hearts of the proud are envy and frequent anger.

THOMAS À KEMPIS

Grieving Love

*For I wrote to you out of
great sorrow and anguish of heart—
along with many tears—
not to make you sad but to let you know
how much love I have for you.*

2 CORINTHIANS 2:4 ISV

Where there is love to God, there is a grieving for our sins of unkindness against Him. A child who loves his father cannot but weep for offending him. The heart that burns in love melts in tears. I must not abuse the love of so dear a Savior! Did not my Lord suffer enough upon the cross, but must I make Him suffer more? Shall I give Him more gall and vinegar to drink? How disloyal and insincere have I been! How have I grieved His Spirit, trampled upon His royal commands, slighted His blood! This opens a vein of godly sorrow and makes the heart bleed afresh.

Peter thought how he was taken up into the mount of transfiguration where Christ showed him the glory of heaven in a vision. That he should deny Christ after he had received such striking love from Him, this broke his heart with grief. He went out and wept bitterly.

Let us test our love to God. Do we shed the tears of godly sorrow? Do we grieve for our unkindness against God, our abuse of mercy, our lack of improvement of talents? How far are they from loving God who sin daily and their hearts never smite them! They have a sea of sin and not a drop of sorrow.

THOMAS WATSON

Stolen Love

For our gospel came not unto you in word only,
but also in power, and in the Holy Ghost,
and in much assurance.

1 THESSALONIANS 1:5 KJV

Some people seem to feel that they must be on probation and must prove to the Lord that they are reformed before they can claim His blessing. But they may claim the blessing of God even now. Jesus loves to have us come to Him just as we are—sinful, helpless, and dependent. We may come with all our weakness, our folly, our sinfulness, and fall at His feet. It is His glory to encircle us in the arms of His love and cleanse us from all impurity.

Here is where thousands fail. They do not believe that Jesus pardons them personally, individually. They do not take God at His Word. It is the privilege of all who comply with the conditions to know for themselves that pardon is freely extended for every sin. Put away the suspicion that God's promises are not meant for you. They are for every repentant transgressor. God does not deal with us as finite men deal with one another. His thoughts are thoughts of mercy, love, and tenderest compassion.

Satan is ready to steal away the blessed assurances of God. He desires to take every glimmer of hope and every ray of light from the soul, but you must not permit him to do this. Can you believe that when the poor sinner longs to return, longs to forsake his sins, the Lord sternly withholds him from coming to His feet in repentance? Away with such thoughts! He hates sin, but He loves the sinner.

ELLEN G. WHITE

Love Does not Complain

Be hospitable to one another without grumbling.

1 PETER 4:9 NKJV

A child who complains about a parent wounds that parent's heart often beyond words. Some people are always complaining, nothing ever pleases them, and no kindness seems ever to be appreciated. We know how uncomfortable the company of such people makes us. We know, on the contrary, how life is brightened by the presence of one who never complains but who finds something to be pleased with in all circumstances.

Far more misery than we imagine is caused in human hearts by the grumbling of those they love. I believe the continual murmuring of His children wounds the heart of our Father in heaven. How often is it despairingly said of fretful, complaining people upon whom every care and attention has been lavished, "Will nothing ever satisfy them?"

I remember hearing of a dear girl who was obliged to undergo a serious and very painful treatment for some disease, and the doctors had dreaded the thought of her groans and outcries. But to their amazement not even a moan escaped her lips, and all the time she smiled at her father who was present, and uttered only words of love and tenderness. The doctors could not understand it. When the worst was over, one of them asked how it could have been. She said, "I knew how much my father loved me, and I knew how he would suffer if he saw that I suffered, so I tried to hide my suffering. I smiled to make him think I did not mind."

Can any of us do this for our heavenly Father?

HANNAH WHITALL SMITH

Love for Rich and Poor

Those who despise their neighbors are sinners,
but happy are those who are kind to the poor.
PROVERBS 14:21 NRSV

Love your neighbor. Perhaps he rolls in riches, and you are poor and living in your little hut beside his lordly mansion. You see every day his estate, his fine linen, and his sumptuous banquets. God has given him these gifts. Do not covet his wealth and think no hard thoughts concerning him. Be content with your own lot, if you cannot better it, but do not look upon your neighbor and wish that he were as yourself. Love him, and then you will not envy him.

Perhaps, on the other hand, you are rich, and near you besides the poor. Agree that you are bound to love them. Some may call them your inferiors. In what are they inferior? God has made of one blood all people who dwell upon the face of the earth. It is your coat which is better than theirs, but you are by no means better than they. Take heed that you love your neighbor although he is in rags or sunken in the depths of poverty.

But perhaps you say, "I cannot love my neighbors because for all I do they return ingratitude and contempt." So much the more room for the heroism of love. Would you be a feather-bed warrior instead of bearing the rough fight of love? If rough is your path of love, tread it boldly. If your neighbors are hard to please, seek not to please them but to please God. Love your neighbor, for in so doing you are following the footsteps of Christ.

CHARLES HADDON SPURGEON

Christian Work Requires Love

There is no fear in love;
but perfect love casteth out fear.
1 JOHN 4:18 KJV

Love is the only power in which Christians really can do their work. Love is a fire that will burn through every difficulty. You may be a shy, hesitating person who cannot speak well, but love can burn through everything. A lady had been asked to speak at a rescue mission where there were a number of poor women. As she entered, she saw a woman sitting outside in deplorable condition, and asked, "Who is that?"

The female supervisor answered, "She has been into the house thirty or forty times, and she has always gone away again. Nothing can be done with her. We have been waiting for you, and you have only an hour for your speech."

The lady replied, "No, this is of more importance." She went outside where the woman was sitting and said, "My sister, what is the matter?"

"I am not your sister" was the reply.

Then the lady laid her hand on her and said, "Yes, I am your sister, and I love you." She so spoke until the heart of the poor woman was touched. The conversation lasted some time, and those inside were waiting patiently. Ultimately the lady brought the woman into the room. She would not sit on a chair but sat down on a stool beside the speaker's seat. And that love touched the woman's heart. She had found one who really loved her, and that love gave access to the love of Jesus. I plead that God would begin with us now and baptize us with heavenly love!

ANDREW MURRAY

Love and the Nature of Faith

I will sing of the LORD's great love forever;
with my mouth I will make your faithfulness known
through all generations.

PSALM 89:1 NIV

The only bond which unites us with God is union with Christ. But the faith which unites us with Christ grows out of a genuine feeling, which is called love. Such faith does not merely believe in Christ. It embraces Him with the soul. Therefore, love expresses well the power and the nature of faith. Truly, if God begins to love us only when we already love Christ, it follows that our love comes before God's grace and that the beginning of our salvation is in us. But many passages in scripture cry out against such a statement. The promise of God is "I shall make them to love Me."

We are said to be loved of God when we love Christ, because when we love Christ, we receive a pledge that God loves us as Father; whereas, before we loved Christ, He terrified us as a hostile judge.

I do not concede that the Spirit asks no more from us than what is within our ability. Rather, He shows us where we must turn when we lack the strength to obey Him. When we hear Christ exhort us to perseverance, we must not rely on our own energy and industry; we must rather pray to Him who commands us to confirm us in His love.

JOHN CALVIN

Claim God's Love

They that be whole need not a physician,
but they that are sick.
MATTHEW 9:12 KJV

Have you never tasted the luxury of indulging in hard thoughts against those who have, as you think, injured you? What a positive fascination it is to brood over their unkindness, to pry into their malice, and to imagine all sorts of wrong things about them. It has made you wretched, of course, but it has been a fascinating sort of wretchedness that you could not easily give up.

Like this is the luxury of doubting. Things have gone wrong with you in your experience. What is more natural than to conclude that for some reason God has forsaken you and does not love you? How irresistible is the conviction that you are too wicked for Him to care for or too difficult for Him to manage. You do not mean to blame Him or accuse Him of injustice, for you feel that His indifference toward you is fully deserved because of your unworthiness. This very ploy leaves you at liberty to indulge in your doubts under the guise of a just and true recognition of your own shortcomings.

The poor little lamb that has wandered from the flock and gotten lost in the wilderness might as well say, "The shepherd does not love me nor care for me nor remember me, because I am lost. He only loves and cares for the lambs that never wander." But Jesus says He came not to save the righteous but sinners. Your very sinfulness and unworthiness is your chief claim upon His love and His care.

HANNAH WHITALL SMITH

Divided Love

"No servant can serve two masters;
for either he will hate the one and love the other,
or else he will be loyal to the one and despise the other.
You cannot serve God and mammon."

LUKE 16:13 NKJV

God will not accept a divided heart. He must be absolute monarch. There is not room in your heart for two thrones. Christ said: "No man can serve two masters." Notice that He did not say, "No man shall serve," but "No man can serve." That means more than a command. It means that you cannot mix the worship of the true God with the worship of another god any more than you can mix oil and water. It cannot be done. There is not room for any other throne in the heart if Christ is there. If worldliness should come in, godliness would go out.

The road to heaven and the road to hell lead in different directions. Which master will you choose to follow? Be an out-and-out Christian. Him only shall you serve. Only in this way can you be well pleasing to God. Will you incur God's displeasure by rejecting Christ, too? He died to save you. Trust Him with your whole heart, for with the heart man believeth unto righteousness.

I believe that when Christ has the first place in our hearts—when the kingdom of God is first in everything—we shall have power, and we shall not have power until we give Him His rightful place. If we let some false god come in and steal our love away from the God of heaven, we shall have no peace or power.

DWIGHT LYMAN MOODY

Love in Nature and in God's Word

I will sing of your love and justice.
I will praise you, LORD, with songs.

PSALM 101:1 NLT

The poet and the naturalist have many things to say about nature, but the Christian enjoys the beauty of the earth with the highest appreciation. The Christian recognizes His Father's handiwork and perceives His love in flower and shrub and tree. No one can fully appreciate the significance of hill and vale, river and sea who does not look upon them as an expression of God's love to man.

God speaks to us through His thoughtful workings and through the influence of His Spirit upon the heart. In our circumstances and surroundings, in the changes daily taking place around us, we may find precious lessons if our hearts are but open to discern them.

God speaks to us in His Word. Here we have in clearer lines the revelation of His character, His dealings with men, and the great work of redemption. Here is open before us the history of patriarchs and prophets and other holy men of old. We see how they struggled through discouragement like our own, how they fell under temptation as we have done and yet took heart again and conquered through the grace of God—and we are encouraged in our striving after righteousness.

As we read of the precious experiences granted them, the light and love and blessing it was theirs to enjoy, and the work they wrought through the grace given them, the Spirit that inspired them kindles in our hearts a desire to be like them in character—like them to walk with God.

ELLEN G. WHITE

The Path of Love

All the paths of the LORD are steadfast love and faithfulness,
for those who keep his covenant and his decrees.
PSALM 25:10 NRSV

By faith we receive the love of God, and by love we give it out again. We must do so freely, after the example of Christ and without any other motive save our neighbor's benefit. We must bestow pure love ourselves—all that we have and all that we are able to do, even on our enemies to bring them to God.

Christ did not do His deeds to obtain heaven. Heaven was His already. He did them freely for our sakes and to bring the favor of God to us and us to God. No natural son does his father's will because he would be heir. He is already heir by birth. His father gave him that out of pure love before he was born. Servants work for hire, children for love. So a Christian acts freely, considering nothing but the will of God and the value he can give his neighbor.

A gentle pastor, Jesus brings the Spirit of God, which loosens the bonds of Satan and couples us to God and His will through strong faith and fervent love. The poor and wretched sinner feels so great mercy, love, and kindness in God that he is sure in himself that it is not possible for God to forsake him or withdraw His mercy and love. He boldly cries out with Paul, saying, "Who shall separate us from the love that God loves us with?" In all tribulations, a Christian perceives that God is His Father and loves him even as he loved Christ.

WILLIAM TYNDALE

Light and Love

> *"And this is the judgment,*
> *that the light has come into the world,*
> *and people loved darkness rather than light*
> *because their deeds were evil."*
>
> JOHN 3:19 NRSV

The design of Christian redemption is to remove everything that is unheavenly, gross, dark, wrathful, and disordered from every part of this fallen world. And when you see every kind of evil, misery, and wickedness, you see that which Christ came into the world to remove. He came not only to give a new birth to fallen man but also to deliver all outward nature from its present vanity and evil and set it again in its first heavenly state.

All of nature's gross, divided elements declare that they are what they are because the light and love of heaven is not working and manifest in them.

Man has no possibility of attaining to any heavenly perfection and happiness except in the way of the gospel. There is no possibility of any other way because there is nothing that can possibly change the first properties of life into a heavenly state. Therefore the "Word was made flesh" and must of all necessity be made flesh if man is to have a heavenly nature.

Now as all evil, sin, and misery have no beginning nor power of working but in their divided, contrary properties, so it is certain that man has nothing to turn to, seek or aspire after but the lost spirit of love. Therefore it is that God only can be his redeemer because God only is love, and love can be nowhere else but in God and where God dwells and works.

WILLIAM LAW

God Loves You

"Look at the birds of the air;
they do not sow or reap or store away in barns,
and yet your heavenly Father feeds them.
Are you not much more valuable than they?"
MATTHEW 6:26 NIV

When I read in the Bible that God is love, I am to believe it just because it is written, and not because I have had any inward revelation that it is true. The Bible says that He cares for us as He cares for the lilies of the field and the birds of the air. The Bible says that the very hairs of our head are all numbered. I am to believe these statements just because they are written, no matter whether I have any inward revelation of it or not.

True humility accepts the love that is bestowed upon it and the gifts of that love with a meek and happy thankfulness, while pride shrinks from accepting gifts and is afraid to believe in the goodness of the one who gives them. Were we truly humble, we would accept God's love with thankful meekness.

It will sometimes look to us impossible that the Lord can love such disagreeable, unworthy beings as we feel ourselves to be. We must ignore these insinuations against the love of God as we would any insinuations against the love of our dearest friend. The fight to do this may sometimes be very severe. We must at once assert in definite words in our own hearts, and if possible aloud to someone, that God does love us. Our steadfast faith will unfailingly bring us, sooner or later, a glorious victory.

HANNAH WHITALL SMITH

Seek Perfection, Seek Love

And don't be wishing you were someplace else
or with someone else.
Where you are right now is God's place for you.
Live and obey and love and believe right there.

1 CORINTHIANS 7:17 TM

For one seeking Christian perfection, God is always in all his thoughts. He walks with God continually, having the loving eye of his soul fixed on Him and everywhere seeing Him who is invisible. And loving God, he loves his neighbor as himself. He cannot speak evil of his neighbor any more than he can lie either to God or man. He cannot utter an unkind word of anyone because love keeps the door of his lips. He ceases not to pray for them although they reject his love.

Love has purified his heart from envy, malice, wrath, and every unkind temper. It has cleansed him from pride. And indeed all possible reasons for contention on his part are cut off. His one intention at all times and in all places is not to please himself but to please Him whom his soul loves.

All the commandments of God he accordingly keeps and that with all his might because his obedience is in proportion to his love. And loving God with all his heart, he serves Him with all his strength. He continually presents his soul and body as a living sacrifice, holy, acceptable to God. Entirely and without reserve he devotes himself, all he has, all he is, to His glory. All the talents he has, every power and faculty of his soul, every member of his body, he constantly employs according to his master's will.

JOHN WESLEY

This Open Sore of the World

Perhaps this is the reason he [Onesimus]
was separated from you for a while,
so that you might have him back forever,
no longer as a slave but more than a slave,
a beloved brother.

PHILEMON 15–16 NRSV

When I came, the chief presented me with a slave girl about ten years old. I thanked him and said that I thought it wrong to take away children from their parents. I wished him to give up this system altogether. He urged that she was to be a child to bring me water and that a great man ought to have a child for the purpose, yet I had none.

I replied that I had four children and should be very sorry if my chief were to take my little girl and give her away, and that I would prefer this child to remain and carry water for her own mother. He thought I was dissatisfied with her size and sent for one a head taller. After many explanations of the repugnance of slavery, and how displeasing it must be to God to see His children selling one another and giving each other so much grief as this child's mother must feel, I declined her, also.

To take her away and probably never be able to secure her return would have produced no good effect on the minds of the natives. They would not then have seen evidence of our hatred to slavery.

All I can say in my solitude is: May heaven's rich blessing come down on everyone—American, English, Turk—who will help heal this open sore of the world.

DAVID LIVINGSTONE

Feelings of Love

Learn to love appropriately.
You need to use
your head and test your feelings.
PHILIPPIANS 1:9 TM

Our feelings are very deceptive because they are affected by the state of our health, changes in the weather, and the presence or absence of those whom we love. There may be causes that account for our depression. It may be that Christ would teach us to distinguish between love and the emotion of love, between joy and the rapture of joy, between peace and the sense of peace. Or perhaps He may desire to ascertain whether we cling to Him for Himself or for His gifts.

Children greet their father from the window as he turns the corner and comes down the street. He hears the rush of their feet along the hall as he inserts his latchkey in the door. But one day he begins to question whether they greet him for the love they bear for him or for the gifts with which he fills his pockets. One day, therefore, he gives them due notice that there will be no gifts when he returns at night. Their faces fall, but when the hour of return arrives, they are at the window as usual, and there is the same trampling of little feet to the door. "Ah," he says, "my children love me for myself," and he is glad.

Our Father sometimes cuts off the supply of joy and suffers us to hunger so that He may know what is in our hearts, and whether we love Him for Himself. If we still cling to Him, He is glad and restores comforts to His mourners with both hands.

F. B. MEYER

Compassionate Advocate

Finally, all of you, live in harmony with one another;
be sympathetic, love as brothers, be compassionate and humble.
1 PETER 3:8 NIV

An advocate is one who pleads the cause of another, who uses his influence in behalf of another by his request. Unless he himself is clear of the crime of which the criminal is accused, an advocate is not the proper person to represent him before a throne of mercy.

He must be the compassionate friend of the sinner—not of his sins but of the sinner himself. This distinction is very plain. Everyone knows that a parent can be greatly opposed to the wickedness of his children while he has great compassion for their person. He is not a true friend to the sinner who really sympathizes with his sins. Would you call a man your friend who wished you to commit murder or robbery, to tell a lie, or to commit any crime?

No! No man is a true friend of a sinner unless he is desirous that he should abandon his sins. If any person would have you continue in your sins, he is the adversary of your soul. Instead of being in any proper sense your friend, he is playing the devil's part to ruin you.

Christ is the compassionate friend of sinners, a friend in the best and truest sense. He does not sympathize with your sins, but His heart is set upon saving you from your sins. I said He must be the compassionate friend of sinners. His compassion must be stronger than death, or He will never meet the necessities of the case.

CHARLES FINNEY

What Would Jesus Do The Railroad Superintendent

> For the LORD loves justice;
> he will not forsake his faithful ones.
>
> PSALM 37:28 NRSV

Alexander Powers said, "The company gives me the use of this room, and I am going to fit it up with tables and a coffeemaker in the corner. My plan is to provide a good place where the men can come and eat their lunch and to give them, two or three times a week, the privilege of a fifteen-minute talk on some subject that will be a real help to them in their lives. They are as a whole entirely removed from church influence.

"I asked, 'What would Jesus do?' Among other things it seemed to me He would begin to act in some way to add to the lives of these men more physical and spiritual comfort. It is a very little thing, this room and what it represents, but I acted on the first impulse, to do the first thing that appealed to my good sense."

Later certain papers had fallen into his hands of the violation of the Interstate Commerce Law. What business of his was it? But if he saw a man entering his neighbor's house to steal, would it not be his duty to inform the officers of the law? Was a railroad company such a different thing? Was it under a different rule of conduct, so that it could rob the public and defy law and be undisturbed because it was such a great organization?

Alexander Powers handed in his resignation and placed his evidence against the company in the hands of the commission, and it is now for them to take action upon it.

CHARLES SHELDON

Truth in Love

I do not hide your righteousness in my heart;
I speak of your faithfulness and salvation.
I do not conceal your love and
your truth from the great assembly.
PSALM 40:10 NIV

Jesus did not suppress one word of truth, but He uttered it always in love. He exercised the greatest tact and thoughtful, kind attention in His conversation with the people. He was never rude, never needlessly spoke a severe word, and never gave needless pain to a sensitive soul. He spoke the truth but always in love.

He denounced hypocrisy, unbelief, and iniquity, but tears were in His voice as He uttered His scathing rebukes. He wept over Jerusalem, the city He loved which refused to receive Him. They had rejected Him, the Savior, but He regarded them with tenderness. His life was one of self-denial and thoughtful care for others. Every soul was precious in His eyes.

Such is the character of Christ as revealed in His life. From the Father's heart, the streams of divine compassion manifest in Christ flow out to the children of men. God permitted His beloved Son, full of grace and truth, to come from a world of indescribable glory to a world blighted with sin, darkened with the shadow of death and the curse. He permitted Him to leave the bosom of His love, to suffer shame, insult, humiliation, hatred, and death.

The Father loves us, not because of the great atonement of Jesus, but He provided the atonement of Jesus because He loves us. Christ was the medium through which He could pour out His infinite love upon a fallen world.

ELLEN G. WHITE

Love Generates Love

But speaking the truth in love,
we must grow up in every way
into him who is the head, into Christ.
EPHESIANS 4:15 NRSV

We love because He first loved us. Contemplate the love of Christ, and you will love. Stand before that mirror, reflect Christ's character, and you will be changed into the same image. There is no other way. You cannot love to order. You can only look at the lovely object and fall in love with it and grow into likeness of it. And so look at this perfect character, this perfect life. Look at the great sacrifice as He laid down Himself, all through life and upon the cross of Calvary, and you must love Him. And loving Him, you must become like Him.

Love generates love. It is a process of induction. Put a piece of iron in the presence of a magnetized body, and that piece of iron for a time becomes magnetized. It is charged with an attractive force in the mere presence of the original force. As long as you leave the two side by side, they are both magnets alike. Remain side by side with Him who loved us and gave Himself for us, and you, too, will become a center of power, a permanently attractive force; and like Him you will draw all people unto you, like Him you will be drawn unto all people. That is the inevitable effect of love. There is no mystery about it. We love others, we love everybody, we love our enemies because He first loved us.

HENRY DRUMMOND

Vain Love

"But strive first for the kingdom of God and his righteousness, and all these things will be given to you as well."
MATTHEW 6:33 NRSV

What good does it do to speak learnedly about the Trinity if, lacking humility, you displease the Trinity? Indeed it is not learning that makes a man holy and just, but a virtuous life makes him pleasing to God. I would rather feel contrition than know how to define it. For what would it profit us to know the whole Bible by heart and the principles of all the philosophers if we live without grace and the love of God? Vanity of vanities and all is vanity, except to love God and serve Him alone.

This is the greatest wisdom—to seek the kingdom of heaven through disdain of the world. It is vanity, therefore, to seek and trust in riches that perish. It is vanity, also, to court honor and to be puffed up with pride. It is vanity to follow the lusts of the body and to desire things for which severe punishment later must come. It is vanity to wish for long life and to care little about a well-spent life. It is vanity to be concerned with the present only and not to make provision for things to come. It is vanity to love what passes quickly and not to look ahead where eternal joy abides.

Try to turn your heart from the love of things visible, and bring yourself to love things invisible. For those who follow their own evil passions stain their consciences and lose the grace of God.

THOMAS À KEMPIS

Jesus' Gift of Love

Christ loved the church and gave himself up for her.
EPHESIANS 5:25 NRSV

So great and wonderful was the love of Jesus toward us that He actually gave Himself for us and to us. The one thing that is necessary is that we should rightly understand and firmly believe His surrender for us. Yes, Jesus gives Himself to prepare for Himself a pure people, a people of His own, and a zealous people. When I receive Him, when I believe that He gave Himself to do this for me, I shall certainly experience it. I shall be purified through Him, shall be held fast as His possession, and be filled with zeal and joy to work for Him.

The more I understand and contemplate Jesus' surrender of Himself for me, the more I give myself again to Him. The surrender is a mutual one. The love comes from both sides. His giving of Himself makes such an impression on my heart that my heart with the same love and joy becomes entirely His. I know that I have Jesus wholly for me and that He has me wholly for Him.

Through faith I live in Jesus who loved me and gave Himself for me. And I say, "No longer do I live, but Christ liveth in me." In His great love, the Father gave the Son. It was out of love that Jesus gave Himself. The taking, the having of Jesus is the entrance to a life in the love of God: This is the highest life. Through faith we must press into love and dwell there.

ANDREW MURRAY

Love and Goodness of the Father

"He is good; his love endures forever."
2 CHRONICLES 5:13 NIV

One of the most illuminating names of God is the one especially revealed by our Lord Jesus Christ, the name of "Father." God had been called throughout the ages by many other names that expressed other aspects of His character. Christ alone has revealed Him to us under the all-inclusive name of Father—a name that holds within itself all other names of wisdom and power, and above all of love and goodness. The name embodies for us a perfect supply for all our needs. Christ, who was the only begotten Son in the bosom of the Father, was the only one who could reveal this name, for He alone knew the Father. "As the Father knoweth me," He said, "even so know I the Father."

When our Lord was teaching His disciples how to pray, the only name by which He taught them to address God was, "Our Father which art in heaven." This surely meant that we were to think of Him only in this light. Millions upon millions of times during all the centuries since then, this name has been uttered by the children of God everywhere. Yet how much has it been understood? If all who used the name had known what it meant, then it would have been impossible to misrepresent His character. The doubts about His love and care that have so distressed the souls of His children would not have crept in. It is inconceivable that a good father could forget or neglect or be unfair to his children.

HANNAH WHITALL SMITH

Love in Three Words

Whoever does not love does not know God,
because God is love.

1 JOHN 4:8 NIV

My subject is the greatest sentence that was ever written. That sentence is in the Bible. The Bible has a way of putting more in a single sentence than other writers can put in a whole book. This sentence has in it but three words: God is love. Each word is a monosyllable. One word has four letters, one three, and one only two. Yet these nine letters, forming three monosyllables, contain so much of truth that the world has been pondering it for centuries and has not got to the bottom of it yet.

"God is love" is the greatest sentence ever written. It sums up the whole contents of the Bible. If I were asked for a sentence to print in letters of gold on the outside of our Bible, a sentence that summed up the whole contents of the Book, it would be this one: "God is love." It is the subject of the first chapter of Genesis, it is the subject of the last chapter of Revelation, and it is the subject of every chapter that lies in between.

The Bible is simply God's love story, the story of the love of a holy God to a sinful world. There is mighty power in that one short sentence, power to break the hardest heart, power to reach individual men and women who are sunk down in sin and to lift them up until they are fit for a place beside the Lord Jesus Christ upon the throne.

REUBEN ARCHER TORREY

Love Balances the Scale

*"You have been weighed on the scales
and found wanting."*
DANIEL 5:27 NIV

Weighed by the laws of God, are you found wanting? One day I was talking to a sea captain. I asked, "Captain, why are you not a Christian?"

"The Golden Rule is a good enough religion for me," he replied.

"Do you keep it?" I asked. He dropped his head. He talked about it, but he did not keep it. Notice that scripture does not merely put the Golden Rule negatively: "Do not do to others whatsoever you would not that they should do to you." The Christian rule is positive. "Do these things to them." Do you do it? Always? Then you are weighed and found wanting.

In Matthew, the Bible tells us to love the Lord our God with all our heart, with all our soul, and with all our mind. This is the first and greatest commandment. How much do you weigh by that law? Put God first in everything—in business, in politics, in social life, in study, in everything. Do you do it? Have you always done it? No, you say, I have not. Then you are weighed and found wanting.

Every one of us is weighed and found wanting. What shall we do then? This is where the gospel comes in. God has weighed the whole world in the balance and found it wanting. In Christ He provided salvation for a wanting world. When we take Christ into the balance with us, then we are weighed and found not wanting.

REUBEN ARCHER TORREY

Love and the Law

Love does no harm to its neighbor.
Therefore love is the fulfillment of the law.

ROMANS 13:10 NIV

The Ten Commandments are not ten different laws. They are one law. If I am being held up in the air by a chain with ten links and I break one of them, down I come just as surely as if I break the whole ten. If I am forbidden to go out of an enclosure, it makes no difference at what point I break through the fence. The golden chain of obedience is broken if one link is missing.

Now face these Ten Commandments honestly and prayerfully. See if your life is right and if you are treating God fairly. God's statutes are just, are they not? If they are right, let us see if we are right. Let us get alone with God and read His law—read it carefully and prayerfully. Ask Him to forgive us our sin, and ask what He would have us to do. If God should weigh us by them, would we be found wanting or not wanting?

If the love of God fills your heart, you will be able to fulfill the law. Love summarizes the Ten Commandments. Love to God will admit no other god. Love to God will never dishonor His name. Love to God will reverence His day. Love to parents makes one honor them. Hate, not love, is a murderer. Lust, not love, commits adultery. Love will give but never steal. Love will not slander or lie. Love's eye is not covetous.

DWIGHT LYMAN MOODY

Love Is Humble

*Be humble and gentle. Be patient with each other,
making allowance for each other's faults because of your love.*
EPHESIANS 4:2 NLT

If we love God, we shall spread abroad His goodness to raise His name and esteem and induce others to fall in love with Him. Love cannot be silent. We shall be as so many trumpets, sounding forth the freeness of God's grace, the superiority of His love, and the glory of His kingdom. Love is like fire. Where it burns in the heart, it will break forth at the lips. It will be elegant in setting forth God's praise. Love must have vent.

When our union with Christ is perfect in glory, then our joy will be full. He who loves Christ loves His appearing.

Love will stoop and submit to anything whereby it may be serviceable to Christ. As we see in Joseph of Arimathea and Nicodemus, both of them honorable persons, one takes down Christ's body with his own hands and the other embalms it with sweet odors. It might seem much for persons of their rank to be employed in that service, but love made them do it. If we love God, we shall not think any work too insignificant for us by which we may be helpful to Christ's members. Love is not squeamish. It will visit the sick, relieve the poor, wash the saints' wounds. The mother who loves her child will do those things for her child which others would scorn to do. He who loves God will humble himself to the most undignified task of love for Christ and His members.

THOMAS WATSON

The Loving Father

I will be a father to him, and he shall be a son to me
I will not take my steadfast love from him

1 CHRONICLES 17:13 NRS

In our Lord's last prayer (John 17:1), He says that He has declared to us the name of the Father so we may discover the wonderful fact that the Father loves us as He loved His Son. Now which one of us really believes this? We have read this chapter, suppose, more often than almost any other chapter in the Bible. Yet do any of us believe that it is an actual, tangible fact that God loves us as much as He loved Christ? If we believed this to be the case, could we ever have an anxious or rebellious thought again? We would be absolutely and utterly sure always, under every conceivable circumstance, that the divine Father who loved us just as much as He loved His only begotten Son would care for us in the best possible way. He could tell us emphatically not to be anxious about anything because He knew His Father and knew that it was safe to trust Him completely.

"Your heavenly Father," Jesus says, "cares for the sparrow and the lilies, and of course therefore He will care for you who are of so much more value than many sparrows." How supremely foolish it is for us to be worried about things, when Christ has said that our heavenly Father knows that we have need of all these things! For being a good Father, He must in the very nature of the case supply it, when He knows our need.

HANNAH WHITALL SMITH

Honor, Obey, Love

Children, obey your parents in the Lord: for this is right.
Honour thy father and mother; which is the
first commandment with promise.
EPHESIANS 6:1–2 KJV

Abraham Lincoln used to say: "All I have I owe to my mother." I would rather die a hundred deaths than have my children grow up to treat me with scorn and contempt. I would rather have their esteem and favor than the esteem of the whole world. Any man who seeks the honor and esteem of the world and doesn't treat his parents right is sure to be disappointed.

If your parents are still living, treat them kindly. Do all you can to make their declining years sweet and happy. Bear in mind that this is the only commandment that you may not always be able to obey. As long as you live, you will be able to serve God and obey all the other commandments. But the day comes to most people when Father and Mother die. What bitter feelings you will have when the opportunity has gone by if you fail to show them the respect and love that is their due!

Joseph wasn't satisfied until he had brought his old father down into Egypt. He was the greatest man in Egypt next to Pharaoh. He was arrayed in the finest garments and had Pharaoh's ring on his hand and a gold chain about his neck. Yet when he heard Jacob was coming, Joseph hurried out to meet him. He wasn't ashamed of the man with his shepherd's clothes.

DWIGHT LYMAN MOODY

Love Beyond Law

"You have loved righteousness and hated wickedness,
therefore God, your God
has set you above your companion.
by anointing you with the oil of joy."

HEBREWS 1:9 NIV

The scriptures reveal to us glimpses of the delight, satisfaction and joy our Lord has in us. That we should need Him is easy to comprehend; that He should need us seems incomprehensible. That our desire should be toward Him is a matter of course, but that His desire should be toward us passes the bounds of human belief. And yet over and over He says it, and what can we do but believe Him?

At every heart He is continually knocking and asking to be taken in as the supreme object of love. In a thousand ways He makes this offer of oneness with Himself to every believer. But all do not say, "Yes," to Him. Other loves and other interests seem to them too precious to be cast aside. They miss an unspeakable joy.

You, however, are not one of these. From the very first eagerly and gladly to all His offers your soul has cried out, "Yes Lord, yes!" What to them is lawful, love has made unlawful for you. To you He can make known His secrets, and to you He looks for an instant response to every requirement of His love. Your love and devotedness are His precious reward for all He has done for you. Do not let there be neither a day nor an hour in which you are not intelligently doing His will and following Him wholly. This personal service to Him will give a halo to your life.

HANNAH WHITALL SMITH

Love and Law

For the LORD is righteous, he loves justice;
upright men will see his face.
PSALM 11:7 NIV

Did Christ really mean it when He taught in the ideal prayer that God's will was to be done on earth even as it is done in heaven? He also says, "If a man loves Me, he will keep My words." There must be something therefore to ease the apparent hopelessness of doing this will of God.

It is a privilege to do the commandments. It consists partly in forgetting that they are laws—in changing their names: commandment, precept, testimony, statute, into this—the will of God. And as my soul trembles at the fearfulness of will, love comes with its calm power. Where God's law is, is God's love. Look at law—it withers your very soul with its stern inexorable face. But look at love or look at God's will, which means look at love's will, and you are reassured, and your heart grows strong. God's will, then, is as great as God, as high as heaven—yet as easy as love. For love knows no hardness and feels no yoke.

Give me love, pure, burning love and loyalty to Him, and I shall climb from law to law through grace and glory to the place beside the throne where the angels do His will. There are two ways, therefore, of looking at God's will—one looking at the love side of it, the other at the law; the one ending in triumph, the other in despair; the one a liberty, the other a slavery.

HENRY DRUMMOND

Teach Us How to Lov

> *"The Father himself loves you becaus*
> *you have loved m*
> *and have believed that I came from God.*
>
> JOHN 16:27 NI

As one said in prayer, "We thank You, Father, that You have give us Your Son to teach us how to love." Yes, God would let us know that He Himself is love, and that if we would be His children, we too, must love Him and love one another. He reveals His love t draw us into fellowship with Himself and make us like Him.

God's love, as displayed in Christ, teaches us what love is The question is often asked, "How shall I love?" Look at the lov of Christ and drink in its spirit. Man is prone to love himsel supremely. But here is a totally different sort of love from that This love commends itself in that while we were yet sinners Christ died for us. How forcibly does this rebuke our selfishness How much we need this lesson, to subdue our narrow selfish ness and shame our unbelief!

How strange it is that people do not realize the love of God The wife of a minister who had herself labored in many revival said to me, "I never, until a few days ago, knew that God is love I never understood it in all its interconnections before."

I assure you, the love of Jesus is a great thing to see as it is When love becomes a reality to the soul and you come under it powerful sympathy, then you will find in the gospel the powe of God unto salvation.

CHARLES FINNE

Love and Spiritual Sickness

O taste and see that the LORD is good;
happy are those who take refuge in him.
PSALM 34:8 NRSV

Sometimes when people are sick, they lose interest in eating. They do not find a savory relish in their food. When Christians find no sweetness in God's promises, it is a sign of a spiritual sickness. At one time they did find comfort in drawing near to God. His Word was as honey, very delicious to their soul, but now it is otherwise. They can taste no more sweetness in spiritual things than in the white of an egg. To lose the taste indicates the loss of the first love. They have no appetite, they do not so prize Christ, and they have no strong affections to the Word. Sadly, their love is decaying.

When Christians grow more in love with the world, it indicates a decrease of spiritual love. Their thoughts and interests are still bound to the earth. It is a sign they are going down the hill quickly and their love to God is declining. When rust attacks a metal, it takes away the brightness and corrodes the metal. In the same way, when the world clings to people's souls, it not only hinders the shining luster of their graces, but by degrees it corrodes them.

Love is a grace that Christians do not know how to be without. A soldier may as well be without his weapons, an artist without his pencil, a musician without his instrument as a Christian without love. How careful then should we be to keep alive our love for God!

THOMAS WATSON

The Highest Gift

And if I have prophetic powers,
and understand all mysteries and all knowledge,
and if I have all faith, so as to remove mountains,
but do not have love, I am nothing.

1 CORINTHIANS 13:2 NRSV

Love is the highest gift of God. All visions or revelations are little things compared to love. All other gifts are either the same with or infinitely inferior to it. There is nothing higher in religion. If you look for anything but more love, you are looking wide of the mark. You are getting out of the royal way. Moreover when you are asking others, "Have you received this or that blessing?" if you mean anything but more love, you mean wrong. You are leading them out of the way and putting them upon a false scent. Settle it then in your heart that from the moment God has saved you from all sin, you are to aim at nothing more except more of that love described in the thirteenth chapter of First Corinthians. You can go no higher than this until you are carried into Abraham's bosom.

Beware of judging people to be either right or wrong by your own feelings. Beware of thinking, *Because I am filled with love, I need not have so much holiness. Because I pray always, therefore I need no set time for private prayer. Because I watch always, therefore I need no particular self-examination.* Let this be our voice: "I prize Your commandments above gold or precious stones. What love have I unto Your law!"

I appeal to you: Beware of bigotry. Beware of self-indulgence, yes, and making a virtue of it.

JOHN WESLEY

Love of Idols

> *"You shall not make for yourself an idol*
> *in the form of anything in heaven above*
> *or on the earth beneath or in the waters below.*
> *You shall not bow down to them or worship them."*
> EXODUS 20:4–5 NIV

What is an idol? An idol is anything that takes the place of God. It is anything that is the supreme object of our affection. God alone has the right to the supreme place in our hearts. Everything and everyone else must be subordinate to Him.

Many a man makes an idol of his wife. Not that a man can love his wife any too much, but he can put her in the wrong place. He can put her before God. When a man regards his wife's pleasure before God's pleasure, when he gives her the first place and God the second place, his wife is an idol.

Many a woman makes an idol of her children. Not that we can love our children too much. The more dearly we love Christ, the more dearly we love our children, but we can put our children in the wrong place. We can put them before God and their interests before God's interests. When we do this, our children are our idols.

Many a man makes an idol of his reputation or his business. Reputation or business is put before God.

One great question for us to decide: Is God absolutely first? Is He before wife, before children, before reputation, before business, before our own lives?

REUBEN ARCHER TORREY

Love in a Locket

If anyone says, "I love God,"
yet hates his brother, he is a liar.
For anyone who does not love his brother,
whom he has seen, cannot love God,
whom he has not seen.

1 JOHN 4:20 NIV

There lived once a young girl whose perfect grace of character was the wonder of those who knew her. She wore on her neck a gold locket that no one was ever allowed to open. One day in a moment of unusual confidence, one of her companions was allowed to touch its spring and learn its secret. She saw written these words: "Whom having not seen, I love." That was the secret of her beautiful life.

You all know what it is to be hungry for love. Your heart seems unsatisfied until you can draw something more toward you. There have been times when I have had an unspeakable heart-hunger for Christ's love. My sense of sin is never strong when I think of the law; my sense of sin is strong when I think of love. It is when drawing near the Lord Jesus Christ and longing to be loved that I have the most vivid sense of unsymmetry, of imperfection, of absolute unworthiness, and of my sinfulness. Character and conduct are never so vividly set before me as when in silence I bend in the presence of Christ, revealed not in wrath but in love to me. I never so much long to be lovely, that I may be loved, as when I have this revelation of Christ before my mind.

HENRY DRUMMOND

Charity of the Souls

Let him know,
that he who converteth a sinner from the error
of his way shall save a soul from death,
and shall cover a multitude of sins.
JAMES 5:20 ASV

Charity is much more valuable when it extends to the souls of men. Is not the soul more valuable than the body? The soul is of infinite value and of infinite concern. Therefore we should extend our charity whenever we see it needful. Likewise we should reprove, rebuke, and exhort with all godliness and love.

We may have a great deal of charity and concern for the bodies of our fellow-creatures yet have no thought or concern for their immortal souls: But, oh, how sad is it to have charity for the body of our fellow-creatures while we have no concern for their immortal souls. You may love to spend a merry evening with them, but you cannot bear the thought of going to a sermon or a religious society with them. No, you would sing the songs of the drunkard, but you will not sing hymns with them.

You will be so uncharitable as to join hand in hand with those who are hastening to their own damnation, while you will not be so charitable as to assist them in being brought from darkness to light and from the power of Satan unto God. Therefore let me advise you to be charitable to the souls of one another; that is, by advising them with all love and tenderness to follow after Christ and the things which belong to their immortal peace before they be forever hid from their eyes.

GEORGE WHITEFIELD

An Example of Love

Let no one despise your youth,
but set the believers an example
in speech and conduct,
in love, in faith, in purity.
1 TIMOTHY 4:12 NRSV

Be an example in love not in what you say, but in deed by directing of your goods to the poor and needy. Let your charity go to people of poor circumstances and treat them with respect. The salvation of their souls is equal to that of the kings of the earth. In heaven the distinction is lost forever.

Be an example in spirit. Always cherish a meek, gentle, and quiet spirit—a humble, loving, heavenly, and praying spirit. Such a spirit will almost silence the tongue of slander or cause its poisoned darts to fall harmless at your feet. Be an example in faith; prove to all by your works, your zeal, and labors of love that you heartily believe what you profess and teach to others. To teach the truth in a dull style lessens the force of truth and pours contempt upon its glory. But the truth presented in the spirit of faith will have a different effect on the hearers. Be an example in purity—purity of heart and life. Avoid impurity in word and action as well as in thought. In all things show yourself a pattern in every good work.

Serve God and pray for the promise of the Spirit. Then will you love your God and Savior. Then you will love your fellow Christians who bear the image of God. Then you will have the spirit of Jesus to love the fallen world and, like Him, to sacrifice all for their salvation.

BARTON W. STONE

Love and Contentment

Whoever loves money never has money enough;
whoever loves wealth is never satisfied with his income.
ECCLESIASTES 5:10 NIV

If you find yourself getting very miserly, begin to dispense your wealth, like a wealthy farmer in New York State I heard of. He was noted as a cheapskate before he was converted. Soon after, a poor man who had lost his home to a fire and had no provisions came to him for help. The farmer thought he would be liberal and give the man a ham from his smokehouse. On his way to get it, the tempter whispered to him, "Give him the smallest one you have."

He had a struggle whether he would give a large or a small ham, but finally he took down the largest he could find. "You are a fool," the devil said.

"If you don't keep still," the farmer replied, "I will give him every ham I have in the smokehouse!"

Contentment is the very opposite of covetousness, which is continually craving for something it does not possess. Do not worry about the future because God has promised never to leave or forsake you. What does the child of God want more than this? I would rather have that promise than all the gold of the earth.

Is the covetous person ever satisfied with his possessions? Riches are like a mirage in the desert that has all the appearance of satisfying and lures the traveler on with the promise of water and shade. But the traveler only wastes his strength in the effort to reach it. Riches never satisfy. The pursuit of them always turns out to be a snare.

DWIGHT LYMAN MOODY

Love That Thirsts for God

As the deer pants for streams of water,
so my soul pants for you, O God.
PSALM 42:1 NIV

If we love our friend, we love his company. His presence is comfortable; his absence is painful. When he comes to us, we entertain him with gladness. Should he die, we would mourn, and probably overmourn. To be separated from a faithful friend is like the rending of a member from our body. Would not our desire after God be such, if we really loved Him? Yes, and it would be much more because He is above all friends most lovely.

May the Lord teach us to look closely to our hearts and take heed of self-deceit in this point. Whatever we pretend, if we love father, mother, husband, wife, child, friend, wealth, or life itself more than Christ, we are yet none of His sincere disciples. When it comes to the trial, the question will not be, "Who has preached most, heard most, or talked most?" But the question will be "Who has loved most?" Christ will not take sermons, prayers, or fastings instead of love.

I dare not conclude that we have no love at all when we are so loath to die, but I dare say that were our love more, we should die more willingly. Where we love most heartily, we shall think most sweetly and most freely. I fear most Christians think higher of the love of a hearty friend than of the love of God. What wonder, then, if they love their friends better than God and trust them more confidently than God, that they had rather live with them than with God.

RICHARD BAXTER

Power of Pure Love

Hearken, my beloved brethren;
did not God choose them that are poor
as to the world to be rich in faith,
and heirs of the kingdom which
he promised to them that love him?
JAMES 2:5 ASV

Jesus has always many who love His heavenly kingdom, but few who bear His cross. He has many who desire consolation, but few who care for trial. He finds many to share His table, but few to take part in His fasting. All desire to be happy with Him; few wish to suffer anything for Him. Many follow Him to the breaking of bread, but few to the drinking of the cup of His suffering. Many honor His miracles, but few approach the shame of the Cross. Many love Him as long as they encounter no hardship. Many praise and bless Him as long as they receive some comfort from Him. But if Jesus hides Himself and leaves them for a while, they fall either into complaints or into deep dejection.

Those, on the contrary, who love Him for His own sake and not for any comfort of their own, bless Him in all trial and anguish of heart as well as in the bliss of consolation. Even if He should never give them consolation, yet they would continue to praise Him and wish always to give Him thanks. What power there is in pure love for Jesus—love that is free from all self-interest and self-love!

THOMAS À KEMPIS

Courageous Love

> *[God] extended to me steadfast love*
> *before the king and his counselors,*
> *and before all the king's mighty officers.*
> *I took courage, for the hand*
> *of the LORD my God was upon me,*
> *and I gathered leaders*
> *from Israel to go up with me.*
>
> EZRA 7:28 NRSV

Love is brave. It turns cowardice into courage. Love will make a Christian venture upon the greatest difficulties and hazards. The fearful hen will fly upon a dog or snake to defend her young ones. Love infuses a spirit of gallantry and fortitude into a Christian. He who loves God will stand up in His cause and be an advocate for Him.

He who is afraid to own Christ has but little love to Him. As the sun expels fogs and vapors, so divine love in a great measure expels fear. Does he love God who can hear His blessed truths spoken against and be silent? He who loves his friend will stand up for him and vindicate him when he is reproached. Love animates a Christian. It fires his heart with zeal and steels it with courage.

Many, being drunk with the wine of prosperity, when the honor of God is wounded and His truths lie bleeding, are not affected by it. If we love God, our hearts ache for the dishonor done to God by wicked men. To see the banks of religion broken down and a flood of wickedness coming in, if there be any love to God in us, we shall lay these things to heart.

THOMAS WATSON

Love, Trust, and Authority

*"In everything do to others as
you would have them do to you;
for this is the law and the prophets."*
MATTHEW 7:12 NRSV

Parents! Be sure that you look on your children as the gifts of God. Remember that if He gives you many mouths to feed, He will send the means to feed them. Be careful, also, that your own hearts and lives are full of praise and prayer. What you are, the children will become. Would that mothers especially realized how they transmit their characters. But remember that you must be obeyed in the home. But if you would rule well, you must obey. The man who is himself under authority can say, "Go, come, do this or that," with the calm assurance of being obeyed.

Parents, be warned. If your children disobey and violate the rules of your home, you must insist on penitence, confession, and apology. The relaxation of the bonds of authority in our homes is one of the saddest symptoms of national decay.

You must show yourself worthy to lead and rule your home. Your character must be such as to command respect. Those whom God has put into your charge require that you do not use your authority for selfish or capricious ends. Above all, love is the source of the truest authority. We count nothing hard or irksome that we do for those we love. Show love, and you will win love; and on love will be built respect, reverence, and obedience. Christ's golden rule holds good in every phase of life.

F. B. MEYER

Love That Unsettles Us

For I the LORD love justice
I hate robbery and wrongdoing
ISAIAH 61:8 NRSV

We have been considering the unfathomable love and care of God. It might seem to those who do not understand the deepest way of love that no trials or hardness could ever come into the lives of His children. However, if we look deeply into the matter, we shall see that often love itself must bring the hardness.

If love sees those it loves going wrong, it must because of its very love do what it can to save them. The love that fails to do this is only selfishness. Therefore, just because of His unfathomable love, the God of love, when He sees His children resting their souls on things that can be shaken, must necessarily remove those things from their lives so that they may be driven to rest only on the things that cannot be shaken. This process of removing is sometimes very hard.

When we talk of building upon the rock of Christ, we need to be shaken from off every other foundation in order that we may be forced to rest on the foundation of God alone. And this explains the necessity for those shakings. The Lord sees that we are building our spiritual houses on flimsy foundations, which will not be able to withstand the storms of life. Not in anger but in tender love, He shakes our earth until all that can be shaken is removed and only those things on a firm foundation are left behind.

HANNAH WHITALL SMITH

First Love, Last Love

"I know your deeds, your love and faith,
your service and perseverance,
and that you are now doing more than you did at first."
REVELATION 2:19 NIV

Look back through all of your experiences and think of the ways that the Lord your God has led you and how He has fed and clothed you every day. He has borne with your ill manners. He has put up with all your murmurings and all your longings after sensual pleasures. He has supplied you with spiritual nourishment from heaven. Think of how His grace has been sufficient for you in all your troubles. His blood has been a pardon to you in all your sins. His rod and His staff have comforted you.

When you have looked back upon the love of the Lord, then let faith survey His love in the future, for remember that Christ's covenant and blood have something more in them than the past. He who has loved you and pardoned you shall never cease to love and pardon. He is alpha, and He shall be omega, also. He is first, and He shall be last. When you shall stand in the cold floods of Jordan, you need not fear because death cannot separate you from His love. Now, soul, is not your love refreshed? Does not this make you love Jesus? Does not a flight through limitless plains of His love inflame your heart and compel you to delight yourself in the Lord your God? Surely as we meditate on the love of the Lord, our hearts burn within us, and we long to love Him more.

CHARLES HADDON SPURGEON

Love for Eternity

"Those who love their life lose it,
and those who hate their life
in this world will keep it for eternal life."
JOHN 12:25 NRSV

There is no love of God without patience, and no patience without meekness and sweetness of spirit. Humility and patience are the surest proofs of the increase of love. Humility alone unites patience with love. True humility is a kind of self-annihilation, and this is the center of all virtues.

God is the first object of our love. Its next responsibility is to bear the shortcomings of others. We should exercise our love toward them who most shock our way of thinking, our temper, our knowledge, or the desire we have that others should be as virtuous as we wish to be ourselves.

In souls filled with love, the desire to please God is a continual prayer. As the furious hate that the devil bears us is termed the roaring of a lion, so our vehement love may be termed crying after God. God only requires that our hearts be truly purified and that we offer Him continually the wishes and vows that naturally spring from perfect love.

We should be continually laboring to cut off all the useless things that surround us. The best means of resisting the devil is to destroy whatever of the world remains in us. In that way we can raise for God, upon its ruins, a building all of love. Then shall we begin in this fleeting life to love God, as we shall love Him in eternity.

JOHN WESLEY

What Would Jesus Do?

Jesus looked at him and loved him.
"One thing you lack," he said.
"Go, sell everything you have and give to the poor,
and you will have treasure in heaven.
Then come, follow me."

MARK 10:21 NIV

Rachel Winslow said, "I am a little in doubt as to the source of our knowledge concerning what Jesus would do. Many perplexing questions in our civilization are not mentioned in the teachings of Jesus. How am I going to tell what He would do?"

"There is no way that I know of," replied Henry Maxwell, the pastor, "except as we study Jesus through the medium of the Holy Spirit. We shall all have to decide what Jesus would do after going to that source of knowledge."

"What if others say of us, when we do certain things, that Jesus would not do so?" asked the superintendent of railroads.

"We cannot prevent that. But the standard of Christian action cannot vary in most of our acts."

Donald Marsh, president of Lincoln College, asked, "And yet what one church member thinks Jesus would do, another refuses to accept as His probable course of action. Will it be possible to reach the same conclusions always in all cases?"

Mr. Maxwell answered, "No, I don't know that we can expect that. But when it comes to a genuine, honest, enlightened following of Jesus' steps, I cannot believe there will be any confusion either in our own minds or in the judgment of others. We must be free from fanaticism on one hand and too much caution on the other. If Jesus' example is the example for the world to follow, it certainly must be feasible to follow it."

CHARLES SHELDON

Love and Grace

*And I ask him that
with both feet planted firmly on love,
you'll be able to take in with all Christians
the extravagant dimensions of Christ's love.*

EPHESIANS 3:17–18 TM

What does growing in grace mean? To say that grace is free, unmerited favor only expresses a little of its meaning. It is the wondrous, boundless love of God poured out upon us without limit, not according to our deserving but according to His infinite heart of love.

I sometimes think we give a totally different meaning to the word "love" when it is associated with God. We well understand in its human application. Put together all the tenderest love you know of, the deepest you have ever felt, and the strongest that has ever been poured out upon you, then multiply it by infinity, and you will begin to have some faint glimpses of what the love of God in Christ Jesus is. And this is grace.

To be planted in grace is to live in the very heart of this love, to be enveloped by it, to be steeped in it, to revel in it, to know nothing else but love only and love always, and to have no shadow of a doubt but that it will surely order all things well. It is to be so satisfied with His skill and wisdom that not a question will cross our minds as to His modes of treatment. It is to grow as the lilies grow without a care and without anxiety, to grow because we live and therefore must grow, to grow because He who has planted has made us to grow.

HANNAH WHITALL SMITH

Assured Love

To those who have been called,
who are loved by God the Father
and kept by Jesus Christ: Mercy, peace and love
be yours in abundance.
JUDE 1–2 NIV

When I recall a prominent Christian friend, I am conscious of the sweet and gracious perfume that was ever rising from his full and ever-moving life. At the heart of this busy worker was the restful lover. He moved about in assured and certain warfare because his soul was ever feasting in a companionship of love with his Lord. I like this sentence of his: "What a thrill it gives me to meet with one who has fallen in love with Jesus!" Yes, that is the speech of a lover who is himself in love with the Lord. It is the thrill of sympathetic vibrations. It is the thrill of one who is already in love with Jesus and who delights to see Jesus come to His own. This renowned Christian's sort of warfare finds its explanation in the lover's thrill, and in a lover's thrill has its secret in the lover's tranquility.

But why should I keep upon these high planes of renowned and prominent personalities? Get a person who is restfully intimate with his Lord and you have a person whose force is tremendous! Such people move in apparent ease, but it is the ease that is linked with the infinite; it is the very peace of God. They may be engaged in apparent trifles, but even in the doing of the trifles there emerges the health-giving currents of the kingdom of God.

JOHN HENRY JOWETT

Love and the Child of God

My little children,
let us not love in word,
neither in tongue;
but in deed and in truth.

1 JOHN 3:18 KJV

Suppose you go and watch workmen at their task. The majority do their work in an uninterested, mechanical sort of way. They come exactly at the hour in the morning and throw down their work to a second exactly when the closing bell has rung. Perhaps you observe an uncomfortable turning of the head occasionally as if some eye were upon them, then a dogged going on of their work again as if it were always done under some restraint.

But among the workmen you notice one with cheerfulness about him. You see him at his place sometimes even before the bell has rung, and if unfinished work is in his hands when closing time has come, he does not mind an extra five minutes when all the others are gone. His work seems better done despite the ease and lightheartedness that mark him.

Now the difference between them is this. The first set of men are hired workmen. The man by himself is the owner's son. Not that he is outwardly different; he is a common workman like the rest. They work for wages and keep the workshop laws in terror of losing their place. But the son keeps them, and keeps them better, not for wages but for love.

So the Christian keeps the will or the laws of God because of the love of God. Not because they are workshop regulations framed and hung up before him at every moment of his life, but because they are his Master's will.

HENRY DRUMMOND

Love and the Dark Shadow

Into the upright there ariseth light in the darkness:
he is gracious, and full of compassion, and righteous.
PSALM 112:4 KJV

God has bound our hearts to Him by unnumbered gifts in heaven and on earth. Through the things of nature, He has sought to reveal Himself to us. Yet these but imperfectly represent His love. Although all these evidences have been given, the enemy of God blinded the minds of men so that they looked upon God with fear. They thought of Him as severe and unforgiving. Satan led men to conceive of God as one who is a severe judge, a harsh and exacting creditor. He pictured the Creator as a being who is watching with jealous eye to discern the errors and mistakes of men so that He may visit judgments upon them.

It was to remove this dark shadow by revealing to the world the infinite love of God that Jesus came to live among men. He went about doing good and healing all who were oppressed by Satan. There were whole villages where there was not a moan of sickness in any house, for He had passed through them and healed all their sick. His work gave evidence of His divine anointing. Love, mercy, and compassion were revealed in every act of His life. His heart went out in tender sympathy to the children of men. He took man's nature so that He might reach man's wants. The poorest and humblest were not afraid to approach Him. Even little children were attracted to Him. They loved to climb upon His knees and gaze into the pensive face, compassionate with love.

ELLEN G. WHITE

The Physician's Lo

For the LORD corrects those he love
just as a fath
corrects a child in whom he deligh

PROVERBS 3:12 N

A good physician acts with the same goodwill toward his patie
when he orders bitter remedy as when he gives pleasant remed
Suppose the good physician to have such intense love for you
to force medicines down your throat that can alone save you
life. Suppose he should declare himself so scrupulous towar
you that he would not spare you to escape his bitter medicin
then you would have a true and just representation of those bi
ter portions that God forces fallen man to drink.

What a gross mistake it is to conclude that wrath must b
in the Deity because He chastens. You have God's own Word fo
it that nothing but His love disciplines. How is it possible fo
words to give stronger proof that God is pure love, that he h
no will toward fallen man but to bless him with works of lov
What can infinite love do to give greater proof that all that
does proceeds from love?

To say "If God is all love toward fallen man, how can H
threaten or chastise sinners" is as absurd as to say "If the ab
physician is all love, goodness, and goodwill toward his patien
how can he apply painful remedies?" So absurd is this reasonin
that the very lack of this chastisement would be the greatest
all proof that God was not all love and goodness toward man.

WILLIAM LA

Grow in Love

*Let them give thanks to the LORD for his unfailing love
and his wonderful deeds for men, for he satisfies the thirsty
and fills the hungry with good things.*

PSALM 107:8–9 NIV

Let me exhort Christians to increase your love to God. Let your love be raised up higher. Our love to God should be as the light of the morning: First there is the daybreak, then it shines brighter at noon. They who have a few sparks of love should fan those divine sparks into a flame. He who has a little gold would have more; you who love God a little, labor to love Him more. A godly man is contented with a very little of the world, yet he labors to add one degree of love to another.

When I see the almond tree bud and flourish, I know there is life in the root. Where we see love to God increasing and growing larger, we may conclude it is true and genuine. The disciples' love to Christ at first was weak; they fled from Christ. But after Christ's death, love grew more vigorous, and the disciples made an open declaration of Him.

If our love to God does not increase, it will soon decrease. If the fire is not stoked, it will quickly go out. Therefore Christians should above all things endeavor to cherish and excite their love to God. This encouragement will be out of date when we come to heaven, for then our light shall be clear and our love perfect; but now it is time to motivate ourselves so that our love to God may increase yet more and more.

THOMAS WATSON

Love Written on Our Heart.

> *"I will put my laws in their mind*
> *and write them on their hearts.*
> HEBREWS 8:10 N

Service can become bondage if it is done purely as a matter c duty. Instead of saying the "May I" of love, the soul finds itse saying the "Must I" of duty. One dear Christian expressed it t me this way. "When I was first converted," she said, "I was s full of joy and love that I was only too glad to do anything fc my Lord. But after a while, my joy faded away and my lov burned less fervently. I found myself involved in lines of servic that were gradually becoming burdensome to me."

Or if this does not describe your case, perhaps another pic ture will. You do love your work in the abstract. But in doing i you find so many responsibilities connected with it and so man doubts as to your own capacity that it becomes a very heavy bu den. You have known this was the wrong way to feel and hav been ashamed of it, but you have seen no way to help it. Yo have not loved your work.

If a man's will is really set on a thing, he regards with a sul lime indifference the obstacles that lie in the way of his reaching i What we need in the Christian life is to want to do God's will . much as other people want to do their own will. And this is wha God has promised. He says He will write His laws on our heart We shall love His law because anything written on our hearts w must love.

HANNAH WHITALL SMIT

Love Yet Incomplete

They will betray their friends, be reckless,
be puffed up with pride,
and love pleasure rather than God.

TIMOTHY 3:4 NLT

You say, "I am not satisfied with my love for Christ." What! Did you expect to be satisfied? Is it your love to Christ or His love to you that is to bring you peace? God's love to sinners, as such, is our resting place. There are two kinds of love in God—His love of compassion to the unbelieving sinner and His love of delight to His believing children.

A father's love to a wayward child is quite as sincere as his love to his obedient, loving child at home, though it is a different kind. God cannot love you as a believer until you are such. But He loves you as a poor sinner. And it is this love of His to the unloving and unlovable that affords the sinner his first resting place. Herein is love: not that we loved God, but that He loved us.

"I am not satisfied with my repentance," you say. It is well. What should you have thought of yourself had you been satisfied? What pride and self-righteousness would it indicate if you said, "I am satisfied with my repentance—it is of the proper quality and amount." If satisfied with it, what would you do with it? Would you base your peace upon it? Would you pacify your conscience with it? Would you go with it instead of the blood to a holy God? If not, what do you mean by the desire to be satisfied with your repentance before having peace with God?

HORATIUS BONAR

The Love of Old

> *In his love and mercy he redeemed them*
> *he lifted them up and carried them all the days of old*
>
> ISAIAH 63:9 NI

We are all prone to think that the earliest days were the best. I is quite possible they were. But we must carefully distinguis between the exchange of the freshness and novelty of our firs love for a deepening and maturing love. The stream may babbl so cheerily, but there may be more water in the river. We lose th green spring, but is it not better to have the intense light c autumn in which the fruits ripen? There may not be so muc exhilaration, but there may be stronger, deeper experiences. W should not reckon our position in God's sight by our rapture and count ourselves going backward because they have gone There is something better than rapture—the peace of a settle understanding and unvarying faith.

Still, if you have left the old place at the feet of Christ an your love is cooling and your spirituality waning, I beseech yo Go back! Remember from what place you have fallen, repen and do the first works. Jesus yearns to reinstate you. He has per mitted this restless longing for the past to come that it may b with you as in the months of old. His lamp shall shine abov your head again. The secret of the Lord shall be upon your ten your steps shall be washed with butter, and the rock pour ou rivers of oil. Your roots shall spread to the waters, and the dev shall lie all night upon your branch.

F. B. MEYE

Personal Responsibility

*For the Son of man is come to seek
and to save that which was lost.*
LUKE 19:10 KJV

I have often thought that the reason why so many pray only in form and not in heart for the salvation of souls is that they lack love like God's love for the souls of the perishing. They lack a sense of personal responsibility for the lost.

You must see impressively that souls are precious. Without such a sense of the value of souls, you will not pray with fervent, strong desire. Without a just apprehension of their guilt, danger, and remedy, you will not pray in faith for God's interposing grace.

Indeed, you must have so much of the love of God—a love like God's love for sinners—in your soul that you are ready for any sacrifice or any labor. You need to feel as God feels. He so loved the world that He gave His only begotten Son, that whosoever should believe in Him might not perish.

You need so to love the world that your love will draw you to make similar sacrifices and put forth similar labors. Love for souls, the same in kind as God had in giving up His Son to die and as Christ had in coming cheerfully down to make Himself the offering, each servant of God must have. Otherwise, your prayers will have little heart and no power with God. This love for souls is always implied in acceptable prayer, that God would send forth laborers into His harvest.

CHARLES FINNEY

Seek Love

And hope does not disappoint us, because God's love has been poured into our hearts through the Holy Spirit that has been given to us.

ROMANS 5:5 NRSV

Has our daily habit been to seek being filled with the Holy Spirit as the Spirit of love? Has it been our experience that the more we have of the Holy Spirit the more loving we become? In claiming the Holy Spirit, we should make this the first object of our expectation. The Holy Spirit comes as a Spirit of love. May God help us to get hold of this simple, heavenly truth that a fruit of the Spirit is love. As the Holy Spirit gets real possession of one's life, the heart will be filled with real, divine, universal love.

When the body is divided, there cannot be strength. In the time of great conflicts, one of the mottoes is: "Unity gives strength." It is only when God's people stand as one body, one before God in the fellowship of love, one toward another in deep affection, one before the world in love—it is only then that they will have power to secure the blessing which they ask of God. Remember, if a jar that ought to be one whole is cracked into many pieces, it cannot be filled. You can take a part of a jar and dip out a little water into that, but if you want the container full, it must be whole. Give yourselves up to love, and the Holy Spirit will come. Receive the Spirit, and He will teach you to love more.

ANDREW MURRAY

The Right Spur

A wise child loves discipline,
but a scoffer does not listen to rebuke.
PROVERBS 13:1 NRSV

A person's body is like clothes with which the soul is covered. It is a horse that bears his master through many perils. And from this horse—a person's body—many things are required if the horse will bear his master out of perils. For no knight can safely fight against his enemy unless his horse is obedient to him. The soul cannot fight against the wiles of the devil if the flesh, which is his horse, lives in lusts.

As soon as a man begins to live wisely and flees all the lusts, desires, and vanities, which he before was used to and loved, and bows himself under the yoke of God's holy doctrine; then his enemies begin to contrive by wiles, frauds, and temptations to make him fall. Therefore, his horse needs to be submissive and help his master to overcome his enemies. If the soul and the body are well agreed and help one another in this spiritual contest, the devil shall soon flee and be overcome.

This is the right spur that should quicken your horse to speed in its way—that you learn to love Jesus Christ in all your living. This love would move such a person to live more virtuously and to flee from sin a hundred times more than any dread of the pain of hell. For perfect love puts out all dread and cleanses the soul from filth, and makes it to see God and to flee often to heaven in its desires, hoping to dwell there forever.

JOHN WYCLIFFE

Sin Against Love

But you, O Lord,
are a God merciful and gracious,
slow to anger and abounding in
steadfast love and faithfulness.

PSALM 86:15 NRSV

It has sometimes been taken for granted that a bad temper is a positive acquisition to the intellect. Its fieriness is supposed to kindle the system into intense and vigorous life. Now of course passion has its legitimate place in human nature, and when really controlled instead of controlling, it becomes a powerful stimulus to the intellectual faculties. However, a quick temper really incapacitates sound judgment. Decisions are struck off at a white heat without time to hear explanations. Then it takes a humbler spirit than most of us possess to reverse them when once they are made.

A peculiarity of the sin of temper is that its worst influence is upon others. It is generally the weak who are the sufferers because temper is the prerogative of superiors. Subordinates have not only to bear the brunt of the storm, but to sink their own judgment and spend their lives in ministering to what they know to be caprice. When the young are disciplined by the iron instead of by the Golden Rule, the consequences are still more fatal. They feel that they do not get a fair hearing.

In its ultimate nature, bad temper is a sin against love. And however impossible it may be to realize that now, however we may condone it as a pardonable weakness or small infirmity, a sin against love is a sin against God, for God is love. He who sins against love, sins against God.

HENRY DRUMMOND

Follow in the Footsteps of Love

Let the morning bring me
word of your unfailing love,
for I have put my trust in you.
Show me the way I should go,
for to you I lift up my soul.

PSALM 143:8 NIV

A higher form of faith is that faith which grows out of love. A child trusts his father because he loves him. Blessed are they who have a sweet faith in Jesus. They cannot help trusting Him because they so much love Him.

When a patient believes in a physician, he carefully follows his prescriptions and directions. There is no physician like Jesus. We put ourselves into His hands, accept whatever He prescribes, and do whatever He bids. We feel that nothing can be wrongly ordered while Jesus is the director of our affairs. He loves us too well to let us perish or suffer a single needless pain.

When a traveler trusts a guide to conduct him over a difficult pass, he follows the track that his guide points out. We trust Jesus to save us. He gives us directions as to the way of salvation. We follow those directions and are saved. Let not my reader forget this. Trust Jesus, and prove your trust by doing whatever He bids you.

Faith has the power of working by love. It influences the affections toward God and draws the heart after the best things. He who believes in God will beyond all question love God. Faith is an act of the understanding. To love God and to love man is to be conformed to the image of Christ.

CHARLES HADDON SPURGEON

Delightful Gifts

> *Rather, the LORD's delight is in*
> *those who honor him,*
> *those who put their hope in his unfailing love.*
>
> PSALM 147:11 NLT

God is not hard to please, nor is true human love, for it is a dim reflection of His own. We do not estimate our love gifts by their intrinsic value but rather by the love they express. God wants our love, He wants our sympathy, He wants the gifts and offerings that are prompted by love.

We seemed to be reminded of the delight often taken by bride and bridegroom in spreading out for inspection the love gifts of their friends so that as many as possible may share their gratification in them. Several may have sent similar gifts, but each is set out to the best possible advantage with the name of the giver attached. And while the intrinsic value of each is not lost sight of, it is the expression of the loving thought that is most prized.

Again we were reminded of our frequent absence from home and children. Wifely letters have cheered and interested us, depicting with motherly tenderness the gifts the children had brought her on her birthday or other occasion. The letters have a fullness of detail that showed alike the pleasure of the writer and her consciousness of the enjoyment with which the account would be read.

God delights in the offering of His servants. He would say, "Behold the love gifts of My people! How many and how precious the offerings of each, and how great the value of the whole!"

HUDSON TAYLOR

Love Drives Out Sin

Blessed is the man who perseveres under trial,
because when he has stood the test,
he will receive the crown of life that God
has promised to those who love him.
JAMES 1:12 NIV

Love to God will never let sin thrive in the heart. Some plants will not thrive when they are near together. The love of God withers sin. The flower of love kills the weed of sin. We should labor for that grace that is destructive to sin! Love to God is an excellent means for growth of grace. What can more promote and augment grace than love to God? Love is like watering of the root, which makes the tree grow.

The eye has seen rare sights; the ear has heard sweet music. But the eye has not seen, nor ear heard, nor can the heart of man conceive what God has prepared for them who love Him! Such glorious rewards are laid up that, as Augustine says, faith itself is not able to comprehend. God has promised a crown of life to them who love Him. This crown encircles within it all blessedness, riches, glory, and delight. It is a crown that fades not away.

Love to God is armor of proof against error. For want of hearts full of love, people have heads full of error; unholy opinions are for want of holy affections. People given up to strong delusions because they receive not the love of truth. The more we love God, the more we hate those opinions that would draw us off from God.

THOMAS WATSON

Gifts of Love

How great is the love the Father has lavished on us,
that we should be called children of God!

1 JOHN 3:1 NIV

God shows His love by His gifts. Suppose on his coronation day, King Edward, after all the ceremonies were over, had taken his carriage and had ridden down to the East End of London and had seen some ragged, wretched boy. Suppose his great heart of love had gone out to that boy, and stepping up to that poor wanderer, he had said: "I love you, and I am going to take you in my carriage to the palace. I am going to dress you fit to be a king's son, and you shall be known as the son of King Edward the Seventh." Would it not have been wonderful? But it would not have been as wonderful as that the infinitely holy God should have looked down upon you and me in our filthiness and rags and depravity, and that He should have so loved us that He should have bestowed upon us to be called the sons of God.

I have a friend in the university. We thought a good deal of each other, but I did not know how much he loved me. Years after, he learned that I was in a position in which I needed fifteen hundred dollars. The next day he came to me. "Let me give you that fifteen hundred dollars! You can pay it back later."

He gave me that fifteen hundred dollars, and I have paid it back, but he did not know I would. I knew then that man loved me.

REUBEN ARCHER TORREY

Love and Duty

And walk in love, as Christ also hath loved us,
and hath given himself
for us an offering and a sacrifice to God
for a sweetsmelling savour.
EPHESIANS 5:2 KJV

I once heard a story that brought me such a glimpse of God's love as I never had before. I do not know whether it is true or not. A man was set to watch a railway drawbridge over a river. He threw it open and let vessels through. He heard the whistle of a train up the track and sprang to the lever to bring the bridge back into place. As he was doing so, he accidentally pushed his boy into the river. He heard the boy cry, "Father, save me; I am drowning." What should he do? The man stood at the post of duty and brought the bridge back so that the train could pass over in safety. Then he jumped into the river to save his boy, but it was too late. He sacrificed his boy to do his duty.

When I heard that story, I wondered if it had been my boy what I would have done. That man owed it to those on the train to do what he did. God owed you and me nothing. We were guilty rebels against Him.

What are you going to do with His love? Accept it, or trample it underfoot? Accept Christ, and you accept that love. Reject Christ, and you trample that love underfoot. I cannot understand how any man or woman in their right senses can harden their hearts against the love of God.

REUBEN ARCHER TORREY

Love of Elders

> *"Honor your father and your mother, so that you may live long in the land the LORD your God is giving you."*
>
> EXODUS 20:12 NIV

Let your mind go back to the time when you were ill. Did your mother neglect you? A neighbor came in and said, "Now, Mother, you go and lie down. You have been up for a week. I will take your place for a night." Did your mother do it? No. If the poor worn body forced her to it at last, she lay watching. If she heard your voice, she was at your side directly, anticipating all your wants, wiping the perspiration away from your brow. If you wanted water, how soon you got it! She would gladly have taken the disease into her own body to save you. Her love for you would drive her to any lengths. No matter to what depths of vice and misery you have sunk, she has not turned you out of her heart. She would draw you back by the bands of a love that never dies.

When I was in England, I read of a man who professed to be a Christian, who was brought before the magistrate for not supporting his aged father. My friends, I'd rather be content with a crust of bread and a drink of water than neglect my father or mother. The idea that a professing Christian would neglect a parent! God have mercy on such a godless Christianity as that! It is a withered-up thing. Don't profess to love God and do a thing like that.

DWIGHT LYMAN MOODY

Tailored in Love

When all the people of Israel saw the fire coming down. . .
they fell face down on the ground and worshiped
and praised the LORD, saying,
"He is so good! His faithful love endures forever!"
2 CHRONICLES 7:3 NLT

A great many people are afraid of the consuming fire of God, but that is only because they do not understand what it is. It is the fire of God's love that must in the very nature of things consume everything that can harm His people. If our hearts are set on being what the love of God would have us to be, His fire is something we shall not be afraid of but shall warmly welcome.

Let us thank God, then, that the consuming fire of His love will not cease to burn until it has refined us as silver is refined. For the promise is that He shall sit as a refiner and purifier of silver, and He shall purge us as gold and silver are purged in order that we may offer unto Him an offering in righteousness. He gives us this inspiring assurance that if we will but submit to this purifying process, we shall become pleasant unto the Lord and all nations shall call us blessed.

To be pleasant to the Lord may seem to us impossible when we look at our shortcomings and our unworthiness. But when we think of this lovely, consuming fire of God's love, we can be of good heart and take courage. He will not fail nor be discouraged until all our impurities are burned up, and we ourselves come forth in His likeness and are tailored to His image.

HANNAH WHITALL SMITH

Love Conquers Selfishness

For God did not give us a spirit of timidity,
but a spirit of power,
of love and of self-discipline.

2 TIMOTHY 1:7 NIV

Nothing but love can expel and conquer our selfishness. Self is the great curse, whether in its relationship to God or to our fellowmen or to fellow Christians. But, praise God, Christ came to redeem us from self. Deliverance from selfishness means to be a vessel overflowing with love to everybody all the day. Many people pray for the power of the Holy Spirit, and they get something but so little! They prayed for power for work and power for blessing, but they have not prayed for power for full deliverance from self. A great many of us try hard at times to love. We try to force ourselves to love, and I do not say that is wrong; it is better than nothing. But the end of it is always very sad. "I fail continually," one must confess.

Why is a lamb always gentle? Because that is its nature. Does it cost the lamb any trouble to be gentle? No. Why not? It is so beautiful and gentle. Does a lamb study to be gentle? No. Why does that come so easy? It is its nature.

And how can I learn to love? Never until the Spirit of God fills my heart with God's love, and I begin to long for God's love in a very different sense from which I have sought it so selfishly as a comfort, a joy, a happiness, and a pleasure to myself.

ANDREW MURRAY

Love and Christian Perfection

Therefore, as God's chosen people,
holy and dearly loved,
clothe yourselves with compassion,
kindness, humility, gentleness and patience.
COLOSSIANS 3:12 NIV

But whom then do you mean by one who is perfect? We mean one in whom is the mind which was in Christ and who so walks as Christ also walked. A person who has clean hands and a pure heart and is cleansed from all filthiness of flesh and spirit. This person can now testify to all mankind, "I am crucified with Christ: Nevertheless I live; yet not I but Christ liveth in me."

The person who strives for Christian perfection is holy both in heart and in all manner of conversation. He loves the Lord his God with all his heart and serves God with all his strength. He loves his neighbor; that is, every person as himself, yes, in the same way as Christ loves us. Indeed, his soul is all love and filled with mercy, kindness, meekness, gentleness, and long-suffering. And his life is full of the work of faith, the patience of hope, and the labor of love. Whatever he does either in word or deed, he does it all in the name—in the love and power—of the Lord Jesus. In a word, he does the will of God on earth as it is done in heaven.

This it is to be a perfect man, to have a heart so all-flaming with the love of God as continually to offer up every thought, word, and work as a spiritual sacrifice acceptable to God through Christ.

JOHN WESLEY

Love and the Face of Jesus

*Jesus Christ. . .who loves us and has freed us
from our sins by his blood.*

REVELATION 1:5 NIV

God remained un-Christianized in the old zealous preaching. God remained Jehovah, the I AM that I AM. He was not God in Christ, God made intelligible by Christ, God made lovable by Christ, but God eternal, unchangeable, invisible, and therefore unknowable. In the nature of this God, the outstanding element was vengeance and anger.

A man's whole religion depends on his conception of God, so much so that to give a man religion in many cases is simply to correct his conception of God. But if man's natural conception of God is of a being opposed to him, a being to be appeased, his religion will be a religion of fear. God therefore was a God to be feared, an uncomfortable presence in one's life. He was always in court either actually sitting in judgment or collecting material for the next case.

The repetition that God was love did nothing to dispel this terrible illusion. We cannot love God because we are told to love Him, for love is not made to order. We can believe God's love, but believing love is like looking at heat. We cannot respond to it. To excite love, we need a person, not a doctrine—a father, not a deity. To be changed into the same image we must look at the glory of God in the face of Jesus. The old zealous preaching was defective in not exhibiting God in the face of Jesus.

HENRY DRUMMOND

Love Revealed in Nature

The LORD loves righteousness and justice;
the earth is full of his unfailing love.
PSALM 33:5 NIV

Nature and revelation alike testify of God's love. Look at the wonderful and beautiful things of nature. Think of their marvelous adaptation to the needs and happiness not only of mankind but of all living creatures. The sunshine and the rain, the hills and seas and plains—all speak to us of the Creator's love. God supplies the daily needs of all His creatures.

God made mankind perfectly holy and happy. The fair earth as it came from the Creator's hand bore no blight of decay or shadow of the curse. It is transgression of God's law—the law of love—that has brought woe and death. Yet even amid the suffering that results from sin, God's love is revealed. It is written that God cursed the ground for man's sake. The thorn and the thistle—the difficulties and trials that make his life one of toil and care—were appointed for his good as a part of the training needful in God's plan for his uplifting from the ruin and degradation that sin has wrought.

In nature itself are messages of hope and comfort. There are flowers upon the thistles, and the thorns are covered with roses. "God is love" is written upon every opening bud and upon every sprig of springing grass. The lovely birds with their happy songs, the delicately tinted flowers perfuming the air, the lofty trees of living green—all testify to the tender, fatherly care of our God and to His desire to make His children happy.

ELLEN G. WHITE

Imitate the Love of Jesu

Do not imitate what is evil but what is goo

Few masters could venture to say, "If you would practice m
teaching, imitate my life." But the life of Jesus is the exact tran
script of perfect virtue. He can point to Himself as the model
holiness as well as the teacher of it. The Christian should tak
nothing short of Christ for his model.

As a husband, the Christian is to look upon the portrait
Christ Jesus, and he is to paint according to that copy. The tru
Christian is to be such a husband as Christ was to His churc
The Lord Jesus cherishes for the church a special affectio
which is set upon her above the rest of mankind. A husban
should love his wife with a constant love, for this is the way tha
Jesus loves His church. He does not vary in His affection. H
may change in His display of affection, but the affection itself
still the same. A husband should love his wife with an endurin
love, for nothing shall be able to separate us from the love
God, which is in Christ Jesus our Lord. A true husband loves h
wife with a hearty love, fervent and intense. It is not mere li
service. Jesus has a delighted love toward His spouse: He priz
her affection and delights in her with sweet contentment. B
liever, you wonder at Jesus' love; you admire it—are you imita
ing it? In your domestic relationships, is the rule and measure
your love even as Christ loved the church?

CHARLES HADDON SPURGEO

Home Filled with Love

*He has taken me to the banquet hall,
and his banner over me is love.*

SONG OF SONGS 2:4 NIV

was visiting once in a wealthy house, where there was an adopted girl upon whom was lavished all the love and tenderness and care that human hearts could give. And as I watched that child running about, free and lighthearted with the happy carelessness of childhood, I thought what a picture it was of our wonderful position as children in the house of our heavenly Father. And I said to myself, *Nothing could so grieve and wound the loving hearts around her as to see this little child beginning to be worried or anxious about herself in any way, about whether her food and clothes would be provided for her, or how she was to get her education or her future support. How much more must the great, loving heart of our God and Father be grieved and wounded at seeing His children taking so much anxious care and thought!* And I understood why it was that our Lord had said to us so emphatically, "Take no thought for yourselves."

Who is the best cared for in every household? It is the little children. And the least of all, the helpless baby receives the largest share. As I have read, the baby "toils not, neither does he spin, and yet he is fed and clothed and loved and rejoiced in."

Let the ways of childish confidence and freedom from care, which so please you and win your hearts in your own little ones, teach you what should be your ways with God.

HANNAH WHITALL SMITH

Signs of Love

And they come unto thee as the people cometh,
and they sit before thee
as my people, and they hear thy words,
but they will not do them:
for with their mouth they shew much love,
but their heart goeth after their covetousness

EZEKIEL 33:31 KJV

By seven signs a man may suppose that he has the love of Christ. First, when all coveting of earthly things and fleshly lusts are weakened by Him. For where coveting is, there is not the love of Christ. If a man does not covet, it is a sign that he has love. The second is a burning desire for heaven. For when he has felt anything of heaven, the more he wants. He who has felt nothing desires nothing.

The third sign is if his language has changed. He who used to speak of earth now speaks of heaven. The fourth sign is practicing what is for spiritual good—as when a person, leaving all other things, has good will and devotion to prayer and finds sweetness in doing so. The fifth is when things which are hard in themselves are made easy through love. The sixth is hardness of soul to suffer all anguishes and troubles. He loves God alone. He has no joy but in God. He fears nothing except to offend God. And all his hope is to come from God.

The seventh sign is joyfulness when he is in tribulation and that he thanks Him in all afflictions that he suffers. It is the greatest token that he has the love of God: No tribulation or persecution can bring him down from this love.

JOHN WYCLIFFE

Love and Imperfection

May he reign under God's protection forever.
Appoint your unfailing love and faithfulness
to watch over him.

PSALM 61:7 NLT

Our Savior was deeply serious and intensely in earnest but never gloomy or morose. The life of those who imitate Him will be full of earnest purpose; they will have a deep sense of personal responsibility. But the religion of Jesus gives peace. It does not quench our joy. It does not restrain cheerfulness nor cloud the sunny, smiling face. Christ came not to be ministered unto but to minister. When His love reigns in the heart, we shall follow His example.

If we keep uppermost in our minds the unkind and unjust acts of others, we shall find it impossible to love them as Christ has loved us. If our thoughts dwell upon the wondrous love of Christ for us, the same spirit will flow out to others. We should love and respect one another although we cannot help but see their faults and imperfections. Humility and a patient tenderness with the faults of others should be cultivated. This will kill out all narrowing selfishness and make us largehearted and generous.

The psalmist says, "Trust in the Lord." Each day has its burdens, its cares and perplexities. When we meet one another, how ready we are to talk of our difficulties and trials. So many borrowed troubles intrude, so many fears are indulged, such a weight of anxiety is expressed that one might suppose we had no loving Savior ready to hear all our requests and to be to us a present help in every time of need.

ELLEN G. WHITE

Love without Bondage

But it was because the LORD loved you. .
that he. . .redeemed you from the land of slaver
DEUTERONOMY 7:8 N

God sought, in commending His love to us, to subdue our sla⟩ ish fear. Someone said, "When I was young, I was conscious ⟨ fearing God, but I knew I did not love Him. The instruction received led me to fear but not to love." So long as we think ⟨ God only as one to be feared, not to be loved, there will be prejudice against Him as more an enemy than a friend.

Every sinner sees plainly that God must have good reaso to be displeased with him. The selfish sinner judges God fro⟩ himself. Knowing how he should feel toward one who ha wronged him, he unconsciously infers that God must feel tl same way toward every sinner. When he tries to pray, his hea⟩ won't; it is nothing but terror. He feels no attraction towa⟩ God, no real love.

God would lead us to serve Him in love and not in bon⟨ age. He would draw us forth into the liberty of the sons of Go⟨ He loves to see the obedience of the heart. He would inspire lo⟩ enough to make all our service free, cheerful, and full of joy. you wish to make others love you, you must give them yo⟩ love. In this way God commends His love toward us in order ⟨ win our hearts to Himself, and get us ready and fit to dwell fo ever in His eternal home.

CHARLES FINN

Love That Enables Love

*For this is the message that ye heard from the beginning,
that we should love one another.*

1 JOHN 3:11 KJV

Concerning surrender to the Lord, it was said that the first great blessing of the grace of God was this—the free, complete, everlasting forgiveness of all your sins. For the young Christian it is of great importance that he should always carry the certainty of it about with him. The forgiveness of our sin is complete forgiveness. God does not forgive by halves. The love of God is so great and the atonement in the blood of Jesus so complete and powerful that God always forgives completely. The forgiveness of our sin restores us entirely again to the love of God.

Love to others arises from the love of the Father. Do not attempt then to fulfill the commandment of brotherly love by yourselves. You are not in a position to do this. But believe that the Holy Spirit who is in you to make known the love of God to you also certainly enables you to produce this love. Never say, "I feel no love; I do not feel as if I can forgive this man." Feeling is not the rule of your duty but the command, and the faith that God gives power to obey the command. In obedience to the Father, with the choice of your will and in faith that the Holy Spirit gives you power, begin to say, "I will love him; I do love him." The feeling will follow the faith. Let your love be a helpful, self-sacrificing love like that of Jesus.

ANDREW MURRAY

Love of Souls

Timely advice i
as lovely as golden apple.
in a silver basket
PROVERBS 25:11 NLT

Consider, my fellow Christians, that it was love for souls that brought the blessed Jesus down from the bosom of His Father. Love of souls made Him—who was equal in power and glory— to come and take upon Himself our nature. Love of souls caused the Lord of life to die the painful, ignominious, and accursed death of the cross. It was love to immortal souls that brought this blessed Jesus among us and that we might consider how great the value of souls was and is. It was that which made Jesus to bleed and die. Surely souls must be of infinite worth, which made the Lamb of God to die so shameful a death.

And shall not this make you have a true value for souls? It is of the greatest worth. This, then, is the greatest charity when it comes from love to God and from love to souls. May this make you have so much regard for the value of souls as not to neglect all opportunities for the doing of them good. Therefore let me earnestly beseech you both to consider the worth of immortal souls and let your love extend to them. By your advice and admonition, you may be an instrument in the hands of God in bringing souls to the Lord Jesus. Let me once more beseech each of you to act according to the circumstances of life, which God in His rich and free mercy has given you.

GEORGE WHITEFIELD

Preparation for Meeting God

For these commands and this teaching are
a lamp to light the way ahead of you.
The correction of discipline is the way to life.

PROVERBS 6:23 NLT

For thirty-three years, Jesus had lived among His disciples. They had lately learned to love Him. And just when their friendship was now pledged permanently, the unexpected words come, "I must say goodbye; it is expedient for you that I go away." It was a crushing blow to the little band. They had staked their all upon that love. They had given up home, business, and friends to follow Him. Now He says, "I must go!"

Sooner or later we find out that life is not a holiday but a discipline. Earlier or later we all discover that the world is not a playground. It is quite clear God means it for a school. The moment we forget that, the puzzle of life begins. We try to play in school; the Master does not mind that so much for He likes to see His children happy, but in our playing, we neglect our lessons. We do not see how much there is to learn. Because He loves us, He comes into the school sometimes and speaks to us. Sometimes the voice is like a startling thunderclap during a summer night. The discipline may seem far less than our desert or even to our eye ten times more. But it is not measured by these—it is measured solely by God's love, measured solely that the scholar may be better educated when he arrives at his Father. The discipline of life is a preparation for meeting the heavenly Father.

HENRY DRUMMOND

Conquered by Love

Yet in all these things
we are more than conquerors
through Him who loved us.
ROMANS 8:37 NKJV

If compassion attracts my love, how immeasurably then am I bound to love Him! All the mercies that have filled my life, all the places that I have lived, all the organizations I have associated with, and every change I have passed through—all tell me that the fountain is overflowing with goodness.

My debt of love continually increases! Shall I dare to think of recompensing all Your love with mine? Will my mite compensate You for Your golden mines? Shall I dare to compete in love with You? Dare I set my faint spark against the sun of Your love? Can I love as high, deep, broad, and long as the one who is love Himself? As I cannot match You in the works of power, no more can I match You in love. No, Lord, I yield; I am overcome. When You lead me in triumph from earth to heaven, all who see it shall acknowledge that You have prevailed.

The Lord shall take my body from the grave and make me shine as the sun in glory forever and ever. Is not heaven the place for a meeting of lovers? Is not the life there a state of love? Is not the employment there the work of love where the souls with Christ will take their fill? My soul begins it here. Keep me now in the love of God, and let nothing separate me from it.

RICHARD BAXTER

Sacrificial Love

"No one can serve two masters;
for a slave will either hate the one
and love the other,
or be devoted to the one and despise the other.
You cannot serve God and wealth."

MATTHEW 6:24 NRSV

Do not those who always think of their own profit and gain prove that they love themselves rather than Christ? Where can a man be found who desires to serve God for nothing? And who shall find a man so truly poor in spirit as to be free from every comfort? His value is like that of things brought from the most distant lands.

If a man gives all his wealth, it is nothing. If he does great penance, it is little. If he gains all knowledge, he is still far afield. If he has great virtue and much ardent devotion, he still lacks a great deal and especially the one thing that is most necessary to him. What is this one thing? That is leaving all. He must forsake himself—completely renounce himself—and give up all personal desires. Then when he has done all that he knows ought to be done, let him consider it as nothing. Let him make little of what may be considered great. Let him in all honesty call himself an unprofitable servant.

No one, however, is more wealthy than such a man. No one is more powerful. No one freer than he who knows how to leave all things and think of himself as the least of all.

THOMAS À KEMPIS

Unceasing Love

The steadfast love of the LORD never ceases,
his mercies never come to an end.

LAMENTATIONS 3:22 NRSV

Again I will speak, Lord, and will not be silent. I will speak to the hearing of my God, my Lord, and my King who is in heaven. How great, O Lord, is the multitude of Your mercies that You have stored up for those who love You. But what are You to those who love You? What are You to those who serve You with their whole heart?

Truly beyond the power of words is the sweetness of contemplation You give to those who love You. You have shown to me the sweetness of Your charity, especially in having made me when I did not exist, in having brought me back to serve You when I had gone far astray from You, in having commanded me to love You.

O fountain of unceasing love, what shall I say of You? How can I forget You who has been pleased to remember me even after I had wasted away and perished? You have shown mercy to Your servant beyond all hope and have exhibited grace and friendship beyond his deserving.

It is a great honor and a great glory to serve You and to despise all things for Your sake. They who give themselves gladly to Your most holy service will possess great grace. They who cast aside all carnal delights for Your love will find the most sweet consolation of the Holy Spirit. They who enter upon the narrow way for Your name and cast aside all worldly care will attain great freedom of mind.

THOMAS À KEMPIS

Touching Love

She had heard about Jesus,
and came up behind him in the crowd
and touched his cloak, for she said,
"If I but touch his clothes,
I will be made well."

MARK 5:27–28 NRSV

The God of patience, meekness, and love is the one God of my heart. The whole bent and desire of my soul is to seek for all my salvation in and through the merits and mediation of the meek, humble, patient, resigned, suffering Lamb of God. He alone has power to bring forth the blessed birth of these heavenly virtues in my soul.

He is the bread of God who came down from heaven of which the soul must eat, or perish and pine in everlasting hunger. He is the eternal love and meekness who left the bosom of His Father to be Himself the resurrection of meekness and love in all the darkened, wrathful souls of fallen men.

What a comfort is it to think that this Lamb of God, Son of the Father, light of the world, glory of heaven, and joy of angels is as near to us—is truly in the presence of us—as He is in the presence of heaven. A desire of our heart that presses toward Him, longing to catch one small spark of His heavenly nature, is as sure of finding Him, touching Him, and drawing power from Him as the woman who was healed by longing but to touch the border of His garment.

WILLIAM LAW

Love Crucified

> *"I have been crucified with Christ;*
> *it is no longer I who live,*
> *but Christ lives in me;*
> *and the life which I now live in the flesh*
> *I live by faith in the Son of God,*
> *who loved me and gave Himself for me."*
>
> GALATIANS 2:20 NKJV

He who loves God will have nothing to do with sin unless to give battle to it. Sin strikes not only at God's honor but also at His being. Does he who loves his prince protect a traitor to the crown? Is he a friend to God who loves that which God hates? The love of God and the love of sin cannot dwell together. A man cannot love health and love poison, too. He who allows any secret sin in his heart is as far from loving God as heaven and earth are distant one from the other.

He who is a lover of God is dead to the world. He who is in love with God is not much in love with anything else. The love of God and ardent love of the world are inconsistent. Love to God swallows up all other love. When a man's heart is raised above the world in the admiring and loving of God, how poor and slender are these things on earth below!

Will God ever bestow heaven upon them who so basely undervalue Him, preferring glittering dust before the glorious Deity? What is there in the earth that we should so set our hearts upon it? The world has no real intrinsic worth; it is but paint and deception.

THOMAS WATSON

Sympathetic Love

"In accordance with your great love,
forgive the sin of these people,
just as you have pardoned them from
the time they left Egypt until now."
NUMBERS 14:19 NIV

God shows His love by pardoning sin. God tells us plainly in His Word that He is willing to forgive any sinner who lives, no matter how deep down he has gone, if he will only turn from sin and turn to God.

I have a boy. I love that boy. I believe there is nothing that boy could do but if he repented and turned from it I would forgive him. But I could not forgive him if he held on to his evil way. I could continue to love him and seek to save him, but I could not forgive him. And God cannot forgive us and remain what He is—a holy God—until we are ready to quit our sin.

God shows His love for us by sympathizing with us. There is not a man or woman who is in trouble but God sympathizes with you. Some of you may know what it is to have a child sick for a long time. At first, friends came and sympathized with you, but their sympathy has grown cold. As you have watched day and night, you have said: "There is no one who sympathizes with me." Yes, there is. God sympathizes with you. There are men and women who have a sorrow of such a character that they cannot confide it to any human ear. They say: "Nobody knows it. Nobody sympathizes with me." Yes, there is One who knows, and He sympathizes with you—God.

REUBEN ARCHER TORREY

Love No Other

> *"Be careful to obey all the commands I give you;*
> *show love to the LORD your God by walking*
> *in his ways and clinging to him."*
>
> DEUTERONOMY 11:22 NLT

Does a father cease to give children rules to obey because they love him? Does a nation burn its statute books because the people have become patriotic? Not at all. Yet people speak as if the commandments of God do not hold for Christians because they have come to love God. The Ten Commandments are necessary. So long as we obey, they do not rest heavy upon us. But as soon as we try to break away, we find they are like fences to keep us within bounds. Horses need bridles even after they have been properly broken in.

A great many people say that if they keep the commandments they do not need to be forgiven and saved through Christ. But have you kept them? Young lady, can you say, "I am ready to be weighed by the law?" Can you, young man? Face the Ten Commandments honestly and prayerfully. See if your life is right and if you are treating God fairly. Let us get alone with God and read His law—read it carefully and prayerfully, and ask Him to forgive us our sin and what He would have us to do.

Is your heart set upon God alone? Have you no other god? If we were true to the first commandment, then obedience to the remaining nine would follow naturally. It is because we are unsound in the first that we break the others.

DWIGHT LYMAN MOODY

Love and Obedience

"If you listen to these regulations and obey them faithfully,
the LORD your God will keep his covenant
of unfailing love with you."
DEUTERONOMY 7:12 NLT

A life of obedience may look hard. But to those who know Him, it is the happiest and most restful of lives. He is our Father, He loves us, and He knows what is best. But even God's own children often seem afraid of His will.

A Christian lady expressed to a friend how impossible she found it to say, "Thy will be done." She was the mother of a little boy. Her friend said, "Suppose little Charley came running to you and said, 'Mother, I know you love me, and I am going to trust myself to your love.' You say, 'Now I shall have a chance to make Charley miserable. I will take away all his pleasures and fill his life with every hard and disagreeable thing I can find. I will compel him to do just the things that are the most difficult for him to do and will give him all sorts of impossible commands.' Would you respond in that way?"

The indignant mother replied, "You know I would not. You know I would hug him to my heart and cover him with kisses, and would fill his life with all that was sweet and best."

"And are you more loving than God?" asked her friend.

The Christian mother said, "I see my mistake, and I will not be afraid of saying 'Thy will be done' to my heavenly Father, any more than I would want my Charley to be afraid of saying it to me."

HANNAH WHITALL SMITH

Find God by Love

> *But may all who search for you*
> *be filled with joy and gladness.*
> *May those who love your salvation repeatedly shout,*
> *"God is great!"*
>
> PSALM 70:4 NLT

Do not be surprised if there should be matters in the Bible, in your own life, and in the secular government of the world that baffle your mind. Remember you are only a little child in a class for infants. It is not likely that you can comprehend the whole system of your instructor. God would cease to be God to us if we by searching could find Him out.

But though we cannot find out God by the searching of the intellect, we may know Him by love. "He who loves knows God; for God is Love." There is a way of knowing God which is hidden from the wise and prudent but revealed to babes. Seek to be strengthened with might by His Spirit in the inner person. Let Christ dwell deep in your heart by faith. Take care to obey all His commandments, and then the holy God will come into you. He will give you Himself, and you will know Him as a little child knows its parent, whom it cannot grasp with its mind but loves and trusts and knows with its heart. We cannot find out God by searching, but we can by loving.

We can also find Him in the character and life of Jesus. He who has seen Jesus has seen the Father; why then ask to be shown the Father?

F. B. MEYER

Governed by Love

But the aim of such instruction is love that
comes from a pure heart,
a good conscience, and sincere faith.

1 TIMOTHY 1:5 NRSV

I believe that a person filled with the love of God is still liable to involuntary transgressions—mistakes and whatever infirmities necessarily flow from the body. They are in no way contrary to love, nor therefore, in the scripture sense, sin. Such transgressions you may call sins if you please; I do not. Let those who do not call them sins never think that themselves or any other persons are in such a state as that they can stand before infinite justice without a mediator.

You ask, "But how can being prone to mistakes be consistent with perfect love? Is not a person who is perfected in love under its influence every moment? And can any mistake flow from pure love?"

Many mistakes may consist with pure love. Some may accidentally flow from it. I mean, love itself may incline us to mistake. The pure love of our neighbor, springing from the love of God, thinks no evil, believes and hopes all things. Now this very unsuspicious mind, ready to believe and hope the best of all people, may cause us to think some people are better than they really are. Here then is a clearly apparent mistake accidentally flowing from pure love.

We can avoid setting perfection too high or too low by keeping to the Bible and setting it just as high as the scripture does. It is nothing higher and nothing lower than this—the pure love of God and man. It is love governing the heart and life.

JOHN WESLEY

Love Beyond Reason

The LORD is slow to anger,
abounding in love
and forgiving sin and rebellion.

NUMBERS 14:18 NIV

A student went to a professor of theology and asked him how long it took him to understand the atonement, the love and forgiveness of God. The professor thought a moment and looked him in the face. "Eternity," he said. "Eternity, and I shall not understand it then."

God's love—how could we understand? God's forgiveness—how could we understand? We need not be distressed if we do not understand them. Most things in religion are matters of simple faith. But when we come to the atonement, we want to see through it and understand it—as if it were finite like ourselves, as if it could ever be compassed by our narrow minds—as if God did not know that we never could fathom it when He said "Believe it," instead of "Understand it."

We are not rationalists when we come to the love of God, or to faith or to prayer. We do not ask for a theory of love before we begin to love, or a theory of prayer before we begin to pray. We just begin. When they brought the sick man once to Jesus, He just said, "Man, your sins are forgiven you," and the man just believed it. He did not ask, "But why should You forgive me?" The fact is, if we would come to Christ just now, we should never ask any questions. If you will not receive salvation as a fact, receive the Lord Jesus Christ as a gift.

HENRY DRUMMOND

Love and Answered Prayers

But I pray to you, O LORD,
in the time of your favor;
in your great love, O God,
answer me with your sure salvation.

PSALM 69:13 NIV

We must pray to God if love for God is to exist. Faith, hope, patience, and all the strong, beautiful, vital forces of piety are withered and dead in a prayerless life. The life of the individual believer, personal salvation, and personal Christian graces have their being, bloom, and fruitful results in prayer.

Almighty God is the very highest model, and to be like Him is to possess the highest character. Prayer molds us into the image of God and at the same time tends to mold others into the same image just in proportion as we pray for others. Prayer means to be Godlike, and to be Godlike is to love Christ and love God, to be one with the Father and the Son in spirit, character, and conduct.

God has much to do with believing people who have a living, transforming faith in Jesus Christ. These are God's children. A father loves his children, supplies their needs, hears their cries, and answers their requests. A child believes his father, loves him, trusts in him, and asks him for what he needs, believing without doubting that his father will hear his requests. God has everything to do with answering the prayer of His children. Their troubles concern Him, and their prayers awaken Him. Their voice is sweet to Him. He loves to hear them pray, and He is never happier than to answer their prayers.

EDWARD MCKENDREE BOUNDS

What Would Jesus Do—
The Novel Writer

Keep your lives free from the love of money,
and be content with what you have.

HEBREWS 13:5 NRSV

His book was nearly done now. He had not forgotten the question "Would Jesus do this?" Would He write this story? It was a social novel written in a style that had proved popular. It had no purpose except to amuse. Its moral teaching was not bad, but neither was it Christian in any positive way.

"What would Jesus do?" He felt that Jesus would never write such a book. The question intruded on him at the most inopportune times. He became irritable over it. The standard of Jesus for an author was too ideal. Of course Jesus would use His powers to produce something useful or helpful or with a purpose. What was he, Jasper Chase, writing this novel for? Why, what nearly every writer wrote for—money and fame as a writer. There was no secret with him that he was writing this new story with that object. But he was urged on by his desire for fame as much as anything.

He turned to his desk and began to write. When he had finished the last page of the last chapter of his book, it was nearly dark. "What would Jesus do?" He had finally answered the question by denying his Lord. It grew darker in his room. Jasper Chase grew into a cold, cynical, formal life, writing novels that were social successes, but each one with a sting in it, the reminder of his denial, the bitter remorse that, do what he would, no social success could remove.

CHARLES SHELDON

Obligations of Love

*By this we know that we love the children of God,
when we love God, and keep his commandments.*

1 JOHN 5:2 KJV

Jesus loves you with more than the love of friendship. As a bridegroom rejoices over his bride, so does He rejoice over you. Have you never longed to lavish your love and attentions upon someone far off from you in position or circumstances? Have you not felt a capacity for self-surrender and devotedness that has seemed to burn within you like a fire and yet had no object upon which it dared to lavish itself?

If, then, you are hearing the sweet voice of your Lord calling you to Himself, will you shrink or hesitate? No! You will spring out to meet His dear call with an eager joy. Even His slightest wish will become a binding law to you, which it would fairly break your heart to disobey. You will glory in the very narrowness of the path He marks out for you and will be sorry for the poor ones who have missed this precious joy.

The obligations of love will be to you its sweetest privileges. The perfect happiness of perfect obedience will dawn upon your soul, and you will begin to know something of what Jesus meant when He said, "I delight to do Your will, O My God." And do you think the joy will be all on your side? The Lord has joy in those who have surrendered themselves to Him and who love to obey Him.

HANNAH WHITALL SMITH

Inner Love

> *"For the Father loves the Son,*
> *and shows Him all things that He Himself does;*
> *and He will show Him greater works*
> *than these, that you may marvel."*
>
> JOHN 5:20 NKJV

The outer life of a man is not the man, just as the paint on a piece of wood is not the wood. The portrait of a man is not the man. It is but a skillful arrangement of colors that look like the man. The man who loves God with all his heart is in a right state; the man who does not love Him in this way is in a wrong one. He is a sinner because his heart is not right with God. He may think his life a good one, and others may think the same. But the outward good cannot make up for the inward evil. The good deeds done for his fellowman cannot offset his bad thoughts of God. And he is full of these bad thoughts so long as he does not love the infinitely lovable and infinitely glorious God with all his strength.

However favorably a good outward life may dispose himself and others to look upon his case, the verdict will go against him. There is another and yet worse charge against him. That his heart is not right with God is the first charge against him. That his heart is not right with the Son of God is the second. And it is this second that is the crowning, crushing sin, carrying with it more terrible condemnation than all other sins together.

HORATIUS BONAR

Prayer and Love

*Praise be to God, who has not rejected my prayer
or withheld his love from me!*
PSALM 66:20 NIV

The ministry of prayer has been the secret power of all of God's saints. We have not the natural ability always to judge kindly, justly, truly, and act the Golden Rule. Prayer enables us to act in all these things according to the divine will. By prayer, the ability is secured to feel the law of love, to speak according to the law of love, and to do everything in harmony with the law of love. We need divine aid to act brotherly, wisely, nobly, and to judge truly and charitably.

Are we praying as Christ did? Are our pleas and spirit the overflow of His spirit and pleas. Does love rule the spirit—perfect love? As our great example in prayer, our Lord puts love as a primary condition—a love that has purified the heart from all the elements of hate, revenge, and ill will. Love is the supreme condition of prayer, a life inspired by love.

Answered prayer is the spring of love and is the direct encouragement to pray. A few short, feeble prayers have always been a sign of a low spiritual condition. People ought to pray much and apply themselves to it with energy and perseverance. Eminent Christians have been eminent in prayer. The deep things of God are learned nowhere else. Great things for God are done by great prayers. A person who prays much studies much, loves much, works much, and does much for God and humanity.

EDWARD MCKENDREE BOUNDS

The God of Comfort

Let your steadfast love become my comfort
according to your promise to your servant.

PSALM 119:76 NRSV

Among all the names that reveal God, the "God of all comfort" seems to me one of the loveliest and the most absolutely comforting. The words "all comfort" admit of no limitation and no deductions. But it often seems that a large number of the children of God are full, not of comfort but of the utmost discomfort. This discomfort arises from anxiety as to their relationship to God and doubts as to His love. They torment themselves with the thought that they are too good-for-nothing to be worthy of His care, and they suspect Him of being indifferent to their trials and of forsaking them in times of need. They are anxious and troubled by their indifference to the Bible, lack of fervency in prayer, and coldness of heart. They are tormented with regrets over their past and with anxieties for their future.

They feel unworthy to enter God's presence and dare not believe that they belong to Him. They can be happy and comfortable with their earthly friends, but they cannot be happy or comfortable with God. And although He declares Himself to be the God of all comfort, they continually complain that they cannot find comfort anywhere. Their sorrowful looks and the doleful tones of their voices show that they are speaking the truth.

Such Christians spread gloom and discomfort around them wherever they go. And the manifestly uncomfortable religious lives of so many Christians is, I am very much afraid, responsible for a large part of the unbelief of the world.

HANNAH WHITALL SMITH

God's Patient Love

Bear in mind that our Lord's patience means salvation,
just as our dear brother Paul also wrote you
with the wisdom that God gave him.

2 PETER 3:15 NIV

God's love is a most patient love. How rare to find a parent so loving his child as never to be impatient. How many of you parents can say that you love all your children so well that you have never felt impatient toward any of them—so that you can take them in your arms under the greatest provocations and love them down, love them out of their sins, love them into repentance and into an obedient spirit? Of which of your children can you say, "Thank God, I never fretted against that child." Often have I heard parents say, "I love my children, but how my patience fails me!"

But God never frets. He is never impatient. His love is so deep and so great that He is always patient.

Sometimes when parents have unfortunate children—poor objects of compassion—they can bear with anything from them. But when they are very wicked, they seem to feel that they are quite excusable for being impatient. In God's case, these are not unfortunate children but are intensely wicked—intelligently wicked. But His amazing patience—so set upon their good, so desirous of their highest welfare—that however they abuse Him, He sets Himself to bless them still and weep them down, and melt them into penitence and love by the death of His Son in their stead!

CHARLES FINNEY

Halfway Love

LORD, I have loved the habitation of Your house,
and the place where Your glory dwells.

PSALM 26:8 NKJV

In giving ourselves to God, we must necessarily give up all that would separate us from Him. Whatever shall draw away the heart from God must be given up. Wealth is the idol of many. The love of money, the desire for wealth, is the golden chain that binds them to Satan. Reputation and worldly honor are worshiped by others. The life of selfish ease and freedom from responsibility is the idol of some. But these slavish bands must be broken. We cannot be half the Lord's and half the world's. We are not God's children unless we are His entirely.

There are those who profess to serve God while they rely upon their own efforts to obey His law, to form a right character, and to secure salvation. Their hearts are not moved by any deep sense of the love of Christ, but they seek to perform the duties of the Christian life as that which God requires of them in order to gain heaven. Such religion is worth nothing.

When Christ dwells in the heart, the soul will be so filled with His love, the joy of communion with Him, and the contemplation of Him that self will be forgotten. Love to Christ will be the spring of action. Those who feel the constraining love of God do not ask how little may be given to meet the requirements of God. They do not ask for the lowest standard but aim at perfect conformity to the will of their Redeemer. A profession of Christ without this deep love is mere talk, dry formality, and heavy drudgery.

ELLEN G. WHITE

Love and Meekness

learned God—worship when my pride was shattered.
Heart-shattered lives ready for love
don't for a moment escape God's notice.

PSALM 51:17 TM

No person can attain any degree of true love to Jesus unless he is truly meek. For a proud person seeks to have his own will and so shall never come to any degree of God's love. The lower that soul sits in the valley of meekness, the more streams of grace and love come to him. And if the soul be high in the hills of pride, the wind of the enemy blows against him all matter of goodness. Therefore as Augustine says, "Whoever wishes to attain to the bliss that is in heaven above, let him set his foundation here low in meekness." Nothing more overcomes the devil than meekness, and therefore he hates it so much.

By two things principally may a man know whether he is meek. If his heart is not moved though his own will be contradicted and criticized—and when he is despised, falsely accused, and slandered. If his will stands unmoved, not desiring revenge, and his mouth be shut from answers that are not meek. For he who has entered truly into God's love is not grieved with whatever slander, shame, or reproof he suffers for the love of his Lord. He is glad that he is worthy to suffer pain for Christ's love. Christ's disciples went in joy when they were worthy to suffer wrongs for the name of Jesus.

JOHN WYCLIFFE

Love—The Cure for Anger

> But when the kindness and love of
> God our Savior appeared. . .
> He saved us through the washing of
> rebirth and renewal by the Holy Spirit
>
> TITUS 3:4–5 NI

Nothing in the world causes such rankling, abiding, unnecessary pain as anger. And Christ's words therefore when He refers to the breach of the law of love are most severe. "If any man offend one of these little ones," He says, "it were better for him that a millstone were hanged about his neck and that he were cast into the depths of the sea."

Christianity professes to cure anything. The process may be slow, the discipline may be severe, but it can be done. But is not temper a constitutional thing? Is it not hereditary, a family failing, a matter of temperament, and can that be cured? Yes, if there is anything in Christianity. If there is no provision for cure, then Christianity stands convicted of being unequal to human need.

It is quite useless by force of will to seek to empty the angry passions out of our life. Who has not made a thousand resolutions in this direction, only and with unutterable regret to see them dashed to pieces with the first temptation? The soul is to be made sweet not by taking the acidulous fluids out but by putting something in—a great love, God's great love. This is to work a chemical change upon them, to renovate and regenerate them, to dissolve them in love's own rich, fragrant substance. If a man let this into his life, his cure is complete; if not, it is hopeless.

HENRY DRUMMOND

A Knowledge of Love

Christ's love makes the church whole.
His words evoke her beauty.
Everything he does and says is
designed to bring the best out of her.
EPHESIANS 5:26 TM

Many are the ways in which God is seeking to make Himself known to us and bring us into communion with Him. Nature speaks to our senses without ceasing. The open heart will be impressed with the love and glory of God as revealed through the works of His hands. The listening ear can hear and understand the communications of God through the things of nature. The green fields, the lofty trees, the buds and flowers, the passing cloud, the falling rain, the babbling brook, and the glories of the heavens speak to our hearts and invite us to become acquainted with Him who made them all.

Our Savior bound up His precious lessons with the things of nature. The trees, the birds, the flowers of the valleys, the hills, the lakes, and the beautiful heavens, as well as the incidents and surroundings of daily life, were all linked with the words of truth so that His lessons might be often recalled to mind. God would have His children appreciate His works and delight in the simple, quiet beauty with which He has adorned our earthly home. He is a lover of the beautiful. Beyond all that is outwardly attractive, He loves beauty of character. He would have us cultivate purity and simplicity, the quiet graces of the flowers.

ELLEN G. WHITE

The Heavenly Father's Love

The LORD bless thee, and keep thee:
The LORD make his face shine upon thee,
and be gracious unto thee: The LORD lift up his
countenance upon thee, and give thee peace.

NUMBERS 6:24–26 KJV

We have dwelt upon the meaning of blessing, the moving of the heart toward an object of affection and contentment, and noticed that when love overflows, loving words, loving embraces, or loving gifts instinctively follow.

Considered as a father's blessing, could anything be more appropriate than "The Lord bless you and keep you"? Is not this just what every loving father seeks to do, to bless and keep his children? He does not find it an unwelcome task but his greatest delight.

Nor may we confine ourselves to paternal love in thinking of this subject. Rather take it as embracing also the love of the mother. We all know how the mother-love delights to lavish itself on the objects of its care. With a patience that never tires, an endurance almost inexhaustible, and a care all but unlimited, how often has the mother sacrificed her very life for the welfare of her babe. But strong as is a mother's love, it may fail. God's love never fails.

"Jehovah, the Father, bless you and keep you." It is an individual blessing, and it includes every form of blessing, temporal as well as spiritual. He wants us His children to know and to enjoy the love that is the source of all blessing, the love that can never by finite words express its fullness, the love that eternal ages will never exhaust!

HUDSON TAYLOR

Love Revealed

"I made your name known to them,
and I will make it known,
so that the love with which you have loved me
may be in them, and I in them."

JOHN 17:26 NRSV

What a mystery is love! If human love is mysterious, divine love is an ocean too deep for the plummet of man and too broad to be bounded by the thought of the loftiest intelligence in the universe. God is not only love, but He is love revealed. The perfect love of God toward man is designed to call forth perfect love toward God in man's heart. The mirror on which His love is reflected is broken into uneven planes and reflects a distorted image—the human soul at its best is shattered by infirmities and incurable imperfections.

The history of God's communication with men is the chronicle of His love. This will be our textbook forever. We can contemplate no more sublime and ennobling theme. The brightness of the material universe pales before the splendors of the divine character—that central fire which melts the hearts of sinners on earth.

In love revealed, there are ceaseless wonders. Our surprise is ever new when we discover that God so loves us that He gave His well-beloved Son to the humiliation of the manger, the agonies of Gethsemane, the mockery of the trial before Pilate, and the ignominy of Calvary. But this was but the beginning of His generosity. The loving Father has bestowed an abiding gift—the Holy Spirit—to whisper in the ear of spiritual death the words of life, to pardon penitence, and to fully restore the lost image of God.

DANIEL STEELE

The End of the Law

> Jesus said. . .
> " 'Love the LORD your God with all your heart. . . .
> Love your neighbor as yourself.'
> On these two commandments
> hang all the Law and the Prophets."
>
> MATTHEW 22:37–40 NKJV

All the divine precepts are referred back to love. Every commandment harks back to love. Love in this context of course includes both the love of God and the love of our neighbor. Therefore whatsoever things God commands and whatsoever things are not positively ordered but are strongly advised as good spiritual counsel—all of these imperatives are rightly obeyed only when they are measured by the standard of our love of God and our love of our neighbor.

This applies both in the present age and in the world to come. Now we love God in faith; then, at sight. Love comes at last to that fullness which cannot be surpassed. Who then can explain how great the power of love will be when there will be no sinful desire for it to overcome? For then the supreme state of true health will have been reached when the struggle with death shall be no more.

But somewhere this book must have an end. But since I have judged that your zeal in Christ ought not to be spurned, and since I believe and hope for good things for you through the help of our Redeemer, and since I love you greatly, I have written this book for you—may its usefulness match its length!—on faith, hope, and love.

AUGUSTINE

About the Compiler

John Hudson Tiner has written several books for Barbour Publishing including *Prayers and Promises for Men* and the best-seller *My Final Answer—Celebrity Edition*. He is the author of textbooks, curriculum material, character-building biographies, and high-interest-level Bible-study books. He has written more than seventy books, and his material has been translated into several languages. *Show Me Your Love* is his first compiled book. He and his wife, D. Jeanene Tiner, a photo-grapher, have been married for forty-two years, and they have two children and three grandchildren.

Scripture Index